My Curious and Jocular Heroes

My Curious and Jocular Heroes

*Tales and Tale-Spinners
from Appalachia*

L OYAL J ONES

**UNIVERSITY OF
ILLINOIS PRESS**
Urbana, Chicago, and Springfield

Publication of this book was supported by a grant from the L. J. and Mary C. Skaggs Folklore Fund.

Library of Congress Cataloging-in-Publication Data
Names: Jones, Loyal, 1928– author.
Title: My curious and jocular heroes : tales and tale-
    spinners from Appalachia / Loyal Jones.
Description: Urbana : University of Illinois Press,
    2017. | Identifiers: LCCN 2017019624 (print) | LCCN
    2017035042 (ebook) | ISBN 9780252099694 () | ISBN
    9780252041136 (hardback) | ISBN 9780252082672
    (paperback)
Subjects: LCSH: Folklore—Appalachian Region.
    | Tales—Appalachian Region. | Folk music—
    Appalachian Region. | Storytelling—Appalachian
    Region. | Storytellers—Appalachian Region. | Oral
    tradition—Appalachian Region. | BISAC: SOCIAL
    SCIENCE / Sociology / Rural. | BIOGRAPHY &
    AUTOBIOGRAPHY / Cultural Heritage. | MUSIC /
    Genres & Styles / Country & Bluegrass.
Classification: LCC GR108.15 (ebook) | LCC GR108.15
    .J66 2017— (print) | DDC 398.20974—dc23
LC record available at https://lccn.loc.gov/2017019624

Contents

Acknowledgments

First of all, I want to thank Elizabeth DiSavino, of the Berea College Music Department, for preparing the musical scores for the ballads and songs of all my heroes in this book, including the transcription from sound recordings of Josiah Combs and Bascom Lunsford. I acknowledge also the work of John M. Forbes, formerly of the Berea College Music Department, for notating other Lunsford songs, and Buell C. Agey, of West Virginia Wesleyan University, for notating the songs collected on recordings by Leonard Roberts.

I am grateful for the help I had from the following persons: Karen Paar, of the Bascom Lamar Lunsford Collection in the Southern Appalachian Archives of the Ramsey Center at Mars Hill University; Fred Hay and Dean Williams, of the Cratis D. Williams Papers, W. L. Eury Appalachian Collection, at Appalachian State University; and Harry Rice and Sharyn Mitchell, for collections of Lunsford, Combs, Williams, and Roberts, in the Southern Appalachian Archives at the Hutchins Library, Berea College.

Then there were the acquaintances, members of the families of those whom I wrote about, who delivered up important information and who became my friends: particularly Jo, Nelle, and Kern Lunsford; Libby, Sophia, and David Williams; and especially Edith Roberts, Lynneda Roberts Stansbury, and Rita Roberts Kelly, who worked on the Roberts genealogy and bibliography. I also want to thank Carl Lindahl, a fellow admirer and scholar of Leonard Roberts, for his help. I knew the late Norris Combs over a shorter period of time, but he was helpful to me in several ways. He made major efforts in publishing Josiah Combs's massive genealogy of the Combs family and in editing others of his uncle's works for possible publication.

I also acknowledge the helpfulness of two readers of my manuscript, Norm Cohen and Stephen Wade, who suggested many ways it could be improved. Lastly, I appreciate the kindness and helpful assistance from the staff of the University of Illinois Press: Laurie Matheson, Julianne Laut, Jennifer Comeau, Roberta Sparenberg, and Kevin Cunningham. I especially thank my vigilant copy editor, Jane Lyle, who improved my syntax and held my nose to the grindstone until I fully documented the main quotations and other sources.

Introduction

I grew up in the mountains of North Carolina at a time when the oral tradition was the source of a great deal of our knowledge and pleasure. My family and friends and neighbors exchanged ideas, jokes, and stories, sometimes songs and tunes, and there were some who stored them in memory for further use.

Eventually, I began to meet people in the wider world who shared my enthusiasm for the doings of the common folk whom I grew up among. One was a fifth-grade teacher who taught us songs by having us all sing them together, and told or read us interesting stories like "Three Billy Goats Gruff." Then, Richard Chase came and told the Old World tales at the nearby John C. Campbell Folk School—he who published *The Jack Tales* (1943) and *Grandfather Tales* (1948), as well as other works. He also taught us folksongs and singing games.

I met Bascom Lamar Lunsford at the State Fair. Lunsford collected ballads, songs, tunes, and stories before there were tape recorders, by committing them all to memory. He later recorded what he called his "memory collection" for Columbia University (1935) and the Library of Congress (1949).

I became friends with Kentuckian Leonard Roberts, who was a pioneer collector and publisher of Old World folktales and riddles, as well as ballads and lyric songs, and who was a master storyteller. We once attended the National Folk Festival in Nashville together.

Cratis Williams, another Kentuckian, became my treasured mentor. He was the father of Appalachian studies with his massive (1,661-page) New York University dissertation, "The Southern Mountaineer in Fact and Fiction." He was a scholar and teacher, a singer of the old ballads, and a teller of folktales and some of the funniest jokes I ever heard. He was also an attentive listener to Appalachian folk speech.

I became acquainted with the works of Josiah H. Combs, also born in Kentucky, who in 1902 began three years of study at Hindman Settlement School, where I, many years later, served nineteen years on the board of directors. Josiah later graduated from Transylvania University and got a doctorate from the Sorbonne, thanks to his service in France in World War I and the meeting of his French bride, Charlotte Bernard. He taught languages, collected stories and songs, gave ballad recitals, was an authority on Kentucky mountain speech, and was a great raconteur.

These last four scholars came from rather modest circumstances, but their families were part of the Appalachian middle class—about which not much has been written—and all became scholars of Appalachian folkways and made major contributions to the arts, culture, and values of Appalachian people. They inspired me and entertained me, and they also taught me a lot more than I learned in formal schooling. Most of the latter I have forgotten, but I have continued to remember what they taught because it was about me and my people, who have often been ridiculed for their shortcomings.

The purpose of this book is to introduce Lunsford, Combs, Williams, and Roberts to new generations, along with some of the treasured lore that they collected, made sense of, performed with great enjoyment, and preserved for the rest of us. They are "my curious and jocular heroes." In the Southern Mountains there are still two meanings for the adjective "curious," as there were in Middle English. It usually means "inquisitive, eager to learn." However, in terms of personality, it can also mean "strange" or "odd" or just being different from most other people. I added that word carefully to the title of this work to signify how I felt about these four unusual fellows. They each had a rare intelligence and a vast, often subtle, sense of humor, although prudes might complain that their interests included materials that ranged into "off-color" matters. But I want the reader to know that they were rare human beings who were interested in pretty nigh everything about the people they grew up among, who happen to be my people as well. I have met a lot of other "curious" folks along the way, several poets who were just born to be different, and with that difference they looked at all things slaunchwise and helped us to see them in a different way. Over the years, I met other folklorists and learned a lot from them. All of them were different from the general run of people in their individual ways, and I came to treasure that in them, but most of all I loved the way they interacted with people—any kind of people—accepting them and cherishing their ways and lore. For folklorists, it did not matter whether the people they met ever took strong steps to "improve" themselves, which was the mission of most of the religious and educational missionaries whom I also knew and observed. What some of the missionaries did not seem to comprehend was that they were not likely to achieve success with people who felt they were being perceived as unworthy in their present state.

Growing up where I did, I was a natural absorber and teller of stories of all kinds, not just the off-color ones, but also such as "Like Meat Loves Salt" (the tale said to have inspired Shakespeare's *King Lear*), "Jack the Giant Killer," the jokes about the city slicker versus the rube, numbskull stories, and hunting and fishing tales. I heard some of the old ballads—stories-in-song-about-love-gone-wrong, such as "Barbara Allen," "Pretty Polly," and "Poor Omie Wise," as well as those about horrendous accidents like "The Wreck of the Old Ninety-Seven" and "The Titanic," and a few that were bawdy but funny.

The Englishman Cecil Sharp came through our community before I was born and collected songs from Hannah Smith (whose son Franklin, my elementary school principal, once paddled me when he heard me reciting a naughty verse). One of the songs that Hannah Smith gave Sharp was "The Cuckoo," but I can't remember now whether her bird "warbled" or "wobbled" as she flew.

Most of the stories and songs I heard came from the people in the community, but also increasingly from a newfangled invention, the radio, which brought the nation and the world into our landlocked area. I still remember the thrill and the wonder of that hard-earned Sears, Roebuck Silvertone radio, with its twenty-pound battery (we didn't yet have electricity), bringing us the *Grand Ole Opry* from Nashville's WSM, with Bradley Kincaid singing "Barbara Allen" and other traditional ballads and songs. At nighttime, when the reception was good, we could bring in WLS in Chicago and its *National Barn Dance*, WSB in Atlanta, and WBT in Charlotte. Much of this music and humor was familiar because talented mountain boys and girls had taken advantage of the stations' need for talent to help fill the radio hours. Radio also brought us regional, national, and world news, and some new kinds of music and stories.

When I was a teenager and beginning to feel my oats, I somehow came into possession of a book entitled *Anecdota Americana*, with a subtitle that announced it as a collection of "vernacular tales," teaching me a new word. They were bawdy, and I was startled to find them in print. To my great chagrin, the book soon disappeared from its hiding place, no doubt consigned to the fire by my good Baptist mother. It was not something I could inquire about, but it was a remembered loss. Now, with the use of the internet, I find that *Anecdota Americana* was compiled by one William Passemon, with a scholarly preface by a J. Mortimer Hall, and that it was published in Boston, of all places, in 1927, the year before I was born. The publisher, Humphrey Adams, it was noted, did the deed for a perhaps fictional group, the Association for the Asphyxiation of Hypocrites, who added these words: "This book is inscribed to all prudes, puritans, hypocrites, censors, and moralists, that have ever been, are, or shall be." (These words are similar to some written some years later by Josiah Combs and quoted elsewhere in this volume.) The initial printing was a mere 850 copies, and it is a wonder to me now that I somehow, briefly, had one. It gave a defense of off-color stories as a counterweight to the religious, legislative, prudish, and elitist pressures to suppress any mention of what we have to admit are natural parts of our lives. Also, I remember that the editor opined that at least some of these jokes could be told in polite company with a modicum of decorum and tact (although my vocabulary at the time did not contain these last two nouns).

I have probably heard many of the stories from *Anecdota Americana* elsewhere in my life as a collector, teller, reader, and listener of jokes, tales, and stories, but its importance to me was that it made the first impression on me that some of this material was important knowledge about otherwise obscured aspects of the human experience. Just a few years ago, I rediscovered a little black book in which, as a teenager, I had compiled the punch lines of many jokes, but sadly I found that I could not remember all the preceding narratives that went with the punch lines. I do remember many of them and have since heard some of the jokes over and over again.

Much later, I came across a book by the Ozark folklorist Vance Randolph, who singlehandedly did for the Ozarks what it has taken platoons of scholars to do for the Appalachians. He published four volumes of Ozark folksongs and a dozen or more books on the folktales and jokes of his region, as well as articles about the speech and folk culture of the Ozarks. This book was entitled *Pissing in the Snow and Other Ozark Folktales*, published by the University of Illinois Press, with a splendid introduction by the distinguished folklorist Rayna Green, then head of the Division of Home and Community Life at the Smithsonian National Museum. She earlier had written on women's bawdry. Randolph had collected many off-color tales and ballads that could not be published along with his other works during his publishing career. However, after *Pissing in the Snow*, and after his death, at least three other books were published from what he had collected, two of them with the term "unpublishable" in the titles. Most folklorists, including Rayna Green, agree that such material should have been part and parcel of his other folklore, and not published separately, but conventional mores in earlier times dictated otherwise.

All of this leads up to the point that my four heroes also collected suggestive and obscene songs and stories, even though only three made any attempt to publish them. Josiah Combs, an avowed atheist, with the help of his nephew Norris Combs, prepared a manuscript that was rejected although complimented by a literary agent. Leonard Roberts, who came out of a strict Church of Christ background (although he later became a Presbyterian), included some off-color stories in his doctoral dissertation that were eliminated from the published work, *South from Hell-fer-Sartin* (University of Kentucky Press, 1955). The posthumous books from the papers of Cratis Williams, who grew up among conservative United Baptists but later became a Unitarian, had a great repertory of off-color stories. Bascom Lunsford, born into the Victorian age and a Methodist, was restrained in his presentations. The ballad "Katy Morey" and the story "Who Is Your Paw?" are about the only examples of his "suggestive" material.

The reader is hereby warned that I have included several suggestive or obscene songs, stories, articles, and jokes at the ends of the essays about my heroes. However, I think that this material is funny and revealing about these four Appalachian scholars and performers, and also about the human race.

Loyal Jones
Berea, Kentucky

Bascom Lamar Lunsford

It was said that Bascom Lamar Lunsford would cross hell on a rotten rail to learn a funny story, a song, or a banjo or fiddle tune. All his life he not only learned and remembered these things, he was accomplished in performing them. In his time, there was no reliable recording machine, and so he had to learn and remember everything. As a result of this passion, I believe he recorded for posterity more material than any other American, and he logically called this bounty his "memory collection."

Bascom was born in the town of Mars Hill, Madison County, North Carolina, on March 21, 1882. His father, James Bassett Lunsford, was born in eastern Tennessee but moved with his family to western North Carolina before they moved on to Texas. In the Civil War, he served in the Douglas Artillery Battery attached to the 4th Texas Brigade throughout the four years of the Civil War, taking part in major battles and skirmishes, including Chickamauga, Missionary Ridge, and Atlanta. He was wounded in the Battle of Elkhorn Tavern (Pea Ridge) in Arkansas in March 1862 but recovered for the Battle of Richmond, Kentucky, in August of the same year, where he had a horse shot out from under him.

Bascom's mother, Louarta Leah Buckner, was the granddaughter of staunch Unionist Thomas Shepherd Deaver, one of the founders of Mars Hill College, a Baptist school, in a county that was split between Unionists and Confederates. To this day it is called "Bloody Madison," from the execution of thirteen Unionist civilians by a detachment of Confederate soldiers in 1863, with additional bloodletting during and after between the two factions.

James Bassett Lunsford was mostly a self-educated schoolteacher. He carried books with him throughout the Civil War, and he had a love of history and fiddle music. Bascom's mother was a singer of the old ballads and hymns.[1]

Since J. B. Lunsford's education was hard-won, he prized it highly, and he and Louarta dedicated themselves to the intellectual development of their nine children: Gudger, Blackwell, Bascom, Florida Belle, Zilpah, Jennie, Azalea, Kern, and Josepha. All were encouraged to memorize poetry to recite in the home, to tell stories and sing songs, and to learn to play musical instruments. "The house would be called to order," Bascom remembered, "and all would come in and take part. If we had visitors, they could take part just the same. It went on that way . . . as long as we stayed together as a family."[2] The schools in the county also had the custom of reserving Friday afternoons for "declamation." This was an entertainment session at which the students were allowed to recite poems, present musical numbers, or tell entertaining, enlightening, or amusing stories. Bascom acquired a banjo, his brother Blackwell a fiddle, and they played instrumental tunes and sang ballads, hymns, and lyric songs at these family and school events. Such sessions were an important part of their educational experiences.

Lunsford later moved the family near Rutherford College in neighboring Burke County so that the children could further their education. Gudger became a teacher and superintendent of schools in Louisiana, and Blackwell followed him there as a teacher and later a school principal. Florida Belle became a nurse but also studied piano and art and wrote poetry. Zilpah taught school but also became a nurse and an artist. Jennie taught school as well, but later moved to Washington, D.C., and became an occupational therapist. Azalea, too, was a teacher; she studied voice and sang in church choirs. They were part of the mountain "middle class."

Bascom would go on to become a teacher in a one-room school, an apple tree salesman, a college teacher, a lawyer, and a newspaper publisher, among other things, but mainly he was a collector and performer of folklore—ballads and songs, fiddle and banjo tunes, jokes, folktales, and square dance calls. He later started the first festival in the country with "folk" in its name, the Mountain Dance and Folk Festival in Asheville.

His first visit with an informant was at the age of seven, when his father took him to see his mother's brother, Osborne Deaver, "a great fiddler of the old school." Even though Uncle Osborne was a rural farmer and storekeeper at the time, he had served in the Republican administrations in Washington after the Civil War, up until Democrat Grover Cleveland was elected president in 1884. Bascom remembered that his mother had often hummed or sung tunes and songs that she had learned from her brother. "One can imagine my deep interest when . . . I was able to see my aged uncle take his precious violin from the black wooden case . . . , draw the bow across the catgut and glide sweetly into some of the old favorites I could recognize."[3]

When Bascom and Blackwell first acquired their instruments, the elder Lunsford took them to visit other notable musicians in the community or invited such people to their family gatherings, so that the boys could learn from them. Soon Bascom was seeking out additional people who knew the old tunes and songs and who had unusual techniques on stringed instruments. The boy made the banjo his primary instrument, although he also became a fiddler. He commented,

> The banjo brings out the balladry in my system, so at an early age I was a full-fledged ballad singer of the southern Appalachian type. Whereupon, I began the erection of a musical layer-cake, with work and school as a filling, and such social ingredients as bean stringin's, butter stirrin's, apple peelin's, tobacco curin's, candy breakin's, corn shuckin's, log rollin's, quiltin's, house raisin's, serenades, square dances, shoe-arounds, shindigs, frolics, weddings and school entertainments. . . . These contacts brought about the exchange of song ballets between the young people with whom I mingled.[4]

Lunsford collected a great repertory of songs of all types, and he had a strong appreciation for the gifts these musicians gave to him. He always remembered from whom he had learned them, and in later years he made sure that their names were attached to the songs and tunes that he performed. However, he was interested in more than just the rich musical heritage of the Appalachian people. He loved the humorous jokes and stories that were told at almost all gatherings, many of which helped to define rural people of his day and to contrast them with those who lived in towns and cities. He also learned minute details about home life, farming techniques, tools, and the many social affairs that he listed above. Later in life he wrote a hundred-page unpublished manuscript entitled "It Used to Be:

The Memoirs of Bascom Lamar Lunsford," about the way of life he knew as a boy in the waning years of the nineteenth century and at the beginning of the twentieth.[5]

Bascom attended Snow Hill Elementary School in Madison County, where he first saw Nellie Triplett, whom he later married. He also studied at Camp Academy in Leicester, where he was taught by its founder, A. C. Reynolds, who later was offered a teaching job at Rutherford College, where he taught Bascom again at that level. After his freshman year at Rutherford College, Bascom took a teaching job in Madison County, where his two brothers and his sister Jennie were already teaching. He later spoke in detail about the parties and other gatherings that he attended that year in the homes of local people, where they made music, sang, danced, and told stories.

After this year of teaching, Bascom was offered a job with a nursery company, selling fruit trees. He traveled by horseback and buggy to farmsteads in western North Carolina, eastern Tennessee, and the mountain counties of Georgia and South Carolina, taking orders. He stayed with local families when night came, usually sending them a free apple tree afterwards to thank them for the hospitality they had extended to him and his horse. He carried his banjo along and entertained with songs and stories, and found that many of his hosts were musicians and storytellers also. He later described these visits:

> A singing at Sam Higdon's at Ellijay, near the home of Jim Corbin, the noted banjo player, or a square dance at Bascom Picklesimer's on Tesantee, and like events tended to keep me satisfied in the field as a nursery salesman. I recall one occasion in Rabun County, Georgia, I spent the night at the home of Ed Lovell. A fellow sojourner by the name of Brown entertained us during the evening by singing "Lord Lovell." Probably the name of our host brought the old song to mind.[6]

After a year, he joined a man who was in the honey business, establishing bee yards on mountain farms and then collecting the honey for retail sale. Sourwood trees are abundant in the southern Appalachians, with their white springtime blossoms that bees visit to make their celebrated sourwood honey, and so it was a good business. As he promoted bees, he also stayed overnight with numerous families on his circuits and learned additional lore.

Bascom courted Nellie Triplett, from the Leicester community, for several years, and in the summer of 1906, when there was a large honey flow, he had enough cash so that they could get married. They settled in a rented house on the side of Hanlon Mountain, on South Turkey Creek across the valley from the farm where she had grown up. That fall, however, they moved to Rutherford College so he could finish his course of study.

Bascom graduated in 1909, then taught in McDowell County schools the following year. After that, he became supervisor of boys at the North Carolina School for the Deaf in Morganton and began to study law on his own. In 1912 he enrolled at Trinity College (later Duke University) Law School as a second-year student. He received his degree in 1913, and after passing the bar that same year, he took a job as solicitor of Burke County. Additionally, he began teaching English at Rutherford College. There he gave his first formal lecture, in formal attire, "North Carolina Folklore, Poetry and Song." A handbill announcing the event warned, "Those who have scruples against a hearty laugh should stay away."[7] Bascom commented on this lecture,

> My work had given me more confidence in myself. Whether this was well-founded or not, I don't know. So I had arranged a discourse of more than an hour's length on no less a subject than "North Carolina Folklore, Poetry and Song," and while I had slipped away a time or two to deliver it at schools where the teacher was kind enough to take the risk, I really gave it its initial test at Rutherford College. To my surprise and to the startling of the students and the "natives," it went over. The parts of it pertinent to ballads and folksongs, the part I was on nettles about, such as singing with a banjo accompaniment "Swannanoa Tunnel," and "Free a Little Bird," was the high spot in the program.[8]

Probably the best thing to come out of his law degree from Trinity was his composition of the song "Old Mountain Dew." He later defended moonshiners in court, and he introduced his composition in this way: "I give the now familiar song 'Old Mountain Dew,' which originally when I wrote it in 1920 was the story of a young man the first time he was charged in court on a liquor count. It is his plea in court."[9] Lunsford recorded the song for Brunswick Records in 1928 (Br 219). Scott Wiseman, of Lulu Belle and Scotty of *National Barn Dance* fame, who was already friends with Bascom, rewrote the verses, and he and Lulu Belle recorded the song for Vocalion

Records in 1935 (Vo 04690), although they were not allowed to sing it on the *National Barn Dance* and WLS, where reference to intoxicants was forbidden. It became popular, and Bascom was pleased with their recording. When Bascom, who was always short on funds, was in Chicago for the National Folk Festival in 1937, he sold the rights to Wiseman for twenty-five dollars so he could buy a train ticket back to Asheville. Wiseman commented:

> I copyrighted my version and turned it over to a publisher [Tree Publishing Co. and Tannen Music, Inc.]. They secured other recordings, and it began to pay substantial royalty through BMI and other publishers. Next time Bascom came to see me, I told him I had made sure his name was kept on the song as co-writer and would see that he received his portion of the royalties. This pleased him tremendously, and we were good friends until his death.[10]

Numerous country entertainers, including Grandpa Jones, Roy Acuff, and Willie Nelson, have recorded this song, and I remember hearing an orchestral version of the tune on the radio.

Lunsford composed other songs and parodies and recorded them along with his folksongs: "'Nol Pros' Nellie" (Brunswick, Br 230, 1928), "Doggett's Gap" (a parody on "Cumberland Gap"; Library of Congress, 9509B1, 1935), "Bryan's Last Battle" (regarding the Scopes Trial, recorded by OKeh in 1925 but never released), and "Fate of Santa Barbara" (about the 1925 earthquake in that city; OKeh, OK 45008, 1925).[11]

Lunsford had other vocational adventures. After two years teaching at Rutherford College, he became an auctioneer (someone once said he could sell a tin dipper to a spring lizard), and he became the editor and publisher of the *Old Fort Sentinel*.

During World War I, Lunsford attempted to enlist but was declared physically unsuitable. He secured a position with the United State Department of Justice as a special agent, mostly chasing draft dodgers. He apparently got his position through the support of the Democratic Party in North Carolina, and this led to his involvement in politics. Beginning in 1920, he managed three successful campaigns for Zebulon Weaver, who served for many years in the U.S. House of Representatives from the Tenth District. In 1924, he managed an unsuccessful campaign to elect Josiah W. Bailey governor. In 1931, Lunsford was elected reading clerk for the North Carolina House of Representatives. In this job, he ran into controversy. Some eastern North Carolina members of the House said that he did not read distinctly, which cut him to the quick, since he prided himself as a public speaker and a reciter of poetry. The problem no doubt came from Lunsford's "mountain" accent, with its hard emphasis on the "r," from those who spoke what they assumed to be the more elegant Piedmont speech, with its disappearing "r." However, it was none other than Sam J. Irvin Jr., then a young member of the House from Morganton (on the dividing line between these two accents), who successfully defended him against a bill of impeachment. Lunsford served out his term but declined to pursue the job further.

Lunsford was also a man of the church. He was baptized into the Newfound Baptist Church when he was eleven, but Nellie was a Methodist, so he joined her church when they married. In 1920, he became field secretary for the Methodist Epworth League in counties east of the Blue Ridge, which acquainted him with new customs and values.

In 1925, Lunsford moved his family back to the mountains, onto the farm that Nellie and her brother had inherited from their parents on South Turkey Creek, near Leicester. By the time they got settled there, Bascom and Nellie had seven children: Lamar, Kern, Ellen, Lynn, Nelle, Merton, and Josepha Belle.

Up to this point, Bascom was mainly interested in collecting songs and stories to add to his repertory as an entertainer, but he increasingly saw the value of these materials as art, history, humor, and literature. He continued to perform wherever there was an opportunity, and soon he came to the notice of people in the North Carolina Folklore Society. In 1922, he recorded some songs on wax cylinders for Dr. Frank C. Brown of Duke University, who credited him on some material in the seven-volume *Frank C. Brown Collection of North Carolina Folklore* (Durham, N.C.: Duke University Press, 1952–64).

In 1924, he went to Atlanta to record two numbers for OKeh Records, and the next year Polk C. Brockman of OKeh set up a studio in Asheville and recorded Lunsford and some other musicians that Bascom had recommended. Dr. Robert Winslow Gordon, who was later to found the Archive of Folk-Song at the Library of Congress, came to western North Carolina in 1925 and sought out Lunsford as an informant, but also to lead him to others who knew the old songs.

Lunsford went to Ashland, Kentucky, in 1928 to record twelve numbers for the Brunswick label, and in 1930 he recorded two humorous numbers for the Columbia Phonograph Company in Atlanta. One was "Speaking the

Truth," an oral version of a sermon supposedly delivered by an illiterate preacher but originally written by the nineteenth-century humorist William P. Brannan; the other was "A Stump Speech in the Tenth District," a preposterous political oration probably composed by Lunsford in celebration of Zebulon Weaver's success (both on Co 15595-D).

In 1928, Bascom was invited by the Asheville Chamber of Commerce to recruit mountain musicians and dancers to perform at the town's new Rhododendron Festival, organized by the Chamber to entertain the tourists who flocked to the Asheville area for the cooler air in summertime before the age of air conditioning. World War II brought an end to the Rhododendron Festival, but Lunsford's Mountain Dance and Folk Festival thrived and has continued to the present. He sought out singers of the old ballads and songs, banjo pickers, fiddlers, and string bands to perform on its stage. He arranged prizes for the best performers in his categories, and he also helped to organize and teach square dance teams in western North Carolina communities to compete for prizes at his festival. This was the first event in America to be called a "folk" festival, and it has served as a model for other festivals throughout the country.

An important scholarly contact was Dr. Dorothy Scarborough. She was a professor of English at Columbia University, but also a literary critic and writer of fiction. She came to the Southern Mountains in 1930 and sought out Bascom. She described this meeting:

> Before I unpacked my bags, I started in search of Bascom Lamar Lunsford . . . the man who is doing more than anyone else in the region to bring the people to realize the interest and value of the native folk arts, singing, fiddle playing, dancing, and so forth. Presently, he came to see me, a man in his forties, with boyish, open countenance, springy step, and in his eye the light of insanity which denotes a folklorist. Here was [a] sympathetic spirit who would not jeer at me for spending my vacation in the arduous work of collecting songs when I might have loafed.[12]

Lunsford steered Scarborough to the Blue Ridge singers he admired the most, and her work was published posthumously in 1937 by Columbia University Press as *A Song Catcher in Southern Mountains*. It is one of the great collections of folksongs from the southern Appalachians.

In 1933, Sarah Gertrude Knott, a Kentuckian who was an avid lover of folk traditions, attended the Mountain Dance and Folk Festival, which inspired her to organize the National Folk Festival the next year. Bascom was her principal advisor, and he would go on to lead many groups from the mountains to her festivals, which were held in various cities across the country. "We couldn't have gotten a National Folk Festival started without Bascom," Knott said.[13] Lunsford himself went on to organize other folk festivals in North Carolina: at the Cherokee Indian Reservation in Cherokee, at Chapel Hill, and at the North Carolina State Fair in Raleigh.

In March 1937, John Lair invited Lunsford to come to Cincinnati to help in organizing the Ohio Valley Folk Festival, which was to be held at Cincinnati's Music Hall. Sarah Gertrude Knott was behind this idea, believing that it would be a good way to discover talent for the upcoming National Folk Festival to be held in Washington, D.C. Lair, a Kentuckian, had earlier been the librarian and then program director at WLS and had moved that year from Chicago to Cincinnati to stage the beginnings of the *Renfro Valley Barn Dance* on WLW, a show that he moved to the actual Renfro Valley, Kentucky, in 1939. Lunsford had earlier taught dancers to do Appalachian square dancing for Lair's radio and stage shows, and he also scouted out musical talent. Lair told me of Lunsford bringing in a mountaineer fiddler, who Lair doubted would go over in Cincinnati, but laughingly recounted,

> He was a tall red-headed boy . . . and I thought he wasn't worth a dime. I wasn't going to go out there on the stage and put him on. . . . So, I said, "Bascom, you're going to have the honor of introducing your own guest tonight." That pleased him. He got out there and told about this boy and sent him out there. He started to fiddle. He hit about four licks and laid his head back and started bellowing out a song, and he just absolutely, completely swept the house. We couldn't get him off the stage to let the other acts on for ten minutes. We missed the boat. He was the biggest hit of the night, and we didn't want to be associated with him.[14]

The festival filled the fifteen-hundred-seat Music Hall for two days, according to folklorist Alan Lomax, and had some two hundred performers. Lomax, who attended the festival, was critical of it in a journal entry. He thought that since Lunsford was working for Lair, whose main interest was commercial radio shows, it was scarcely a folk event at all, but featured mostly music such as "Little Rosewood Casket" and "Maple on the Hill." Lomax further commented that "Lunsford, feeling that the noisier and more spectacular the act, the better pleased [was] his . . . audience, put on a square dance every five minutes." Lomax felt that "Mr. Lunsford had bungled his job." However, he added, "One felt a marvelous release of folk energy. . . . No question that 'hill-billy' music is following a vigorous development on its own, more or less apart from folk music, and this group of performers thoroughly vindicated its independence with tremendous vigor; but it was obvious that these performers knew a great deal about folk material, too, and there was no excuse for a gathering called a Folk Festival, that did not give this material a chance to speak for itself as well."[15]

During Lunsford's association with Lair, his stationery announced that he was "Entertainer and Instructor in Appalachian Balladry and Folk Dancing," with the following associations: "Folk Dance Director of the Renfro Valley Barn Dance"; "Founder and Director of the Mountain Dance and Folk Song Festival" in Asheville; "Executive Committee National Folk Festival, St. Louis, Chattanooga, Dallas, Chicago"; "Member, United States Section, International Commission on Folk Dance Arts."[16]

No doubt being associated with Lair gave Lunsford opportunities to use his talents and knowledge in ways that he otherwise would not have had and made him known to a much wider public, but Alan Lomax was not the only one who criticized Lunsford about his staging of the folk arts and other matters as well. First and foremost, Bascom's intention was to use the Mountain Dance and Folk Festival to present traditional singers, musicians, and dancers with the support of the Asheville Chamber of Commerce. But, of course, he was also active in hyping culture-changing industrial capitalism and its tourism component, which meant selling "The Land in the Sky" as a place for affluent Americans to spend their summers and their money. The contradictions were obvious, but in Lunsford's mind the industrial boom of the twenties made his work even more crucial. Critics saw the work of the Chamber of Commerce as overwhelming and destroying the folk culture while luring Lunsford into organizing a platform to showcase remnants of this culture.

Others, concerned with the folk traditions of the region, saw Lunsford's work as a one-man show. Marguerite Bidstrup, director of the John C. Campbell Folk School at Brasstown, told me that she invited Lunsford to a meeting of the committee that organized the annual Spring Dance Festival at Berea College. When he saw the size of the group, made up of representatives from private schools, he remarked, "Well, I see you work as a group. I work alone." Others were critical of his staging of the festival, which awarded prizes to the best dancers and musicians, who sometimes exhibited showmanship more than tradition. He was also criticized for allowing or promoting clogging, traditionally a solo performance, to be performed throughout the set dances. The clogging also led to heel and toe taps to accentuate the rhythm, which overpowered the music. Both the smooth dance groups and the clog dance groups also began to wear stage clothing, something that Lunsford had earlier discouraged with his performers.

Ethel Capps, former director of the Berea College Country Dancers, offered her opinion of the influence of the Mountain Dance and Folk Festival on traditional styles:

> When you put it on as a show or as a contest where you win money—what happens is that the people who take part and try to win the prize, they just go to all kinds of lengths to get attention. They try to be as exotic and interesting as they can be, far and above what they would be if they were doing it in a natural kind of way. It will change it. It's like putting hormones on a plant. It makes them too big and too important. Sometimes the effect of tourists on an audience is bad.[17]

However, folklorist Michael Ann Williams, who wrote a fine book entitled *Staging Tradition: John Lair and Sarah Gertrude Knott*, stated that musicologist Charles Seeger was more impressed with Lunsford's festival than he was with Knott's National Folk Festival, feeling that Lunsford was "one of the people," whereas Knott's introductions were "looking down from above." Seeger's son Pete, who attended both festivals, liked both Knott's and Lunsford's "fast-paced" staging. However, Williams wrote, "Pete did not like the limited format that Lunsford employed. He had an all-white festival playing mountain music."[18]

Even though Lunsford collected songs in black churches and schools, he did not challenge the rigid segregation system of the South by including black artists in this festival. And though he worked for the very liberal musicologist Charles Seeger and was hospitable to his radical son Pete, he harbored some of the same biases and prejudices against "outsiders" as did most southerners of his time. Roger Sprung, a Jewish banjo player from New York, would sometimes get onstage by joining an invited band. Bascom once threw him bodily off the stage and reportedly called him "Jew-Boy." However, Sprung later did repair work on Bascom's banjo, and he said that they remained friends through the rest of Bascom's life.[19]

Michael Ann Williams also wrote of Lunsford's difficulty during the Folk
Revival:

> [H]e was uncomfortable with the personal and political style of youthful
> revivalists. In addition, a competing folk festival organized along Newport
> lines had its debut in Asheville in 1963 with the support of the Chamber
> of Commerce but, luckily for Lunsford, it lost money and did not survive.
> Lunsford also faced challenges from within. Attendance at the Mountain
> Dance and Folk Festival slumped, and some within the Chamber of Com-
> merce felt he had become too old [to run it]. At least some astute members,
> though, realized that Lunsford *was* the festival and suggested that publicity
> be built around him. He continued to be a presence at the Mountain Dance
> and Folk Festival until his death in 1973.[20]

During the 1960s and early 1970s, liberals and radical activists criticized
Lunsford for not taking a stand on social issues. Some of them seemed
to think that folk music and liberalism were linked together and seemed
surprised when they found that Lunsford was not a social activist like they
were. Perhaps the harshest critic of his conservative outlook was writer
Bill Finger, who published an article in *Southern Exposure* entitled "Bascom
Lamar Lunsford: The Limits of a Folk Hero." Although he praised Lunsford
for knowing the value of regional history and folklore long before others did,
he condemned his lack of a social conscience and his failure to fight against
the exploitive forces that were imperiling the traditional culture. He wrote:
"His was not a voice of political struggle; he did not involve himself in the
labor struggles of the thirties or forties, nor did he often speak out against
the potential dangers of land development. In fact, he disapproved of the
political music of great balladeers like Woody Guthrie and Pete Seeger."
Finger also suggested that "[t]he long verses of the English ballads lacked
the contemporary poignance of protest songs from the textile or paper
mills."[21] It is obvious that some of Bascom's critics were trying to remake
him in their image. He was what he was.

In 1935, at the urging of Dorothy Scarborough, George W. Hibbitt, a
professor in the English Department at Columbia University, invited Lunsford to come to New York and record what Bascom called his "memory
collection." He did so in a two-week session, recording some 315 ballads,
lyric songs, hymns, fiddle and banjo tunes, square dance calls, and stories,
usually with comments on when and how and from whom he had come to

learn each item. It took seventy-nine twelve-inch aluminum disks to hold all of Bascom's memory collection.[22] The *New York Herald Tribune* took notice of his visit:

> Bascom Lamar Lunsford, "minstrel of the Appalachians," who is making phonographic recordings for the Columbia University Library of 300 of the many mountain ballads, fiddle tunes and dance calls he has learned in his native Carolina hills, gave a concert for sixty students of American folklore in Philosophy Hall yesterday.
>
> Mr. Lunsford, who passes more time in collecting folksongs than in his lawyer's office in Asheville, N.C., explained that he had never taken singing lessons because he wanted to show only the folk value and not the entertainment value of his songs. He accompanied himself on the fiddle and the banjo, both of which he plays by ear. . . .
>
> George W. Hibbitt, English instructor, who is conducting the recordings, had him lecture to his class yesterday, and he has given a few informal concerts around the campus.[23]

Also in 1935, Lunsford was recruited by Charles Seeger to work in two New Deal programs, the Works Progress Administration and the Resettlement Administration, to promote the folk arts in southern communities, especially in the Special Skills Division of the Resettlement Administration in North Carolina and the Skyline Farms project in Scottsboro, Alabama. Seeger had a political motive for promoting the arts as part of the New Deal Programs. He believed that "proletarian music is an integral part of the question of social evolution. . . . Music is one of the cultural forms through which the work of humanizing and preparation operates. Thus it becomes 'a weapon in the class struggle.'"[24] Lunsford was to the right of Seeger politically, but he believed some of the same things about the importance of the arts. He was willing to go along with Seeger's ideas about the musical arts of the people, but he later made it known that he disapproved of using the music as an instrument of politics.

In 1939, Lunsford was invited by President and Mrs. Roosevelt to bring singers and dancers to the White House to perform for the visiting King George and Queen Elizabeth of Great Britain. Mrs. Roosevelt wanted to present the royal couple with a cross-section of American music, so among those invited were folklorist Alan Lomax, popular singer Kate Smith, opera baritone Lawrence Tibbett, John Lair of the *Renfro Valley Barn Dance*, and the Coon Creek Girls (the Ledford sisters, Lily May, Rosie, and Susie). Lunsford brought Sam Queen and his Soco Gap Dancers from North Carolina and the Skyline Farms Dancers from Alabama. John Lair related a story about Lunsford at this event:

> When we were in the reception line to meet the king and queen and President and Mrs. Roosevelt, Lunsford told us how well he knew Mrs. Roosevelt. She'd met him down at the White Top Festival in Virginia. But as we began to get close, he got cold feet, and he said, "Now, John, she may not remember me. It's been some time and she may not remember me at all." When we got up close to her, she said, "Why, Bascom!" She threw both arms around his neck and pulled him over. I thought he was going to faint, he was shaking so.[25]

Two events occurred during this day and evening that reveal how much closer to folk roots American governmental leaders were then than they are now. Lily May Ledford of the Coon Creek Girls related the first episode:

> We went over early for a rehearsal. The people in charge wanted us to run through what we were going to do that night. We went through it all. A distinguished-looking gentleman came to the door and listened for a while. He said, "How long have you been playing?" I said I had been playing for a long time. He said, "I play a little myself. Could we play some together? Let me go get my fiddle. I'll be right back." He introduced himself. He said, "I'm Cactus Jack." That's all he said. We went over to another room. He'd play a tune, then I'd play one, and then we'd play one together for quite a long time. It was later I found out that that was the vice president, John Nance Garner. That was Cactus Jack.[26]

That evening, Bascom picked the banjo with the string band while Sam Queen called such square dance figures as "Dive and Shoot the Owl," "London Bridge," and "King's Highway." Afterwards, Cordell Hull, then secretary of state and a former U.S. congressman and senator from Tennessee, came forward and bragged that he could dance any figure that Bascom or Sam Queen could call.[27]

After John Lair moved his *Renfro Valley Barn Dance* to its namesake valley near Mt. Vernon, Kentucky, it became extremely popular over WLW in Cincinnati and later WHAS in Louisville. He started two other radio shows, *Monday Night in Renfro Valley* and the *Renfro Valley Gatherin'*, which aired on Sunday mornings. He also staged other activities, such as harvest festivals, horse shows, and later tent shows that traveled over many states. After concocting the idea for a Red Bud Folk Festival, he hired Lunsford to come and organize it in 1946, with music, dance, and a beauty contest exclusively for red-headed women. Among them was Jean Ritchie, then a social work student and later a Phi Beta Kappa graduate of the University of Kentucky, and it was at this festival that she was first recorded for the Library of Congress by balladeer, actor, and folklorist Artus Moser, whom Lunsford had brought to the event. According to Michael Ann Williams in *Staging Tradition*, Lair and Lunsford showed that they had learned from Sarah Gertrude Knott's experience with her National Folk Festival. They invited a wide variety of amateur artists to come at their own expense to perform. They included an all-black group from a segregated Richmond, Kentucky, school to sing spirituals; a group of dancers from the Cherokee Reservation in North Carolina; groups of singers from Berea College and the Highlander Folk School; gifted fiddlers Bill Hensley and Dock Roberts; and many others.[28] This festival, imaginative as it was, did not endure. The redbud trees were ruled by the weather rather than the calendar, and perhaps there was also a scarcity of red-headed beauties.

In 1949 Lunsford was selected by Duncan Emrich, who directed the Archive of American Folk Song at the Library of Congress, to represent the United States at the International Folk Festival in Venice, Italy, both to perform and to demonstrate and teach Appalachian square dances. It was a huge deal for Bascom. He took fiddler Henry Hudson and Lillie Lee Baker, a Texas dance leader, with him. A particular pleasure, he noted, was riding in a Boeing Stratocruiser at 35,000 feet while picking "Sourwood Mountain" on his banjo. Beatrice McLain, former director of the Southern Folklife Center at the University of Alabama, told me about a square dance that Bascom led in St. Mark's Square while bewildered Venetians watched.

A big thrill was visiting England on his way back from the festival. Because of his love of the British ballads and poetry that he had memorized and frequently quoted, he felt a close friendship with England. While in London he gave a program at the Cecil Sharp House, named for the English dance and song collector who led the folk revival in England and also collected songs and dances in the Appalachians from 1916 to 1918.[29]

In 1949, Emrich invited Lunsford to Washington, D.C., to rerecord his memory collection on newer equipment at the Archive of American Folk Song. In a one-week session, the archive recorded and listed 317 items, although Lunsford claimed 350. This and the earlier recording session at Columbia University, as well as other recordings, show that his total memory repertory indeed was about 350 items. Even though the equipment was supposed to be better at the Library of Congress, the quality of some of the recordings was poor.

Between 1947 and 1976, Bascom recorded forty-five numbers that were released by commercial recording companies on 33⅓ discs: *Smoky Mountain Ballads*, eight numbers (Folkways Records, Folk FP 40, 1953); *Minstrel of the Appalachians*, fourteen numbers (Riverside Records, RLP 12–645, 1956); and *Music from South Turkey Creek*, twenty-five numbers (with George Pegram and Red Parham; Rounder Records, Rounder 0065, 1956).

Although Lunsford spoke with authority on folk subjects, he wrote relatively little. When asked, he would contribute articles explaining his work, and for a time he wrote a regular column for the *Asheville Citizen*. In the mid-twenties, Robert Winslow Gordon, who a few years later would found the Archive of American Folk Song at the Library of Congress, visited Lunsford, who toured him around to meet singers and musicians. Gordon edited a column called "Old Songs That Men Have Sung" in *Adventure* magazine, and he announced in 1926 in that journal that Lunsford had agreed to become the magazine's official collector in western North Carolina. When Bascom was asked, he would write articles explaining his work. For example, the editor of *Southern Life*, a magazine devoted to country clubs and outdoor subjects, asked Lunsford to contribute articles to that publication.[30] He collaborated with fellow North Carolinian Lamar Stringfield, a classical composer, flutist, and symphony conductor, on *30 and 1 Folk Songs from the Southern Mountains* (New York: Carl Fischer, 1929). And with cowriter George Stephens, a long-time admirer and friend, he published a well-illustrated instruction book, *It's Fun to Square Dance: Southern Appalachian Calls and Figures* (Asheville, N.C.: Stephens Press, 1942), which went into many printings. His book of memoirs was never published.

Two film documentaries featured Lunsford. The first, *Music Makers of the Blue Ridge*, premiered on NET in 1964 and was later broadcast on PBS as part of the American Experience series. It was made by filmmakers David Hoffman and Jonathan Gordon, as Bascom took them to visit some of his favorite Blue Ridge musicians and dancers. He had some difficulties with Hoffman and Gordon, partially, perhaps, because both were urban and Jewish, and they differed in their opinions on which artists to film, with Bascom preferring those who best reflected his sense of aesthetics and tradition, and the filmmakers preferring to seek out those who were more colorful and stereotypical.[31] Long after Lunsford's death, Hoffman returned to do another documentary on his life, *Ballad of a Mountain Man* (1989), also included in PBS's American Experience series, with Alan Lomax and Mike Seeger interviewed as the experts on Lunsford's career.

Smithsonian/Folkways brought out a compact disc, *Ballads, Banjo Tunes, and Sacred Songs of Western North Carolina* (SF CD 40082), in 1996, produced by Wayne Martin, director of the Folklife Program of the North Carolina Folk Arts Council, and Jo Lunsford Herron, Bascom's youngest daughter. I did the biographical notes.

The total Lunsford collection at the Library of Congress, including handwritten and printed material, is said to be the largest from a single individual. The bulk of the material Lunsford gathered over a lifetime, including a twenty-eight-by-thirty-inch scrapbook, eight inches thick, containing almost every mention of him in newspapers and other periodicals, is in the Mars Hill University Library. Recently, this scrapbook was professionally cleaned, digitized, sealed, and rebound, at a cost of $10,000. Significant copies of materials, including recordings, are also in the archives of the University of North Carolina at Chapel Hill and at Berea College.

Nellie Lunsford suffered a paralyzing stroke in 1956 and spent the rest of her life in a nursing home, dying in the spring of 1960. Later that year Lunsford married Freda Metcalf English, a Tennessee singer and guitarist who had been a frequent performer at the Mountain Dance and Folk Festival, as well as on area radio stations. Bascom suffered two strokes in 1965 that put an end to his performing career, but he recovered enough to move with Freda into an apartment in West Asheville, where I interviewed him. He was still able to talk fluently and could sing stanzas of songs to illustrate what he was talking about.

All of Bascom and Nellie's children did well. Kern attended nursing schools and became a nurse-anesthetist. Lamar graduated from North Carolina State University and taught vocational agriculture at various high schools. Ellen attended Blanton's Business College and worked as a secretary in a brokerage firm and in governmental offices in Washington, D.C. Lynn graduated from the Carolina School of Commerce and was a high school secretary. Nelle studied at Boyd Business College in Washington, D.C., and was a church secretary. Merton, still living, studied at Berea College and Blanton's Business College. She and her late husband ran a farm on South Turkey Creek. Josepha (Jo) studied at Boyd Business College and American University in Washington, D.C., and was a March of Dimes and Girl Scout executive.

Mars Hill College declared September 6, 1969, to be Bascom Lamar Luns-ford Day in recognition of his contributions to the region. In the evening, a folk festival was held, patterned after the one he had directed in Asheville for forty-one years. Performers responded in large numbers, and a huge crowd assembled. It was such a success that, with Bascom's blessing, it was decided to make it an annual event. Now held during the first week of October and known as the Bascom Lamar Lunsford "Minstrel of Appalachia" Festival, it has been going strong ever since.

On August 2, 1973, Bascom attended his last Mountain Dance and Folk Festival. With burdened step, he was assisted to the microphone as the audience came to their feet, some remembering the early festivals when he had served as master of ceremonies, picked and sung, fiddled, called square dances, and buck-danced with agility and joy. His body was now frail and bent, but he stood with dignity in his white suit and red carnation and greeted the gathering in a surprisingly strong voice. He sang a verse of "Sourwood Mountain," then summoned the fiddlers to play "Gray Eagle" to open the festival. Then he was helped to a seat in the wings, where he listened, watched, and greeted friends and admirers. He attended all three nights of the event and on the last asked for a calendar to see when the next year's festival would be. Presiding onstage was his son Lamar, who had been serving as the festival's primary master of ceremonies since his father's stroke.

Two weeks later, Lunsford grew ill and was taken to a hospital, where his family gathered around, including his ninety-five-year-old brother Black-well, with whom he had first performed the music of the mountains. On September 4, Bascom died. He was ninety-one.

Stories about him appeared in major regional and national publications. Dr. Fred Bentley, the president of Mars Hill College, gave the eulogy at his funeral:

> Bascom Lunsford saw . . . values which to him were as sacred as life itself. . . . his commitment to a cause, a principle, a way of life, preserved what so many were running from and others were seeking to change. He has seen the pendulum make a full swing. The ballads, tales and dances which were expressed by our grandparents, mostly abandoned by their children, are now reborn in their grandchildren. This rebirth could not have occurred had it not been for the man known as "the Minstrel of the Appalachians."[32]

David Whisnant, a professor of English and American studies at the University of North Carolina, summed up the importance of Lunsford's work in an *Appalachian Journal* article, "Finding the Way between the Old and the New: The Mountain Dance and Folk Festival and Bascom Lamar Lunsford's Work as a Citizen":

> The importance of Lunsford's Mountain Dance and Folk Festival extends far beyond its local context in western North Carolina. As the earliest of the folk festivals, it was an important seed-bed for hundreds of other festivals later spread across the United States. . . . It contributed to substantial cultural revitalization inside the region and projected a new image of regional culture to a national and international audience through media coverage and guest appearances by some of its regular performers at the White House and elsewhere. It constituted an important transitional cultural form between "the old and the new"—between the old rural, traditional, community and family-based culture and the emerging urban, industrial, media-dominated mass culture that swept through the mountains as it did through the rest of the country. It furnishes a complex and instructive example of intentional intervention into traditional culture by a forceful entrepreneur.[33]

Forty years after his death, musicians, scholars, and others are still visiting archives to learn about Lunsford and the materials he collected, performed, and passed on through his recordings. People are still writing about him and creating art linked to him. Mars Hill College commissioned playwright Randy Noojin to write a play based on Bascom. *The Memory Collection: The Legend of Bascom Lamar Lunsford* was staged in 2007 by the Appalachian Repertory Theater. In 2011, the Parkway Playhouse in Burnsville, North Carolina, produced *Along about Sundown*, written by two of Bascom's great-nieces, playwrights Sandra Mason and Brenda Lilly. In 2012, Kazoo Films released a narrative feature film, *If I Had Wings to Fly: A New Movie about Old-Time*.[34] It was produced by two film students at New York University, Bruno Seraphin and Harrison Topp. It features Lunsford's voice throughout in speech and song, but the actors and singers are current young musicians from western North Carolina. Edward Herron, Bascom's grandson, has recently signed a contract with Smithsonian/Folkways to do a boxed set of Lunsford's music—180 songs on seven CDs, due out soon.

Bascom Lamar Lunsford's work lives on.

Jokes, Stories, Songs, and Recitations
That Lunsford Liked to Perform

✺ Where the Lion Roareth and the Whang-Doodle Mourneth for Its First-Born

This sermon parody was originally published by the mid-nineteenth-century humorist William P. Brannan in 1865 as "The Hardshell Baptist Strikes Ile." Brannan also wrote "The Harp of a Thousand Strings." Both pieces were learned and performed by humorists and orators and thus became part of the oral tradition. Lunsford recorded the sermon parody, with local references, for the Columbia Phonograph Company in Atlanta in 1930 (150228-2, Columbia 125595-D) and for Columbia University in 1935, from which recordings this text is taken. Benjamin A. Botkin also recorded him performing it in January 1949 in Asheville, and that version can be found in the Benjamin A. Botkin Collection at the Library of Congress.

This type of sermon existed at about the time flatboats were going down the Mississippi, say about 1885. I'm giving it here because, as it sounds—I'm not referring to its meaning here, but as it sounds—as a type of sermon that sometimes might be heard in some communities in the Great Appalachian region.

Imagine a country audience with the minister ready to start his sermon.

Brethern and sistern, I do not come before you this evening to engage in any grammar talk or college highfalutin'. But I come to prepare a pervarse generation for the day of wrath, and my text when you find it you'll find tis somewhere a'twixt the lids of this old Bible from the first chapter of Second Chronicles to the last chapter of Timothy-Titus and when you find it you'll find it in these words: "And they shall gnaw a file and flee into the mountains of Hespudam where the lion roareth and the whang-doodle mourneth for its first-born."

Now my brethern there's different kinds of files. There's the rattail file, and there's the handsaw file, and there's a cross-cut file, and there's the profile and the defile, but the text says that they shall gnaw a file and flee into the mountains of Hespudam where the lion roareth and the whang-doodle mourneth for its first-born.

And my brethern there's different kinds of dams. There's Amsterdam, and then there's Rotterdam, and there's Beaverdam, but the last of all and the worst of all my brethern is I don't give a damn! But the text says that they shall gnaw a file and flee into the mountains of Hespudam where the lion roareth and the whang-doodle mourneth for its first-born.

Now my brethern, this reminds me of the man who lived up on the north fork of Little Pine Creek in Madison County, North Carolina. He had a little mill but it ground a heap of corn. But one night the fountain of the great deep was broken up and the windows of heaven were opened and the rains descended and the winds came and it washed that man's mill dam to kingdom come. And he got up the next morning, and he told the good old wife of his bosom that he wasn't worth a damn. But the text says that they shall gnaw a file and flee into the mountains of Hespudam where the lion roareth and the whang-doodle mourneth for its first-born.

My brethern, this doesn't mean the howling wilderness where John the Hard-Shell Baptist fed on locusts and wild asses, but it means the city of New Orleans, the mother of harlots and hard lots where corn is six bits a bushel one day and nary a red the next. And where thieves and pickpockets go skittering about like weasels in a barnyard, and where honest men are sca'cer ner hen's teeth, and where a woman once took up your beloved teacher and bam-boozled him out of a 127 plunks, in three jerks of the eye, or a twinkling of the sheep's tail, but she can't do it again, Hallelujah!

✺ A Stump Speech in the Tenth District

It is my opinion that Lunsford wrote this mock speech, but it may be that he learned it from someone else. He recorded it for Columbia Records in Atlanta during the same session as the preceding item in 1930 (Columbia 15595-D). The music on this recording was performed by the famous Georgia Skillet Lickers, who happened to be in the studio at the time. This last information came to me in a conversation with Bert Layne, a member of the band. Lunsford also performed a somewhat different version of this speech, obviously from memory, for folklorist Benjamin A. Botkin when he visited Asheville in January 1949. It was published in his A Treasury of Southern Folklore (New York: Crown, 1949), p. 250. It is puzzling that Lunsford did not include it in his recording sessions at Columbia University in 1935 or at the Library of Congress in 1949, or reveal its origin. The piece has some traditional elements; for example, the bit on farm relief was used by Uncle Dave Macon on his 1929 recording Farm Relief (Vocalion 5341). It was a widespread joke of the time.

Gentlemen and fellow citizens of the good old county of Buncombe. The first thing I say is that I want to thank the ladies for bringing me these pretty flowers. The next is that I want to compliment the boys for that splendid fiddling and say that we'll have some more out'n them before we leave. And thirdly permit me to again remind you that I am an independent candidate for the Lower House, and at our next election I expect to represent this district in Congress.

I'm glad to see so many of you farmers out here today. You come, some of you, with your feet on the ground and your hair stickin' out'n the top of your hat a-fightin' for farm relief, when you don't know what you're fightin' for. Looks to me like you've already been relieved of about everything you ever had, but you better leave that to me after I get there.

My platform is like one of your hillside plows. When I gets to one end, I just turn the wing over and plow back t'other way, a simple twist of the wrist. That's all.

Fellow citizens, the Old Tenth is the grandest district in North Carolina. It stretches from the crest of Mt. Mitchell on the east to Hanging Dog Township in Cherokee County on the west, from the Great Smoky Mountain Park on the north to Spicer's Cove in the Dark Corners to the south.

It stretches from the headwaters of the Nantahala to the mouth of South Turkey Creek.

Yes, some of you say that the women are agin' me in this campaign, and I'll tell you fer why. They know they can't brow-beat me around and have me to do things that I han't orter.

But I have stumped every township in this district and here's how I stand. I break even with them in Willyshot. I'll walk away with them in Sugar Loaf. I'm neck and neck with them in Bear Waller, and when it comes to Lower Fork, you boys know I've always stayed with them there.

I want to tell the dear people that this is a momentous campaign and getting more momentous as the day approaches, and let me tell you fer why. You can't beat Hoover on one hand, nor Max Gardner [a former governor of North Carolina] on t'other, but I beg of you don't let 'em beat me.

My opponent claims he's got his preparation for office between college walls. I don't deny it of him, but I got my schoolin' a-plowin' a bull in the meadow where the sun don't shine 'til 10 o'clock of a mornin' and sets before the shank of the evenin', and yet just watch me take my graduatin' exercises a-ridin' that jackass into the Capitol!

Now boys, all of you that are willin' to help me out in this fight and help me put this rotten ring out of business, just come forward, and while the boys play a lively tune get one of these fruit jars. You'll find a two-dollar bill in the bottom of it. Take it out the back way up 'cross the fence into the pasture to the mouth of the Stillhouse Branch, and you boys will know the rest.

❁ Now Brethren, Be Mighty Careful

This story was widely told throughout the country South and implies that not all marriages are idyllic. This and the following stories are from "It Used to Be: The Memoirs of Bascom Lamar Lunsford," pp. 143–55, a copy of which is in the Bascom Lamar Lunsford Collection, SAA 29, Southern Appalachian Archives, Hutchins Library, Berea College, Berea, Kentucky, box 2, folder 5. Most of this collection came originally from the Bascom Lamar Lunsford Collection at Mars Hill University, Mars Hill, North Carolina.

It seems that a man's wife had gotten sick and she died. The neighbors came to help, and they provided for the casket. They came in and made the arrangements, and neighbors were pallbearers. When they had the service, they called on the pallbearers to carry the casket out to the cemetery. They had to go around this little steep hill, and one of the fellows slipped. That let down his part of the load. The other men slipped, and the coffin dropped down, the lid flew off. The woman was jolted, so she raised up and spoke a word or two. Of course, they were scared when she came back to life. They assisted her and carried her home, and people were frightened very much. But she recovered and got well and lived several years after that. Then she grew sick again and lingered along and died. So they had the same friends to come again and they had another casket and they had the funeral service. They called on the same brethren to act as pallbearers, and they started out. Of course, the bereaved husband walked behind the casket with the minister. They got to this same little hill in the turn of the walk, and the husband says, "Now brethren, now be mighty, mighty careful." He says, "You remember what a terrible accident happened here three or four years ago right at this same place."

✸ Is That Your Paw?

Lunsford's story reflects a bit of tragic history. The basic story is widely told, and it profoundly reveals the fact that reality and eulogies often differ.

The flu epidemic of 1918 was a fearful time, because in a small town often there was hardly enough people who were well enough themselves to wait on the sick and bury the dead. From that, this story, they said, originated. The undertakers were busy, ministers were busy, doctors were busy, and nurses were busy, and everybody was busy. A woman lost her husband. They had some small children. Finally they got an undertaker to come out, and they made arrangements about the funeral. Of course, there was going and coming at the churches. It was hard to get even an hour to conduct a funeral. But finally they went out to the funeral with the proper arrangements. The minister [apparently a stranger to the family] began his discourse. He talked about what a good father the deceased had been, what a good provider he was, how well he was thought of among his fellow men and the people he dealt with and the people he'd worked with. He spoke of how good he had been to his family and his church and so on. He spoke very complimentary about this unfortunate man. The woman . . . bent over and spoke to her little son and says, "You look over there, honey, and see if that is really your paw."

✳ Who Is Your Paw?

Jokes like this one reflect on matters that are not always openly discussed.

We were going down the road, and we came to this house. There was a little boy standing by the road just crying and crying.

We stopped, and we heard the biggest racket you ever heard up in the house.

"What's the matter, son?"

"Why, Maw and Paw are up there fightin'."

"Who is your Paw, son?"

"Well, that's what they are fightin' over."

✳ Where's My Big Toe?

Type 366

This type of story was used to frighten children. It and variants such as "Tailypoe" and "The Golden Arm" have been collected over most of the United States and are of Old World origin. Mark Twain gave a version of "The Golden Arm" in How to Tell a Story and Other Essays *(New York: Harper and Brothers, 1897), pp. 7–15, and Stephen Wade informed me that he had told "Tailypoe" thousands of times as part of his* Banjo Dancing *show.*

This is a scary story to tell children along about dark. I heard my mother tell this one about an old man—a crooked old man—who had a wife, a crooked old woman. They'd been living quite a while, a long time, in a little old crooked house. They'd work around in the garden. They planted a long, crooked potato patch up and down the branch, and it crooked along with the branch. One day, they were in the garden digging those potatoes with their crooked hoe. As they were digging, they dug up a long, crooked big toe, and they asked what to do about that.

"Well," they said, "we'll just take it on to the house with the rest of the potatoes."

So they did, and they went on to the house, and they washed the potatoes, and they got out the crooked pot, and they put all the potatoes in that. When they came to the toe, he said, "What'll we do?"

"Well," she said, "let's put it in and cook it with the potatoes."

By the time they put the potatoes on, it was gettin' along toward dark.

They sat there and once in a while they'd take the crooked shovel and they'd rake out some coals and throw 'em over the lid [of the Dutch oven] and talk and wonder when the potatoes would be done. When they got them out, they were ready, and then they found the crooked toe to see if it was done. They said, "Yes, it's done too." They put it out on the plates and put the potatoes out, and about that time, they heard an unusual noise outside, way off, and they listened.

"Where's——my——big——toe?" (in a big quavering voice). "Where's my big toe? Where's my big toe?"

And they said, "What is that?"

"I don't know. What is it?"

"I don't know."

Then it sounded closer. "Where's my big toe?"

And they said, "What could that be?"

"Why, I don't know. What could that be?"

"I don't know."

Well, they went on eating again. Once again, they heard, "Where's my big toe?"

The crooked old woman says, "Go out, old man, and see what that is."

He went out and looked all around, and he come back, and he said, "I didn't see nothing."

"Didn't you see nothing?"

"Naw, I didn't see nothing. You go out there."

She got up, and she went out and looked all around, and she came back in and she said, "Old man, I didn't see nothing."

They started eating again, and again they heard, "Where's my big toe?"

"Well," they said, "let's both go out."

They both went out, and they went all around the house, and they came back in the house, and they looked up the chimney. They saw something up there—big long claws, big long bushy tail, and it had eyes just as fierce as could be that looked like coals of fire, and he says, "What's them big eyes for?"

And it says, "To look you through."

"What's them big claws for?"

"To dig your grave."

"What's them big teeth for?"

"TO CHOMP YOUR BONES!"

✳ A Mortgage on the Hogs

Some of these stories, as well as songs, were first printed in my book Minstrel of the Appalachians: The Story of Bascom Lamar Lunsford *(Lexington: University Press of Kentucky, 2002), with permission. I have edited some of them slightly to make better sense.*

An interesting story happened over at Old Fort, North Carolina. Alec Burnett, a mountaineer, lived up there on Mill Creek. He was a waggish kind of fellow, and he had a habit of drinking. I knew him very well. He had fun wherever he went. He had been down at Old Fort and bought a cow [on credit] from some fellow down about Greenlee by the name of Tooten Williams, I believe. He'd gotten ahold of some booze somewhere along the line. He had a little pistol. It occurred to him that it would be fun to run the cow through Old Fort and fire off the pistol. He did it, and they hailed him before the magistrate and fined him 10 dollars and the cost.

"Well," he said, "I don't have a cent of money."

"Well, can we secure this," the magistrate said, "in something?"

"The cow's not mine."

"Well, haven't you got something else?"

"I've got an old Civil War rifle."

"We'll put that down. Anything else?"

"Well, I've got some hogs."

"Well," he said, "we'll take that. How many?"

"Well," he said, "five, five or six; we'll just say five."

"Well," he said, "all right, we'll take a mortgage on the hogs and the rifle."

So they wrote out the mortgage to secure the amount that he owed, a rifle and five bay hogs . . . with brown noses and short tails, and so on, on Mill Creek. In the fullness of time he defaulted in the payment of the mortgage, and the magistrate asked him about it, and he said, "You'll just have to gather up the hogs. I can't pay." So one morning the officer, the deputy, came up to Mill Creek at his home to get the hogs, and he said, "They're up the hollow here." He says, "All right, we'll have to go up and get them." They started on up there and he passed around the chimney corner and he picked up a mattock. He put it on his shoulder and he walked on up a little higher. He went to go around a turn in Mill Creek, a little walkway making a turn around the hill, and he says, "You'll have to be pretty quiet. Them hogs are pretty wild."

He says, "They are not all that wild, are they?"

"Oh," he said, "yes, they're pretty wild. I guess you know'd they was groundhogs, didn't you?"

"Well," he said, "what about the gun?'

"Well," he says, "the gun, I left that in Seven Pines [the site of a Civil War battle] I set it down agin a tree and run, and you can have it if you want to go after it."

❊ Peach Tree Street

Almost everyone knows about the old Peach Tree Street in Atlanta.

Many of us have heard the old story about the Southerner who's always been used to the comforts of life, but as times grew hard, he got in want. Although he stayed immaculately clean, his clothes were ragged. He never got enough to eat, and he was very much disturbed about it, and he did not know what to do. So, he decided to seek counsel, and he went along the street—Peach Tree Street—to where a stairway led up to some law offices, and he waited around the door. A lawyer came down, and he said, "I would like to talk with you just a little."

The lawyer said, "Well, we'll go back in the office. I was just going out for a little lunch."

"Well," he said, "I wouldn't want to do that. In fact, that's my trouble, I don't have any money, and I never begged in my life. I'm hard put to it now, and I don't know what to do. I'm not sick, but I am weak, and I'm bewildered trying to think what I ought to do, how to get on my feet. I don't want to beg, as I stated. I don't have any acquaintances that can help me. I'm ragged, I'll admit it. I hate to mention it, but I try to stay clean. But I just don't know what to do. If I went to apply for a job in my condition, it would just be impossible to get it, and it would defeat what I would want."

"Well," he says, "we can go up in the office and talk."

"Well," the man says, "I wouldn't want to do that. I—I . . ."

"Well," he says, "I feel like I know your position. Now you've told me a straight story about this, and I believe you. And I believe if I were you in your place, I'd go way down on Peach Tree Street. There's nice homes along there, and I'd go down there, and I'd go up to the front door and ring the bell, and when the lady comes out, you just explain what you have said to me in just the way you have said it. They'll help you, do something for you and fix it where you might be more presentable to talk with somebody else. That's what I'd do."

"Well," the man said, "I'm going to act on your advice."

So he went a little ways down on Peach Tree Street, and he saw a nice home some little distance from the street. He walked up to it and rang the bell. A lady came out and he gave her his story. Well, she was impressed with it, and she felt just about like the man had back at the office. She said, "It may be that I can help you. Come in and sit down." She said, "My husband's got a suit that would just about fit you, and I think I'll let you have it. You can go to that room and put on the suit, and I'll see if I can prepare a little food for you. You go on and prepare."

So he went and changed his clothes, and he looked nice. He came down, and she was surprised with his looks but rather overcome by his saddened condition, and she said, "I think you should stay here until you can get control of yourself and get your morale back. I just think you ought to do that."

He said, "Well, I have no reason to stay here, no excuse."

"Well," she said, "that would be perfectly all right. You ought to do that. Then when you get out, you'll have more confidence in yourself and so on."

About that time, the door opened and the husband came in, and she said to him, "This is my cousin. I haven't seen him since he was a little boy. He's going to stay with us for a few days, and I'll be glad to have him. Now, you boys talk while I go and prepare us something to eat."

So, she turned and went out and left the fellow there as if he were her distant cousin, and the husband looked at him from head to foot, and he said, "Why, damn you, I told you to go *way down* on Peach Tree!"

There were many hard-luck stories told during the Great Depression. I heard Pappy Taylor, an old-time country music performer, tell this one about how poor they were. He said one of his children woke him up one night and whispered, "I think I hear a burglar in the house." He whispered back, "Be real quiet. If he finds anything, we'll get up and take it away from him." Grandpa Jones, of Grand Ole Opry and Hee Haw fame, said his family was so poor that they couldn't afford any clothes for him, but when he got to be sixteen years old, they bought him a hat and let him look out the window.

Social Life on the Farm

All the following items in this category are from Lunsford's memoir "It Used to Be," pp. 34–41.

One of the outstanding things about farm life years ago were the social pastimes connected with the economic life—that is, the custom of work-ings, like corn shuckings.

❋ Corn Shuckings

You haul the corn in from the field in wagons, about twenty bushel to the load, and throw it into piles, sometimes in a kind of circular pile like a half-moon. Then, after all the corn on the farm has been brought in, they send the word around and ask in the neighbors and friends, and anybody they would like, to come. Some of the women, of course, come in also. The younger ones helped shuck the corn, and the older ones prepared food for the crowd. They start early, and the fellow who comes goes right to the pile of corn, wedges in, gets a place to shuck, and starts to work. They'll be fifteen or twenty, twenty-five, or more than that, big piles of corn, and they'll shuck until dinner time. Somebody will say, "Well, all right, they're calling us in." That would mean to get out and go to the spout; that is, the water that would be running down close to the house where they'd put the end of a trough in the branch that would be coming down off a rock-cliff, maybe. Sometimes it was a trough made of planks, sometimes a trench cut in a poplar tree, and sometimes just bark that would be curled over. The water would be running over into a tub. They'd go to the spout and wash. They'd bring the soap gourd out and a few clean towels, and pass them around. They would wash, comb their heads, and then go on to dinner.

It might be that they'd have several tables, and some would have to wait to eat at the second table, and maybe even the third table. Of course, they'd have all kinds of food, various kinds of cornbread, wheat-bread, and biscuits. . . . And they'd have sourwood honey and the ham and the apple jelly and beans—several kinds—leather-britches beans, and shell beans, and pickled beans, and whatever kinds there might be.

Soon as they got through dinner they'd go back to the corn pile. . . . By afternoon some of the young girls and the younger boys would be coming in from farther away. There'd be some corn left, maybe, not shucked, and they'd go back after supper, and they'd finish up. They'd put a girl and a boy, a boy and a girl around the pile by that time, and some of the oldsters would be a little farther around the edges. If the boy should happen to find a red ear, he knew that definitely gave him the constitutional right to kiss his sweetheart, or gave the girl the great privilege of getting kissed, either way you want to put it. When they'd finish up the corn and get ready to put up the shucks, they'd turn around, facing the shucks that had been thrown back of them, and they'd catch up each arm around the right and to the left in a close-contact circle. They'd take up the shucks, roll them into the shuck pen and tramp them down [for cattle fodder]. By that time the fiddlers and banjo-pickers had come.

They'd go around to the house, move out some of the furniture, and start up "Band Box," or "Katy Hibble," or "Cumberland Gap," or "Johnson Boys"—some old-time fiddle tune. A caller of the dance would say: "Big ring; all go left and half way round; and half back; turn and swing your corner lady; all promenade; ladies drop back and swing your partners; swing your opposite and on to the next; drop back, swing, and on to the next; drop back, swing, and on to the next; drop back, swing, and all promenade." And there were many games that they would play at the corn shuckings.

❈ Bean Stringings

Bean stringing is not such a large assemblage, but it is a very good one. In the immediate community they'd gather all the beans from the garden close by. They'd gather the beans from the cornfield where they'd planted beans in the corn [so the vines could run up the cornstalks]. They'd go high on the mountains where the bean vines grew rank, and they'd bring all those green and tender beans down from the high coves in the mountains. They would have quite a number of sacks of beans. They'd have them brought in on the porch, they'd have them in the big house, and they'd have them in the kitchen. Then the young people and some of the nearby oldsters would come in. Some of the boys and girls would come together, and some from over the mountain at the other settlements would come over. They'd get to one side of their friends (sometimes they would couple off), get a pile of beans, and they'd string those beans until all were strung preparatory for pickling or for drying. They'd dry them on a board like they'd dry fruit, or they'd string them on a string. All those strings would be several feet long. They'd put those strings out in the sun. They'd dry them, and they'd be what they called "leather britches" beans. They ate a lot of "leather britches" beans. They have a lot of different kinds of beans. They have what they called the "lazy wife" bean, and I think that came from Kentucky. It's a bean that you plant on the side of the porch and it runs around the edge of the porch, like an ornamental vine. The wife can go out on the porch and pick enough beans for the family from the porch without having to go out to the garden. So we call them the "lazy wife" bean. And they had the "bang belly" beans. Those are the shell beans that have been dried, a small bean like a navy bean.

✳ Making Molasses [Sorghum] and Apple Butter Stirring

There's a butter-stirring that's held when you make molasses. They'd boil the molasses in a boiler over a furnace that's built out doors, or maybe under a little shed. In the making of molasses, the cane is stripped and put in piles. Some boys would strip the cane blades off the cane stalk. Someone would cut the seed off—that is, the end, the tassels, the part that carries the seeds and is about a foot in length. That leaves just the stalk, and they carry those up to the old cane mill.

The cane mill is made of two or three cylinders. It used to be just two. New ones were smaller, but had three. Two cylinders rolling together will draw the cane through, and at the same time mash out the juice which runs into a little trough. The trough goes into a tub with a cloth over it to strain out the trash, or whatever may have fallen into it—pieces of cane stalk or cane blade that may come down into the juice. The way the mill is operated is, at the top of the cylinders there is the king cylinder, so to speak, which is made in a kind of square or V. A long bending or crooked pole is put on top of the cylinder with the heavy end shorter than the longer end. There is a mortised hole in it that fits into the part of the mill that operates the king cylinder. When this long pole is pulled around, it operates the mill. There is a weight on the short end, and a horse is hitched to the long end.

A smaller lead pole leads off from this long end that extends out, to which the horse's bridle is fastened. So the horse imagines that he is being led around the mill. As a matter of fact, he's pulling it, and the line leads off in front of him as a result of his efforts. He goes round in a circular path. The cane is fed through the cylinders, and the juice is pressed out.

After they've gotten the tub full, they put it into the boiler. Someone there, most generally a woman, with what they call a strainer, dips out the impurities and the foam that boils up. She skims that, and that's what is called "skimmings." It's put off to the side. First it's very green, but she keeps doing that until, after a while, it's all golden colored and sweet as honey. And there are some molasses-makers who know how to produce that kind of thing that is just as fine as can be. That goes on for some little while, till they put away several gallons of molasses—a hundred gallons or more. . . .

The last run of the molasses that is boiled is the one that they make the apple butter in. They have had an apple cutting (that's a party of its own, an opportunity for the young people to get together and prepare the apples for both drying and making apple butter). So they pour the apples into the last run in this boiler, and they stir that until it gets to be a fine apple butter. They put in some spices and flavoring. That's wonderful food too.

❄ Candy Pulling

Some of that molasses they have left aside, and they boil it and boil it and boil it until it gets to be a kind of candy. And then's when you have a "candy pulling." The young people get together, and after all the work around the place has been done, they get this candy ready. The more you pull it, the brighter it gets, and the better it gets. You pull it in this sort of way: you take a wisp of this candy—it looks like the golden hair of some blond— and two young people face each other. You put your left hand on the end of this roll of soft and stretchy candy, and you put your right hand about two-thirds of the way down on it. The other party facing—boy or girl—does exactly the same thing. Each one pulls and brings his hands together and then they twist. That puts the candy in two different strands. They twist that around, twist it around, pull it out again, and bring it out just like they did before. And, of course, they carry that on till the small hours of the morning. We've often heard the question, "When are we going to have the next candy pullin'?"

❀ The Quilting Party

An interesting occasion in the old days was the quiltin' party. There's a line from a song, "It was from Aunt Dinah's quiltin' party, I was seeing Nellie home." Of course, you have heard of that for years. The quiltin' party was a party at which people of the house would have laid aside their quilt scraps from making dresses of various kinds. Sometimes they were pretty costly dresses, still that would go into a quilt. And then the children's dresses of calico and gingham and things of that kind would be saved. The older and more inactive women of the household would take time out to sew the scraps together in various patterns (first with fingers and after a while with sewing machines) until they had made a quilt top. When one was finished, they'd begin another. They would make these quilt pieces and quilt squares into certain patterns, and it is a science in itself.

When they'd get ready to make quilts, they'd get the wool or the cotton batting—or whatever it was—and have all that ready. If they didn't have quiltin' frames, they'd go borrow them. I remember having gone to a neighbor's house to borrow the quiltin' frames. (That's always the job for the youngster.) The quiltin' frames are made with small holes every few inches along each of the four sides and put together with pins so that they can tighten the quilt or loosen it as they may desire. . . . They put the quiltin' frames together in an oblong square, and it's swung from the ceiling by cords or rope run through a staple or screw. They put in the first part of a quilt, the lining, and roll out the cotton batting, or wool batting on that. Then they put the quilt top on this and lower the quilt down to where a person can sit in a straight-back chair. At this height one could reach over the top with one hand, push the threaded needle through the other side, reach under and push it back through to the top side. If the quilt is thin, some may be able to sew it all from the top. They sometimes sew it around in a fan shape, mostly starting at one end. Usually three people would be seated on each side. In all, twelve people would be seated around the quilt. If there's a big quiltin' they might have more than one quilt in different rooms.

On these occasions, people who liked to quilt and who could talk and be jolly would be invited. They carried on a lot of fun, and they would have a big feed. All the news about all the people within a wide radius would come out. If the men had work, like log-rolling or house-raising, as was the case of the log-rolling I attended in North Georgia, that would be held at the same time as the quiltin' party. In that case, they'd have to have enough ladies who were not quiltin' to do the housework, prepare the food, cook the meals, wash the dishes, and straighten up the house, in addition to those who . . . would do the quiltin'.

The interesting thing about the old-time quiltin' was that after the work had been done, and they were ready to take the quilt out of the frames, they would manage to induce some young fellow about the place into the room or out in the hall under some false pretext. The young man might be someone at the log-rolling, a member of the family, or some young man who'd been courting and getting along pretty well, and it had been prophesied that he was going to get married pretty soon. They'd have some of the younger members of the party get him in—one or two single ones and maybe the older ones that knew what was coming. They'd get the quilt out of the frames, and they'd wrap this fellow entirely up with the quilt and tell him that this was a sign that he was going to get married to so-and-so. That was something that they always looked forward to, and they'd plan it. Of course, if they could get some of the younger girls to help do that, why, that would add more to the fun.

Ballads and Songs

❋ Old Mountain Dew
Roud 18669

These are Lunsford's original lyrics and tune, taken from his recording at Columbia University in 1935. Lunsford recorded it commercially on Brunswick 219 in 1928, and Lulu Belle and Scotty recorded their revised version on Conqueror 9249 in 1939. Others who recorded it were Roy Acuff, the Delmore Brothers, the Stanley Brothers, Uncle Dave Macon, Grandpa Jones, and Willie Nelson. Later performers added new verses.

On my first day in court I wish to re - port,_____ Now wit-ness my sto - ry so true;_____ When the State closed its case, a young man raised his face, And be - gan all the facts to re - view._____ Oh they call it that old Mount - ain Dew,_____ said those who re - fuse it are few; _____ While I know I've done wrong, the temp - ta - tion is strong, When they call for that old Mount - ain Dew._____

Chorus:

2. The deacon drove by in his auto so shy
   Said his family was down with the flu.
   Said he thought that I ought to give him a quart
   Of that good Old Mountain Dew.
   Yes, he called it that Old Mountain Dew,
   Said those that refuse it are few.
   So, I thought that I ought to just give him a quart
   Of that good Old Mountain Dew.

3. The doctor he phoned just to see me alone
   One night about half past two.
   Said he'd close up his mug if I'd fill up his jug
   With that good Old Mountain Dew.
   Yes, he called it that Old Mountain Dew,
   Said those who refuse it are few.
   So, I closed up his mug when I gave him a jug
   Of that good Old Mountain Dew.

4. The conductor said, with a nod of his head,
   My wife she never knew
   That I take my fun when I'm out on the run,
   So, give me a quart or two

Of that good Old Mountain Dew,
For those who refuse it are few,
But his wife said to me, you can bring me three
Before his train is due.

5. My attorney began to turn the lid on the can,
   I knew my case was lost.
   Said his honor to me,
   I'll set you free if you will pay the cost,
   For they call it that Old Mountain Dew,
   And those that refuse it are few,
   But you acted the man when you took the stand
   To swear what is so true.

❈ Little Marget

(Sweet William and Lady Margaret)

Child 74, Roud 253

*This is one of the ghostly ballads. Lunsford's text and tune are from his 1935
recording at Columbia University. Campbell and Sharp collected versions of the
ballad in Kentucky, Virginia, and North Carolina in 1916. Bascom got his version
at about the same time from a young girl named Loretta Payne on Roaring Fork
in Madison County, North Carolina.*

Lit-tle Mar-get was a-sit-ting in her high hall-door,____ A - comb-in' back her long yel-low
hair; She saw sweet Wil-liam and his new-made bride, A - rid-in' up the road so near.

2. She throwed back her ivory comb,
   Throwed back her long yellow hair;
   Said, "I'll go out and bid him farewell,
   And never more go there."

3. It was all lately in the night,
   When they were fast asleep;
   Little Marget appeared all dressed in white,
   A-standin' at their bed feet.

4. "How do you like that snow-white pillow?
    How do you like that sheet?
    How do you like that fair young lady
    That lies in your arms asleep?"

5. "Oh, well do I like my snow-white pillow,
    Oh, well do I like my sheet;
    Much better do I like that fair young lady
    That stands at my bed feet."

6. He called on his serving man to go
    And saddle the dappled roan;
    He went to her father's house and knocked,
    He knocked at the door alone.

7. "Is Little Marget in the house,
    Or is she in the hall?"
    "Little Marget's in her cold black coffin
    With her face turned to the wall."

8. "Unfold, unfold those snow-white robes,
    Be they ever so fine;
    And let me kiss them cold corpy lips,
    For I know they'll never kiss mine."

9. Oh, once he kissed her little white hand,
    And twice he kissed her cheeks;
    Three times he kissed her cold corpy lips,
    And he fell in her arms asleep.

❋ The Light Is Bad, My Eyes Are Dim

This recitation is from the 1935 Columbia University recordings. There weren't many songbooks in early America, and many people could not read, so the song leader "lined out" the song for the congregation by starting the first line and then chanting each succeeding line for them to sing in unison.

Visualize a country congregation, where an old minister is trying to line out a hymn in an unlit church house on a cloudy day, with a copy of *The Sweet Songster*.

MINISTER:
"This light is bad, my eyes are dim,
I sca'ce can see to read my hymn . . ."

CONGREGATION to the tune of "Amazing Grace":
"This light is bad, my eyes are dim,
I sca'ce can see to read my hymn. . . ."

MINISTER:
"I did not mean to sing a hymn,
I only meant my eyes are dim."

Congregation sings back the minister's lines.

MINISTER:
"Upon the honor of my hat,
I didn't mean for you to sing that."

Congregation again sings his lines.

MINISTER:
"I didn't mean to sing a-tall,
I think the Devil's in you all!"

❀ On a Bright and Summer's Morning
Roud 9137

There are a good many nonsense songs in British and American folklore with exaggerated, contradictory, illogical, or unrelated information in the stanzas. This one is a hunting tale that Bascom sang. Artus Moser collected it from Lunsford in 1946 (Library of Congress LP 21), and Bascom sang it for Kenneth Goldstein in 1956 for Music from South Turkey Creek *(Rounder 0065). It is included also on* Ballads, Banjo Tunes, and Sacred Songs of Western North Carolina *(Smithsonian/Folkways, SF 40082, 1996).*

On a bright and a sum-mer's morn-ing, The ground all cov-ered with snow; I
put my shoul-der to my gun, And a-hunt-in' I did — and a hunt in' I did go.

2. I went up on the mountain,
   Beyond yon high hill;
   Sixteen or twenty,
   Ten thousand I did . . .
   Ten thousand I did kill.

3. The money that I got for
   The venison and skin;
   I hauled up to my daddy's barn,
   And it wouldn't half go . . .
   And it wouldn't half go in.

4. The boys and girls were skatin'
   On a bright and summer's day;
   The ice broke through, they all fell in,
   The rest they run a . . .
   The rest they run away.

5. I went up on the mountain
   Beyond the peak so high;
   The moon came around with lightnin' speed,
   I'll take a ride says . . .
   I'll take a ride says I.

6. The moon went 'round the mountain,
   It took a sudden whirl;
   My foot slipped and I fell out,
   And landed in this . . .
   And landed in this world.

7. The man who made this song and tune,
   His name was Benjamin Young;
   If you can tell a bigger lie,
   I'll say you oughta be . . .
   I'll say you oughta be hung.

✳ Darby's Ram
Roud 126

This is an old English ballad. Llewellynn Jewitt wrote about it in his The Ballads and Songs of Derbyshire *(London: Bemrose and Sons, 1867), 115–19, and* asserted that it had been sung for over a century. It is said that George Washington sang it. Artists who have recorded the song include Tennessee Ernie Ford, Grandpa Jones, and Merle Travis. Lunsford recorded it for Brunswick in 1928 (Br 228, Br 80089), for the Library of Congress in 1949, and for Riverside in 1956 (RLP 12–645). Notable ballad singer Cas Wallin, a Baptist and a native of Madison County, where Bascom was born, sang a satiric verse to this ballad aimed at the Presbyterian missionaries who came to the county to establish a church and school and tried to change the name of his community of "Sodom" to "Revere." He sang: "The horns on that ram, sir / Were too high to reach / And there they built a pulpit / For the Presbyterians to preach."

As I went out to Dar-by all on a mar-ket day; There I saw the big-gest ram that was ev-er fed on hay. And he ram-bled, and he ram-bled, and he ram-bled till the butch-er cut him down.

2. He had four feet to walk, sir,
   He had four feet to stand;
   And every one of them four feet,
   They covered an acre of land.

   Chorus

3. The wool on that ram's back, sir,
   It reached up to the sky;
   The eagles built their nests there,
   For I heard the young ones cry.

   Chorus

4. The old ram had horns, sir,
   That reached up to the moon;
   A man climbed up in January,
   And he didn't get home till June.

   Chorus

5. The butcher that killed this ram, sir,
   Was drowned in the blood;
   The little boy that held the bowl
   Was washed away in the flood.

Chorus

✿ Katie Morey

Laws N24, Roud 674

Apparently the first printed notice of this song was in 1856. It has been referenced to "The Baffled Knight" (Child 74), although scholars disagree as to whether it is a true variant. Lunsford recorded it both at Columbia University in 1935 and at the Library of Congress in 1949, but he did not record it commercially. This version is from the Columbia University recordings. The great folk artist Doc Watson did a splendid version for Vanguard on his Home Again *album (VSD-79239, LP 1967, CD 1996), and you can hear him sing it online.*

Come gen-tle-men and la-dies all, and lis-ten to my sto-ry; I'll tell you of a plan I laid to ruin Miss Ka-ty Mo-rey. Tum-ble did-dy i-sye Ding dye a, Tum-ble did-dy eye di ding dye a

2. I went unto her father's house,
   Just like a clever fellow;
   I told Miss Kate the grapes and plums
   Were gettin' ripe and mellow.

Chorus

3. I told her that my sister Nan
   Was down in yonder valley;
   And wanted her to come down there,
   And spend a half an hour.

Chorus

4. She squeezed my hand most sweet and pleased,
   Said, "One thing I do fear, sir;
   My father's down in yonder field,
   And he will see and hear, sir."

Chorus

5. "So, you go up in yonder's tree,
   And see where he is, sir;
   In yonder's grove we will go,
   And there we'll sport and play, sir."

6. The way I heaved to climb a tree,
   Not being in the least offended;
   And there she stood and gazed at me,
   To see how I ascended.

Chorus

7. "It's your ugly looks I do disdain,
   You look just like an owl, sir;
   You can eat your grapes and suck their stems,
   I'm going to the house, sir."

Chorus

8. Away she heeled across the field,
   And left me half distracted;
   I ripped, I tore, I cussed, I swore,
   To see how Kate had acted.

Chorus

❉ I Wish I Was a Mole in the Ground
Roud 4957

This seemingly innocent song, with its earlier tune and floating verses, has attracted some attention. Harry Smith included Lunsford's 1928 Brunswick recording of this song (Br 219B) on his Anthology of American Folk Music, *and it caught the attention of the Berkeley critic and author Greil Marcus, no doubt leading him to review my book on Lunsford in the* Village Voice.[35]

*Marcus had commented that the discovery of Smith's anthology of down-home folk music was like discovering a whole new continent of people that he had known nothing about. He later wrote about Lunsford and this song in his Lip-*stick Traces: A Secret History of the Twentieth Century *(Cambridge, Mass.: Harvard University Press, 1989), p. 14: "[It] wasn't an animal song. . . . It was an account of everyday mysticism, a man dropping his plow, settling onto the ground, pulling off his boots, and summoning wishes he will never fulfill. . . . Now what the singer wants is obvious, and almost impossible to comprehend. He wants to be delivered from his life and to be changed into a creature insignificant and despised. He wants to see nothing and to be seen by no one. He wants to destroy the world and survive it. That's all he wants. . . . It is an almost absolute negation, at the edge of pure nihilism, a demand to prove that the world is nothing, a demand to be next to nothing, and yet it is comforting." For more discourse on Lunsford and this song, see Greil Marcus,* Three Songs, Three Singers, Three Nations *(Cambridge: Harvard University Press, 2015), pp. 106–47. Another intellectual, Archie Green, labor historian and folklorist, also reviewed my book in* Appalachian Heritage *13, no. 3 (Summer 1985): 66–70, and ended by asking, "Did Bascom Lamar Lunsford find a mole in his natal community, or across the county line at time of death? Who are to be tomorrow's moles? What mountain needs leveling? What mountain needs lifting?" (p. 70). Lunsford got this song from Fred Moody, Haywood County, North Carolina, early in his collecting efforts. I remember Lunsford commenting somewhere that the "bend" mentioned in the song was the bend of the Pigeon River, and that "the rough and rowdy men" were the timber-cutters who had deforested the area in the first quarter of the twentieth century. The reader can hear Bascom's and other versions of the song online.*

2. Oh, Tempe wants a nine-dollar shawl,
   Yes, Tempe wants a nine-dollar shawl;
   When I come o'er the hill with a forty-dollar bill,
   'Tis baby, where you been so long?

3. Oh, where have you been so long?
   Yes, where have you been so long?
   I've been in the bend with the rough and rowdy men,
   It's baby where you been so long?

4. Oh, I don't like a railroad man,
   No, I don't like a railroad man;
   A railroad man will kill you when he can,
   And he'll drink up your blood like wine.

5. I wish I was a lizard in the spring,
   Yes, I wish I was a lizard in the spring;
   If I's a lizard in the spring I could hear my darlin' sing,
   I wish I was a lizard in the spring.

FIGURE 1. Bascom Lamar Lunsford dressed for his first formal lecture, "North Carolina Folklore, Poetry and Song," at Rutherford College, probably in 1915. Courtesy of the Bascom Lamar Lunsford Collection, Southern Appalachian Archives, Mars Hill University, Mars Hill, N.C.

FIGURE 2. Bascom at the Renfro Valley, Kentucky, post office, probably 1946. Courtesy of the Bascom Lamar Lunsford Collection, Southern Appalachian Archives, Mars Hill University, Mars Hill, N.C.

FIGURE 3. Bascom showing his huge scrapbook to his grandchildren. Courtesy of the Bascom Lamar Lunsford Collection, Southern Appalachian Archives, Mars Hill University, Mars Hill, N.C.

FIGURE 4. Bascom leading a square dance in his living room on South Turkey Creek. Courtesy of the Bascom Lamar Lunsford Collection, Southern Appalachian Archives, Mars Hill University, Mars Hill, N.C.

FIGURE 5. Lunsford and his second wife, Freda, celebrate his ninetieth birthday, assisted by Jerry Israel, friend and promoter of Bascom and his work. Courtesy of the Bascom Lamar Lunsford Collection, Southern Appalachian Archives, Mars Hill University, Mars Hill, N.C.

Josiah H. Combs

I never met Josiah Combs, but we were connected through Hindman Settle-ment School in Knott County, Kentucky, where he studied from 1902 until 1905, and for which I, many years later, was a member or chairman of the board for nineteen years. Furthermore, one of my best students, the late Michael Mullins, was the effective long-time executive director of the school. Combs's doctoral diploma from the Sorbonne hung in the school's dining hall, where I vaguely noticed it for several years before I began to pick up other information about him, mainly from the poets Albert Stewart and James Still, who knew him well and told me some of his choice jokes. Finally, I had a hand in getting copies of Combs's papers and his beloved dulcimer for the Berea College Archives.

Combs was born in Perry County, Kentucky, on January 2, 1886. His father was John W. Combs, his mother Clementine Cody Combs. John Combs was elected sheriff of Perry County during the French-Eversole feud, and the family witnessed much of the violence of that era. When Knott County was formed in 1882, the Combses moved there—mainly, Josiah remembered, to get away from the feud—first to Irishman's Creek and then to Hindman, where John Combs built a house and established a store. He also formed the Republican Party in the county and later served as a U.S. commissioner and state senator. Josiah much later wrote, tongue in cheek, of his background: "My own ancestors were of Devonshire provenience, and, along with Sir Francis Drake, of Devon; they were as meek and humble as any man that ever slit a throat or scuttled a ship!"[1] He was proud of this "Old English" heritage, and it influenced his scholarship throughout his years.

Established in 1902, Hindman was the first of the Appalachian settlement schools. Combs spoke fondly of the school and its dedicated teachers. In an article he wrote later for the magazine *Kentucky Explorer*, he described his entry:

> I was sixteen, almost old enough to be out of high school, yet I had never seen one. Miss Pettit [the cofounder] used to tell, even before the school opened, she saw me sitting one day reading and asked me what I was reading. "Hist'ry," said I proudly. Maybe it was that way; I don't remember. I was barefoot, and I was when I entered the school. There was no way of classifying us as to courses, and the teachers hardly knew where to put us. But we soon got put. These teachers I remember as if it were yesterday. . . . I was in a new world.
>
> Along with Miss Pettit, Miss Lucy Furman was one of the most wholesome, one of the finest influences in the school. . . . I learned to respect her right away. She "had a way" with the little boys, and she had a sense of humor. . . . Such was the atmosphere in which Miss Furman found herself working with a "bevy of boys" and meeting and knowing mountain people, and little by little storing away data for her books: *Mothering on Perilous*; *Sight to the Blind*; *The Quare Women*. She was a Godsend to the mountain boys at the school, and it is a pity that her tribe has not increased sufficiently. . . . I owe most of [my] intellectual curiosity to those early years at Hindman.[2]

I learned that Josiah already had a head full of his mother's old British ballads. The directors and teachers had an interest in the ballads and folksongs of the region and had begun a collection of them. Katherine Pettit took down some of his ballads, and later sent these and others she had collected off to the famed Harvard Shakespearean and ballad scholar George Lyman Kittridge, who published them in the American Folklore Society's *Journal of American Folklore*.[3] It is not clear how many of these were from Josiah, for no credit was given to him or others who actually sang them.[4] It was a common practice in scholarly circles at the time to give credit to the collector rather than the singer, perhaps because it was assumed that the native singers had little awareness of the worth of the ballads, and thus the song-stories were credited to the "educated" person who "discovered" them.

Josiah proved to be a very bright student at the school, and with the help of his able teachers, who had graduated from the leading colleges and universities in the East, he learned proper English and the historical background of ballads and other oral traditions of his native land and local culture. He also learned a good many other things from these remarkable teachers. As he wrote in the *Kentucky Explorer* article, "I have said that I was the first 'graduate' of the school. It is necessary to supply the quotation marks, since in the true sense of the word, I did not actually graduate. I simply took what little advanced or high school work that could be offered, and after three years, walked the forty miles to Jackson, took the train to Lexington and entered Transylvania College."[5] When he left Hindman in 1905, Miss Pettit gave him a dulcimer made by local craftsman Edward Thomas (who made and peddled some eighteen hundred of the slender instruments, including one for the Prince of Wales). Josiah played it for the rest of his life in ballad recitals.

Combs described his arrival at Transylvania University this way: "Entering that famous old school . . . I discarded my hip-pocket artillery and 'snake medicine,' and hung my budget of Highland, Elizabethan vernacular on the turnstile at one end of the entrances. A *coup de grâce* to Highland life and customs! I was exasperatingly homesick and disgusted; but one thought obsessed me and burnt to the quick: once in a fight, it would be cowardly to run away. And so I stuck with it."[6] The folklorist D. K. Wilgus reported another version of his college entrance: "In 1905, with a dulcimer and a corn cob pipe and without five dollars in his pocket, he got off the train . . . and crawled under the turnstile," where, he said, "a senior asked me if I had 'matriculated.' I started to hit him, but catching a friendly look in his eyes, I held back."[7]

As it turned out, "the new school was an inspiration," and Combs "went at it with a will. There was Latin, European history, literature, which I devoured in great globs. More books. . . . I think I read them by the square foot in the shelves."[8] He soon caught the attention of the young head of the department, Hubert G. Shearin, who taught English philology. Shearin encouraged him in his interest in folksongs, and led him in a scholarly study of the English language. Combs also took courses in French, Spanish, and German. To support himself, he arose at 3:30 each morning to deliver the *Lexington Herald*. In addition, he edited the school paper, the *Transylvanian*, and he and Shearin prepared the manuscript for *A Syllabus of Kentucky Folk-Songs*, which was published in 1911. The book included "333 items, exclusive of 114 variants," in which they examined the number of syllables in the lines and the rhyming scheme and meter. The collection includes popular songs that had been "'learned by ear instead of by eye,' as existing through oral tradition—song-ballads, love-songs, number-songs, dance-songs, play-songs, child-songs, counting-out rimes, lullabies, jigs, nonsense rimes, ditties, etc.," mostly from eastern Kentucky counties.[9] Combs greatly appreciated Shearin's friendship and scholarly teaching and later commented that Shearin's home was the only one he was invited into during his years in Lexington.

With his college diploma, he taught at high schools in Kentucky, Virginia, Oklahoma, and Tennessee, and at Tahlequah Teachers College in Oklahoma. He also published *The Kentucky Highlanders from a Native Mountaineer's Viewpoint* (Lexington, Ky.: J. L. Richardson, 1913) and a huge and impressive collection of verse, *All That's Kentucky: An Anthology* (Louisville, Ky.: J. P. Morton, 1915).

During these years, he performed lecture-recitals of ballads and stories, and was probably the first Kentucky native to do so as a means of educating a larger audience to the rich folk heritage of the Appalachian portion of his state. Once, carrying his dulcimer, he was accosted by a stranger with "Can you pick that thing?" He replied, "Shore, I can pick 'er. I wouldn't pack 'er if I could'n' pick 'er, and I foller pickin' 'er a lot."[10]

The United States entered the Great War in 1917, and on January 31, 1918, Josiah, at age thirty-two, joined Base Hospital 40, a volunteer army medical unit organized by Dr. David Barrow of Lexington, consisting of 220 soldiers and 30 officers, mostly from Kentucky. They trained at Camp Zachary Taylor near Louisville and sailed from New Jersey to zigzag (evading submarines) their way to Glasgow on the HMS *Scotia*. They marched overland to a place called Sarisbury Court in Hampshire, to property owned by the American Red Cross. There they began clearing land and building a hospital during months of rain and mud. The hospital was to receive American casualties from the battles in France, as well as to serve other Americans stationed in England. Combs would later publish a humorous account of their labors, along with their adventures in the countryside, entitled *The Seige of Sarisbury Court: Which Chronicles the Feat of Base Hospital 40 in Winning the World*

War, "by Ex–Buck Pvt. Josiah H. Combs." This work reflected Combs's huge sense of humor as well as his knowledge of English history and skilled use of the language in prose and verse. He wrote also of the boredom and toil of their lives there, and their cunning in finding ways to relieve tedium in the numerous pubs, but also to deal with the painful knowledge that their work was all in vain. By the time the hospital was finished, the Armistice was signed, and it was no longer needed. Their unit was broken up, with some going to France and some back home to Kentucky. Combs was sent home. *The Seige of Sarisbury Court* was finished and published in 1919.

Back in the States, Combs secured a job with the Young Men's Christian Association and was sent to Moravia, assigned to the Czech Army. He later served as director of publicity and publications for the YMCA in Czechoslovakia.[11]

Through a friend, Josiah began corresponding with a young French woman named Charlotte Bernard, and after an exchange of letters—fifty-some from Josiah alone—their friendship grew romantic, and he proposed marriage. Her parents objected, but she agreed, and Josiah went to France for their wedding on July 12, 1920. They settled in Prague, where for a year he edited the YMCA's journal, the *Czechoslovak American*, and performed other duties. In his spare time, he made a study of the Bohemian language and culture.

Combs had decided that he wanted to earn a doctorate in languages, and, no doubt influenced by Charlotte, he enrolled at the University of Paris. After two years he finished his coursework, then brought Charlotte to the United States, where he taught French and Spanish at West Virginia University from 1922 to 1924 as he worked on his thesis, a study of the folksongs he had been collecting and performing over the years. One summer, they lived in very rural Knott County, Kentucky, where Josiah noted that Charlotte fell in love with mountain people. While there, he taught students at Hindman Settlement School. During this time, he was also collecting additional ballads and songs. They returned to Paris in 1924, and Josiah received his doctorate from the Sorbonne *summa cum laude* in 1925. His thesis, written in French, was entitled "Folk-Songs du Midi des Etats-Unis" (Folk-songs of the southern United States).

Early in his career, Combs published a booklet entitled *Lectures on the Kentucky Highlanders, Folk-Lore, and Dialect of the Southern Mountains, Old Kentucky: Five Lectures by Josiah Combs of the Kentucky Mountains*.[12] The first lecture was "Folk-lore: Dulcimer and Ballad Recital," where he listed twelve ballads of British and American origins (such as "Hiram Hubbard," "Lord Thomas and Fair Ellender," "William Hall," and "Barbara Allen") that he might sing, along with "Jigs, Ditties, Nonsense Rimes." Combs believed that most of the people who settled the Appalachians were primarily of English origin. He ignored the German element, and rejected the theory that the Scotch-Irish from Ulster were prominent and influential in southern speech and folklore.

His second lecture was "Folk-Lore of the Southern Mountains." Here he discussed "Folk-Songs Traditional and Modern," asserting that the ballads that southern highlanders sang were "largely English in origin." He discussed the music of the folksongs and methods of transmission. He also demonstrated dance calls, children's play-party games, rhymes, and riddles. He gave examples of beliefs and superstitions and ended with the primary reason for his lectures: the passing of folklore from the memories of the people of the highlands.

"Dialect: The Language of the Southern Mountains" was the third lecture, starting with the ancestry of the mountaineers: "Pure Old English—Foreign Element Negligible." He delineated between Old English, Middle English, and Elizabethan elements of mountain speech and moved on to slang, peculiar grammatical structure, and glib use of formal terms. He also discussed place names, family and given names, and pronunciation.

His fourth lecture was "The Kentucky Highlanders." He discussed their "Origin, Extent and Nationality," "Old and Middle English," "Folk-Lore and Philology as an Argument," and "The Scotch-Irish Theory," and expounded on their "pure Old English." He moved then to a discussion of "The Mountaineer's Personality and Hospitality," mountain women, lawyers and politicians, the lack of social caste, and "Old English Customs and Superstitions." He remarked on the Highlanders' general and educational outlook and on their religion, and concluded with thoughts on the future of the mountaineer.

His fifth program, "Old Kentucky," consisted of recitations from his own publication *All That's Kentucky*.

During his years of teaching, Combs worked diligently on scholarly projects, as he continued to do in retirement. The most daunting was his genealogical research into the Combs family, from Great Britain to Virginia, into Kentucky, other states, and throughout the world. He worked on this project for more than thirty years until his death in 1960, making use of the work of British and American genealogists, but also visiting archives, libraries, courthouses, and cemeteries, and carrying on a correspondence with numerous people. After his death, his nephew Norris K. Combs (a retired U.S. Navy commander), with Charlotte's help, took up the enormous task of editing his work for publication. *Combs: A Study in Comparative Philology and Genealogy* was published in Pensacola, Florida, by Norris K. Combs in 1976; it was reprinted in Tallahassee by the Rose Printing Company in 1979 and electronically reprinted by the Combs &c. Research Group in 1999 (http://www.combs-families.org/combs/jhc/ms-jhc.html#copy). Combs included humor in his genealogy, such as the brain-twister "I Am My Own Grandfather," which was known and passed around among humorists:

> I married a widow with a grown daughter. My father fell in love with my step-daughter and married her, thus becoming my son-in-law; and my step-daughter became my mother, because she was my father's wife. My wife gave birth to a son, which was, of course, my father's brother-in-law, and my uncle, for he was the brother of my step-mother. My father's wife became the mother of a son. He was, of course, my brother, and also my grandchild, for he was the son of my daughter. Accordingly, my wife was my grandmother, because she was my mother's mother—I was my wife's husband and grand-child at the same time—and as the husband of a person's grandmother is his grandfather—I AM MY OWN GRANDFATHER!

In 1947, songwriters Dwight Latham and Moe Jaffe made this implausible story into a song, "I'm My Own Grandpa." The country comedy team of Lonzo and Oscar pounced on it, and it became a big hit for them the same year. Other country performers, including Homer and Jethro, Willie Nelson, and Ray Stevens, recorded it, as did pop performers Jo Stafford and Guy Lombardo.

The Combs Family Reunion was held for many years the first weekend of August at Buckhorn State Park in Kentucky. Out of it came the Combs &c. Research Group, which worked diligently for several years to correct errors in the genealogy and add new information to it before the electronic edition was put online. One major addition was a name index, including nicknames. At the date of this writing, 543,238 persons have accessed this edition.

Josiah taught French and German for two years at the University of Oklahoma, then moved to Texas Christian University, where he headed the

Department of Foreign Languages from 1927 to 1947. Charlotte explained in a handwritten note that they initially chose the Southwest because of Josiah's nasal catarrh and her weak lungs, but later they went east, where he was professor of French at Mary Washington College of the University of Virginia at Fredericksburg until he retired in 1956, at which time he and Charlotte moved back to Fort Worth, Texas.

In the summer of 1957, D. K. Wilgus, a professor of English and folklore at Western Kentucky College, visited the Combs home in Fort Worth to talk with Josiah about the possibility of translating his Sorbonne dissertation into English so that the English-speaking world could make use of it. Combs was apparently agreeable to the idea. Wilgus also wanted to make copies of Combs's papers for the Western Kentucky University Archives. Combs agreed, and, according to a note handwritten by Charlotte Combs in a published copy of *Folk-Songs of the Southern United States* in the Combs Collection in the Berea College Archives, Wilgus made copies and returned the original papers to Combs.[13]

Wilgus, an Ohio native, was a distinguished folklorist. He had earned three degrees from the Ohio State University and taught folklore at Western Kentucky University for thirteen years. There he founded and edited the *Kentucky Folklore Record* and did extensive fieldwork in Kentucky. In 1963 he was invited to the University of California at Los Angeles, where he and another acclaimed folklorist, Wayland D. Hand, established the prestigious Folklore and Mythology Program, which Wilgus chaired for seventeen years. He was one of the first folklore scholars to include country, western, and blues music in his studies. He also published the definitive and influential study *Anglo-American Folksong Scholarship since 1898* (New Brunswick, N.J.: Rutgers University Press, 1959) and hundreds of scholarly articles. He served, too, as president of both the California Folklore Society and the American Folklore Society.

Wilgus fully intended to sound-record Combs as part of his project to translate and publish his thesis, but he allowed three years to pass before he loaded up his recording equipment on June 2, 1960, to drive to Fort Worth. When he arrived, he found that Combs had died. At this time Wilgus told Charlotte that Josiah had promised him his Edward Thomas dulcimer. Charlotte reluctantly allowed him to take the instrument, but Norris Combs told me that she spoke of her resentment at his asking for it at that critical moment and that she later questioned whether Josiah would have promised the dulcimer to him at all.[14]

The only known recording of Combs was made by folklorists John and Ruby Lomax in Fort Worth in 1940 for the Library of Congress's Archive of American Folk Song. Accompanying himself on his dulcimer, he sang "Lord Thomas" (3950-A1), "Corn Likker" (3950-A2), "Cluck Old Hen" (3950-A3)," "Slago Town" (3950-A4), "Wilma and Dina" (3950-B1), "I'm Climbing up Jacob's Ladder" (3950-B2), "Barbara Allen" (3950-B3), and "Jack Wilson" (3950-B4).[15] Unfortunately, the disk-recording equipment that the Lomaxes used could record only the shorter numbers that Combs selected, and required an abridgment of the two longer ballads, leaving out parts of the stories they told.

Apparently, Wilgus had not gotten far with his project, and with Combs's passing, he asked Charlotte to assist him in translating the thesis and reformulating it into a book. He wrote, "Fortunately, Combs' English manuscript of his thesis survived and, through the courtesy of Mrs. Combs, was used as the base text of this new edition. It is, however, only the 'base,' as it is not a precisely parallel form of the French. The difference between the two texts is one of the conditions which have necessitated difficult editorial decisions."[16] It appears that Wilgus did all of the actual translation from the French. There is no indication that he and Charlotte ever worked together on the translation, since she was in Fort Worth and he was in Los Angeles, and later on she criticized some aspects of it. It was published in 1967 as *Folk-Songs of the Southern United States* by the University of Texas Press for the American Folklore Society.

In his foreword, Wilgus noted that it was a "rare book," in that Combs was closer to his material than most folklorists, and because "few have come as far—from informant to scholar, from the Highlands of eastern Kentucky to the Sorbonne and beyond." He continued:

> While "furriners" like Cecil Sharp and Loraine Wyman were tracking down the "lonesome tunes" in the Highlands, a young mountain boy was bringing them to the lowlands with a blend of defensiveness and self-criticism, grounded in hard-won learning but salted with folk attitudes and anecdotes.[17]

Wilgus restored a whole chapter, "The Highlander's Music," that had not been accepted by Combs's dissertation advisors because music was not their or his field of study, and also perhaps because many of the songs had been previously published in the United States. However, the committee had recommended it to the French publication *Vient de paraître*, and it was published with a foreword by William Aspenwall Bradley, a Paris-based literary agent.[18] A major weakness of the dissertation, and later the book that Wilgus created, was the lack of musical notations to the ballads and songs. Having never learned to read music, Combs had collected and performed the songs entirely within the oral tradition. He no doubt knew the tunes to most of the songs, but he never sought musical notations from his singing. However, his papers do include some musical notations that had been sent to him. Perhaps his doctoral committee's reservations about his venturing into the realm of music had influenced him, but it may have been that he, like Francis James Child, was more interested in the texts than he was in the tunes.

Wilgus also added other material that he thought would be useful to readers of the English edition. His work was a great service to Combs and to scholars, folklorists, and collectors in making this volume available in English. However, Charlotte was critical of his work, and of him as a person. Both were strong personalities, and they seem to have clashed. Some of this animosity may have come from Josiah. Obviously, he and Wilgus had different ideas about folklore because of the different eras in which they were active in the field. For example, Josiah had written and spoken negatively about the use of the banjo for ballad accompaniment, and he detested the use of the word "hillbilly" in reference to his people or their music, whereas Wilgus had embraced so-called "hillbilly music," in which the banjo was employed frequently and raucously, as a subject for study. No doubt they differed over other aspects of folklore because of their age difference and their places of origin. In a copy of *Folk-Songs of the Southern United States* now preserved in the Berea College Archives, Charlotte made extensive comments in the margins, in which she quibbled over Wilgus's versions of events, questioned his factual statements, and also questioned his translation. In one of those marginal notes, she wrote, "Since the publication of this book it has been my desire to have someone with me to read the translation as I read the French text—reason? I do believe that Josiah did not follow exactly the English text which was written years *before* the French."[19] However, despite Charlotte's critical comments, I give Wilgus credit and thanks for his years of scholarly toil in making this work available to the English-speaking world.

In his reformulation of the book, Wilgus decided not to introduce more recent folksong scholarship on such matters as the origins of ballads—whether or not they were mostly "pure Old English" versus Scotch-Irish or Irish—so as to preserve the integrity of Combs's original work, explaining, "Josiah H. Combs, with an intimate knowledge of one continuing folk culture and with a grasp of the scholarly literature, approached the matter with a sturdy common sense."[20] Wilgus's admiration of Josiah is obvious throughout the book. He pointed out that Combs was among a very small number of singers and collectors at that time who were native to the area from which they were collecting, and that his scholarly credentials were of the highest quality.[21] Thus, he emphasized, the book is important folksong scholarship even though younger folklorists might differ with him on such matters as the ethnic origins of the ballads. Combs's annotated list contains 325 songs and rhymes and more than 100 variants.

Full texts are provided for only 58 ballads and songs, 25 of British origin and 33 American. However, each of the songs that Combs collected has his careful annotation in the appendix, indicating the singer, collector, location, and where other printed versions might be found. Not all these songs were collected or known by him, although he wrote that most of them were songs he had collected over fifteen years "from the folksingers themselves." Others came from collector-scholars, some well-known and others not, who were known by Combs, including his own students. Over half of the songs were from Kentucky singers, a third from West Virginia, and the rest from other states.

Combs maintained his interest in folk music through his teaching years, with his ballad recitals. In 1939 he published *Folk-Songs from the Kentucky Highlands*, a collection of sixteen songs with piano accompaniments.

Combs thought that the folksong tradition was dying and that he was preserving the remnants of it. He blamed three institutions for the decline of his beloved music: educational institutions, the industrial corporations that were invading the highlands, and the churches.

But the college and university are not the sole educational institutions which unconsciously militate against the propagation of the folk-song. The Highland schools themselves, whether they be colleges, academies, preparatory schools, church schools, or public schools, are almost without exception sworn enemies of the folk-song. The sole reason seems to be that the songs of the people are not "culture," because they do not appear in the pedagogical *curricula* of a time-worn educational system. . . .

Commerce and industries are not only dispossessing the simple, unsuspecting Highlander of his worldly goods and belongings, but are also driving the folk-song from its once secure habitation. One of the curses of the civilization which is now invading this simple, pure-minded folk is that its vanguard is made up of a type of men who have little or no interest in the welfare of the folk they are despoiling and dispossessing. These jackals of civilization are abusing the confidence of the hillsmen, even debauching them in many instances, and possessing their lumber, coal, and mineral wealth, without according them the right to share in the development of the resources of their own native hills. Many a community of once simple folk, formerly enjoying the simple pleasures afforded by their songs, has several years since heard the clank of the colliery on the hillsides, the shrill notes of the factory whistle, the roaring of the furnace, and the rattle of the locomotive reverberating through the Highland valleys. These things can have only one interpretation for the folk-song: *destruction*. It retreats at their advance, and never returns, save in songs of a greatly inferior type, Negro songs and railroad songs. But the vast reaches of the Southern Highlands are not by any means in the clutches of commerce—not yet. Whenever they shall be, within a generation or two, the destruction of Highland balladry will be complete.

The Primitive Baptist Church, one of the most primitive religious institutions in the United States, is the most deadly enemy of the folk-song. This institution admits no secular literature, oral or written, and long ago excommunicated the folk-song. . . . Once a Highlander who was mighty in the realm of fiddling and ballad-singing decided to align himself with the church. He had been especially proficient at performing on the fiddle that famous air of all the Highlands, "Sourwood Mountain." At his baptism (by immersion) a local wit sat on the bank of the stream and cried out, just as the new communicant disappeared under the water, "Good-bye, Sourwood Mountain!"

Combs reveals some of his biases and prejudices here. He notes three exceptions to his criticism of educational institutions: two Kentucky schools, Hindman and the Pine Mountain Settlement School in Pine Mountain, and the Mount Berry School in Rome, Georgia. They, and other schools,

did indeed prepare collections of folksongs and used them for group singing. They also paid close attention to the handicrafts of the natives, such
as weaving, quilting, and basket-making, and included such arts in their
curriculum and in their "industrial" programs to make items for sale to
support the schools. However, Combs is right in saying that most educa-
tors saw their mission as uplifting students above their traditional culture
and values.[22]

Certainly the industrial age invasion did change the mountain landscape
and its human culture. It decimated the forests, and it opened the coal
mines and brought in the railroads, as well as African American workers
from the South and foreigners from Eastern Europe who joined the native
workforce. Combs reveals a prejudice, shared by most white people of the
time, toward black culture and its songs. He railed also against the phonograph and printed music, with its jazz and ragtime, and against singing
schools promoted by church music publishing companies, but he ignored
in his writings the emerging influence of radio. It is important to note that
the music that he saw as overwhelming the traditional native folksong
traditions has for many years now been a legitimate object of scholarly
folkloric study.

He is also too hard on the Primitive Baptists, perhaps the most traditional of the all the mountain churches. Actually, there are other predestinarian churches in eastern Kentucky that sprang from the Primitive
Baptists, such as the Regular and Old Regular Baptists (meaning that they
are regular predestinarians, not free-will) and even the United Baptists
(formed in the mid-nineteenth century to bring the predestinarian and free-
will Baptists together, but with many drifting back to "primitive" beliefs).
Combs chose to use the *Oxford English Dictionary*'s secondary meaning of
"primitive," "unsophisticated" or "crude," rather than the first meaning,
"original" or "non-derivative."

It should be noted that in more recent times, folklorists and musicolo-
gists have been studying music and other oral expression of such groups as
these Baptists and sharing them in print and recordings. The best example
can be found in a 2015 news release, "New Entries to National Recording
Registry," in which the National Recording Preservation Board announced
a list of twenty-five new recordings to be added to the Library of Congress's National Recording Registry because of their "cultural, artistic and/

or historical significance to American society." One of them was *Old Regular Baptists: Lined-Out Hymnody from Southeastern Kentucky* (Smithsonian Folkways Recordings, 1997; produced by Jeff Todd Titon, Elder Elwood Cornett, and John Wallhausser). Librarian of Congress James H. Billington explains its importance:

> These hymns are considered the oldest type of Anglo-American religious music passed down orally in the U.S. They represent a historic type of singing that can be traced back to the music of the 16th-century parish church and the Protestant reformation. Once a very common way of singing sacred songs in the American colonies, the Old Regular Baptists of southeastern Kentucky are one of the few groups who still worship using this old style of "lining hymn." Lined-out hymns have no written musical notation to guide the singers. A single song leader guides the congregation through the hymn one line at a time. Typically, the leader sings the line quickly and then the congregation repeats the words in unison, but to a tune much longer and more elaborate than the leader's original chant or lining tune. The congregation's response has no regular beat or harmonizing parts and is often very emotional. The intent is not to sing with the unified precision of a practiced choir. The result is heterophonic, a musical texture characterized by the simultaneous variation of a single melodic line sung by many different voices, unique in Western music.

I wish Josiah could have known before he sounded its death knell that the folksong is alive and well (although sometimes on the outskirts of authenticity) at the many festivals throughout the region in our day and time, and the humble dulcimer is being made and played by thousands more people than when he collected and performed songs and wrote his dissertation. Furthermore, in spite of the elitism of the colleges and universities, some are now teaching bluegrass and old-time music. East Tennessee State University, Berea College, and Morehead State University, for example, now have excellent programs in old-time music and bluegrass—the latter of which Combs no doubt would have frowned on because of its loud and aggressive style, and the idea of "folk music in overdrive" would have incensed him.

Combs's primary interest, however, was the English language in England and America. All this time, he was also working on the Combs family genealogy. He was a member of such organizations as the Modern Language Society, the American Dialect Society, the American Folklore Society, and the Kentucky Folklore Society. He contributed articles and word lists to the publications of those groups as well as to other journals. He also contributed to B. A. Botkin's *The American Play-Party Song* (New York: Ungar, 1937). Examples of his work include "A Word List from Georgia," *Dialect Notes* 5, pt. 5 (1920): 183–84; "Language of the Southern Highlanders," *PMLA* 46, no. 4 (1931): 1302–22 (reproduced with permission at the end of this essay); and "Early English Slang Survivals in the Mountains of Kentucky," *Dialect Notes* 5, pt. 4 (1921): 115–17. He also contributed articles and humorous stories to the *Kentucky Folklore Record*.

His contributions came to the attention of H. L. Mencken, editor of *The American Language: An Inquiry into the Development of English in the United States*. Mencken and Combs corresponded over the years (a total of eighty-eight letters from Mencken or his wife, Sara), and Mencken quotes, mentions, or references Combs some twenty times in his work. He included Combs among "that small minority of American scholars who took the national language seriously, and gave it serious scientific study."[23] Josiah and Charlotte became friends of Henry and Sara Mencken, and they visited with one another over the years.

Charlotte noted that Mencken had invited her to be the hostess at a dinner that he was giving at his hotel in Washington, D.C. Another time at the Mencken home, she wrote, "an awful storm came up—lightning, popping. H. L. rushed to the window. Sara said, 'Henry, Henry, get away from that window.' [He replied,] 'Don't you know, this is not the way I will go—but on the scaffold.'"[24] Mencken died before fulfilling a promise to write a preface or foreword to a book by Josiah, and the latter wrote, "It is a matter of deep regret to me that he did not live long enough to add another of his many favors to me. The least I can do is to dedicate the present work to that phenomenal man of letters—with the firm assurance that such an act would comfort him on any scaffold and console him in Valhalla." Mencken had earlier invited Combs to come to work at his journal, the *American Mercury*, but Combs continued with his teaching and scholarly pursuits.[25]

Much of Combs's scholarship is still in manuscript form. He wrote on American dialects, surnames, place names, pronunciation, syntax, slang, idioms, and the language of folksongs. One essay is on the family surname Smith, noting that the word "smith" comes from the old Anglo-Saxon word *smietan*, meaning "to smite" with a hammer. He also listed surnames that are related to smithies in other languages, such as Schmidt in Germany,

LeFèvre in France, and Gowan in Scotland. Some of this work is included at the end of this essay.

Another piece he called "An Excursus into Scatology," and it contains essays, jokes, and lists of obscene words and phrases, attesting to the breadth of Combs's interest in all aspects of the lives and language of the folk from whom he had risen. D. K. Wilgus commented that Combs "was outspoken and 'salty.' Many who disagreed with his pronouncements had the greatest appreciation of his character. Combs was a 'mountain man' to the end. Indeed, the characteristics of the Highlanders that he analyzes include many of his own traits. Although he lived elsewhere . . . he remained stubbornly loyal to his native Highlands, to the ideals and prejudices of his people."[26]

The work for which Combs hoped that Mencken might write a foreword may have been a collection of stories about legal matters, or probably something else that he had worked on for many years and hoped to publish after he retired. This did not happen, but after he died, Norris Combs reorganized a manuscript entitled "Voices from Below: A Journey into Fartology," and said this about Josiah's involvement in the subject: "I must say that Josiah was a man of the highest moral character, as well a complete gentleman. . . . His literary excursion into the interesting world of wind-breaking served as a source of amusing diversion from his more serious work." Josiah's written comment on the above work was "Let no man point a finger at me and exclaim 'He's a charming fellow, but at bottom a very obnoxious fellow.' I am human and nothing human is foreign to me."[27]

Wilgus noted that much of Combs's scholarly work and his stories and comments were "unpublishable," at least in his time. Combs himself commented on "off-color" humor, including his collection of material in "An Excursus into Scatology" and other works that that were never published:

> Look not in the great dictionaries, encyclopedias and slang dictionaries for the scatologia which follows these introductory remarks. For reasons of propriety and conventions, such things do not appear, as a rule, in print for the public eye. . . . They are, however, of more than ordinary human interest, in spite of all the straight-laced Puritans and prurient prudes. Regardless of all the preachments of the past, the present, and of time to come, it is impossible to eradicate the vulgar and the *risque* from the human mentality. . . . A serious and scholarly interest in scatologia in no way implies that

one's proboscis must be continually rooting around in the muck, that one's mind is not necessarily always parked in the sewer or gutter.[28]

Here are some excerpts from Norris Combs's foreword to "Voices from Below," a work that ran to 301 pages:

> Now, in my opinion, no other subject . . . can bring on a smile as quickly as the subject of farting. Yet, as we all know, it is not considered a proper subject of conversation in today's society. Some even consider it vulgar. . . . Be that as it may, my uncle was a very refined man and certainly not one who dealt in off-color topics. It was, and I emphasize the point, a most serious and rewarding endeavor to him and a valid subject for research.
>
> It was only after reading the full manuscript that I began to comprehend the vastness of his research. He . . . had corresponded with people all over the world, some famous, some otherwise. The bibliography lists an astounding one hundred and twenty-three sources of reference. . . . [M]any are from a rare and beautiful little book entitled *Bibliotheca Scatologica*, printed in France in 1849. . . . The bibliography is retained, as its loss, in my opinion, would mean an unforgivable literary sin. Future researchers will be thankful for this action. . . . Undoubtedly, such a list of references has never been compiled on the subject.[29]

Norris sent the manuscript to a literary agent, who wrote a lengthy letter in praise of it but concluded that he would not be able to find a publisher for it.

While Norris was comfortable with Josiah's interest in sexual and scatological matters, other relatives were not, and one even suggested that Charlotte may have influenced him in this interest, apparently believing that the French were far more lenient in such things than were Americans. Josiah ruminated at length on the part of our anatomy called the "arse" in Old English. In one piece he gave these ruminations the title "Some Anal Caterwauling"; another was entitled "Kiss Me, Don't Kick Me." Other off-color manuscripts were "Some Indecent Stag Yarns," "Some Pornographic Pot-Shots," and "Nerissa's Ring: Symbolism, Slang and Story." His comment on one piece was "Let us admit for the sake of argument that its subject matter is obscene; such an admission, however, does not argue that it is vulgar, dirty or nasty. I am ready to defend the thesis that there is such a thing as 'decent' obscenity."

After he retired, he prepared another book manuscript with Norris's help, entitled "May It Please the Court," a collection of stories, jokes, and published items all based on the justice system and the practice of law, mostly from eastern Kentucky, Texas, and Oklahoma. Some of these reflect the lusty side of human nature that brings people before the bar. One publisher had this manuscript set in type before noticing that some of the subject matter might not be appropriate for its readers, and the publication was canceled.

Another manuscript is "Quips and Observations (for My Classes)," which runs to 147 pages and numbers 1,852 entries. These were both original and collected items, some of which Combs read to his classes to amuse them and stimulate their thinking. He commented that he did not try to influence his students in such matters as religion (which he had harsh words for) or politics, and that he would not have read some of the quips to them.

Combs had no use for prudery, elitism, or false airs. Even though he spent most of his life in the towers of higher learning, he remained a mountain man at heart, and much of his scholarship had to do with the common people, their music, jokes, and tales, and their language and how they used it. He took great umbrage when his people were referred to as "hillbillies" or by other demeaning terms. He probably had suffered slights or disdain because of his origins and the people he wrote and taught about. Like other mountain people, he no doubt was acutely sensitive to any condescending look or disparaging word. Among his papers is a note stating his wish that "under no circumstance" should any of his papers go to the University of Kentucky, Louisville's Filson Club, or Indiana University. Wilgus suggests in the foreword to *Folk-Songs of the Southern United States* that the reason for these restrictions was "[t]he rivalry between Transylvania University and the once-arrogant state university, the exclusiveness of the historical club of Louisville's first families, and the impolite rejection of a scholarly note—these could not be forgotten."[30] The last part of Wilgus's comment refers to someone in Indiana University's famous folklore department who had dismissed something that Combs had written. Charlotte wrote "That's right" in one of her marginal notes in *Folk-Songs of the Southern United States*, affirming Wilgus's explanation of Combs's animus toward these three institutions.

Josiah Combs died of a heart attack on June 28, 1960, in Fort Worth, Texas. He was buried in the Sam Houston National Cemetery in San Antonio (section A–H, grave 1413). A smart man with a retentive mind and a superb education, he had lived life with full measure, observing his fellow humans and their beliefs and activities skeptically but with humor. He had complained little about the vagaries of living, and he faced death with equanimity. He was not someone who had relied on supernatural powers: an atheist, he wrote two manuscripts deriding religious beliefs, "Decretum Est" (It is decreed) and "I'll Be Damned." "My simple request," he wrote in the former, "is that I be buried totally and completely without ceremony ordinarily attendant upon such occasions. . . . A plain box—for a plain man. No tears, no flowers."[31]

Norris Combs wrote, "Josiah's death completely devastated Charlotte, and life became difficult. . . . Her love for him could not have been greater." Yet she rallied to assist Wilgus with his translation and reformation of Josiah's dissertation and to help Norris with the Combs genealogy project. She stoutly defended her husband and his work until she died on October 23, 1974. She is buried beside him in the Sam Houston National Cemetery. Josiah and Charlotte had no children.

Addendum

After the death of D. K. Wilgus in Los Angeles in 1989, his widow, Dr. Eleanor Long-Wilgus, also a folklore scholar, called me to ask if Berea College would be interested in receiving copies of the Josiah Combs papers that were part of her late husband's collection. After conferring with Dr. Gerald Roberts, archivist at the Southern Appalachian Archives at the Hutchins Library, I answered yes, indeed. She later called to ask if the college would also be interested in having the Edward Thomas dulcimer that Combs had received from Katherine Pettit at Hindman Settlement School, and of course we were delighted to receive it as well. Eventually, she also donated copies from her late husband's folklore collection relating to his work with Combs. The Josiah Combs Folklore Collection is part of the D. K. Wilgus Folklore Collection, SAA 67, Southern Appalachian Archives, Hutchins Library, Berea College, Berea, Kentucky. Dr. Long-Wilgus, who moved to Chapel Hill, North Carolina, also deposited copies of her husband's papers and the Combs papers in the Southern Historical Collection of the Wilson Library at the University of North Carolina.

Combs's Stories, Scholarship, Wit, and Songs

✳ "Black" Shade Combs

Let us begin this section with a story Combs told about a kinsman in the Kentucky mountains. It is among the papers that Eleanor Long-Wilgus donated to Berea College and was quoted in Combs's Folk-Songs of the Southern United States, *p. xiii.*

"Black" Shade Combs [was] a picturesque mountaineer whose long beard descending swept his rugged breast. "Black" was merely a pseudonym, for Shade was white, with no great claim to education and culture, but blessed with much native wit and intelligence. Shade and some other mountaineers found themselves in Frankfort, stopping at the Capitol Hotel, frequented by the Senators and Representatives, and by the elite. It was dinner time. Directly across the table from Shade sat an elegantly dressed woman, of easy morals and notorious reputation. A waiter comes to the table to take the orders. He addresses the courtesan:

Waiter: "What will you have, Lady?"

Courtesan: "First bring me a thimbleful of honeyed and spiced nectar, as sweet and soothing as an infant's cordial; second, bring me a tiny bowl of potage, seasoned with mushrooms and nightingale tongues; third, bring me a modest portion of asparagus tips, gently smothered with vinaigrette sauce; fourth, bring me a small beefsteak as tender as a chicken's breast; fifth, bring me a soft silk napkin to spread upon my bosom—and please inform me who the gentleman is that sits opposite."

"Black" Shade was thinking, and thinking fast. He drank in the whole import of the woman's obvious satire and contempt. By the time the waiter got around to him he was ready with a retort stinging and terrible.

Waiter: "And what will you have, Sir?"

"Black" Shade: "First, fetch me a pint of moonshine liquor as clear as crystal and as strong as hell; second, fetch me a big bowl of onion soup full of hog kidneys and 'mountain oysters' [hog testicles]; third, fetch me a bowl of hominy swimmin' in hog grease; fourth, fetch me a hunk of beefsteak as tough as a saddleskirt; fifth, fetch me a burlap sack to spread over my hairy breast—and (pointing straight at the woman of easy morals) please inform me who that God damned chippy is that sits opposite me."

Highland Stories

The following stories in this category are from another Combs collection in the Southern Appalachian Archives, the Josiah Combs Papers, SAA 71, box 2. They were published by Combs in the Kentucky Folklore Record *4, no. 2 (1958): 45–61 as "Some Kentucky Highland Stories," with notes by Herbert Halpert, and are used here with permission.*

❋ Y'Ain't A-Comin' Back

The revenue men were looking for a moonshine still. They stopped at the mouth of a creek, where a little boy was shooting marbles in the road, near the cabin. Then, "truth or consequences," with the following dialogue:

DEPUTY COLLECTOR: Sonny, does your daddy have a moonshine still?
BOY: Yeah, he does.
D.C.: Will you show me where it is?
BOY: No I won't.
D.C.: You'll show it to us, now, won't you? (He dangles a gold watch before the boy's eyes. . . .)
BOY: Yeah, I will, fer that.
D.C.: Come on, then, let's go. (He starts up the creek.)
BOY: Wait a minute, y'ain't gimme the watch.

D.C.: Oh, we'll give it to you when we get back.

BOY: No, ye won't; y'ain't a-comin' back.

Halpert, p. 59, referenced Ozark and Illinois versions, and I have heard several versions told.

❀ Trouble to Yourselves

An industrial school was being founded at Hindman, in Knott County [Hindman Settlement School]. The ladies delegated to start the school were from the lowlands. The trip from the nearest railroad, at Jackson, required two days in order to reach Hindman, and the ladies were traveling in a rough jolt-wagon, over rough, dirt roads. They stopped at a mountaineer's home the first night. The beds were in one room. The mountaineer's wife watched, with great curiosity, the ladies undress and put on their sleeping garments before retiring.

"Do ye all do this every night before ye go to bed?" she asked them. On being told that they did, she paused for several seconds, then: "Ye all must be a lot of trouble to yeselves."

Halpert, p. 58, notes that "[a] similar comment is made to a traveling salesman by ranch children" in Oren Arnold, The Wild West Joke Book *(New York: Perma Books, 1957), pp. 21–22.*

❀ Healthy Hogs

The county health officer was making the rounds. At one mountain cabin he could see that several hogs slept under the floor of the cabin. He said to the mountaineer:

"Don't you think that is unhealthy?"

"They ain't a one of them hogs died yet," replied the mountaineer.

Halpert, p. 58, gives a similar punch line in "an older, probably English, jest about Irish peasants. Asked why he let the pig live in his house, the Irishman replied: 'Why not? Doesn't the place afford every convenience?'" Bonnie Collins from West Virginia contributed a version to Loyal Jones and Billy Edd Wheeler, Laughter in Appalachia: A Festival of Southern Mountain Humor *(Little Rock, Ark.: August House, 1987), p. 61.*

❋ The Dilemma

There were two small hotels in the town, facing each other. A traveler rides up and addresses the proprietor of one of them:

Traveler: Say, which one of these hotels is the best?

Proprietor: Stranger, no matter which one you go to—you'll wish you'd gone to t'other one.

Halpert, pp. 59–60, referenced Allan M. Trout in the January 29, 1954, Louisville Courier-Journal, who said that he had asked a man which restaurant in an east Kentucky town was "the best place to eat" and "was given the same answer."

❋ The Necessities of Life

A traveler stopped to chat with a mountaineer who lived on top of the mountain, miles distant from the nearest habitation or country store.

Traveler: Isn't it rather difficult to obtain the necessities of life up here so far from everything?

Mountaineer: Yeah, hit shorely is, and even when you git 'em they ain't fitten to drink.

I once heard another story about bad liquor. This fellow hitched a ride with a mountain man. After a few miles, the driver offered him a drink from a fruit jar. He politely declined. The driver pulled out a pistol, aimed it as at his passenger, and said, "Stranger, around here, if you're offered a drink, you take it." The passenger took a drink and shuddered and gasped. Then the driver handed the pistol to him and said, "Now hold that pistol on me while I take a drink."

❋ On Suicide

Culbert Stamper, of Knott County, thought he was a ladies man, a gay Lothario—until: there appeared a young lady from the lowlands, to teach in the local public school. It was in the days of rubber-tired buggy, patent leather shoes, tight-fitting pants, and the mustache. Culbert suddenly took a liking for the new teacher, her face, dress, carriage and all. He wanted to call on her, but every time he thought of it he could not muster up courage to ask her; for he saw at once that she was "different" from the mountain girls. At long last he overcame his timidity, and bluntly asked the "ferrin" lady for a date. Out of curiosity she accepted. Culbert calls. They sit in the "parlor." Total lack of conversation, for Culbert does not know how to begin, nor what to say. Continued silence. . . . Finally, to start conversation, the new teacher says to Culbert:

"Mr. Stamper, what do you think of a man that commits suicide?"

Culbert lapses into profound meditation, squirming in his chair, crossing first one leg and then the other, then twists both ends of his mustache with his fingers, looks up and replies sententiously:

"Well, Madam, I think he ought to be made to take the child and raise it."

Halpert, p. 60, said that he had collected a similar story in western Kentucky. He notes also, "In Vance Randolph, Funny Stories from Arkansas *(Girard, Kansas, 1943), p. 4, a Justice of the Peace tells a village constable that for a suicide he thinks the law is 'six months in jail an' support the child.'"*

❀ Good-Hearted

Andy was considerate of his beasts of burden. For a day's work once, one of my uncles let him have a bushel of corn. Starting for home in the evening, he placed the sack of corn on his horse's back. "But no," said he, "this old horse has worked hard today; I'll just tote the corn myself." He got up on the horse and had the corn lifted on his own back.

Stories like this one have been collected all over the world, and they have been designated by folklorists as "numbskull" jokes.

❀ Every Opportunity

An old mountaineer, too far along in years to have any sexual interest in women, married a young woman. In time she complained of pains in her abdomen, and a doctor was called.

DOCTOR: She's pregnant.
OLD MAN (HARD OF HEARING): Eh?
DR.: I say, she's pregnant.
OLD MAN: Eh?
DR.: She's going to have a BABY.
OLD MAN: Wall, I ain't surprised; she's had every opportunity.

I've heard several versions of this joke over time, usually told by older men. I'm reminded of another story related to folklorist Bill Lightfoot by his elderly heating-oil deliveryman, John Vickery, in Boone, North Carolina, and reprinted in Loyal Jones and Billy Edd Wheeler, Curing the Cross-Eyed Mule: Appalachian Mountain Humor *(Little Rock, Ark.: August House, 1989), p. 188. Three young city fellows recruit an old man wandering past the golf course to fill in for a missing player. He complies. They play eighteen holes, and he beats them, wins all their money, and then drinks them under the table at the clubhouse. He is asked if his old age has any disadvantages at all. He thinks for a minute and says, "Yeah, I can think of one. This morning when I woke up, I asked my wife to make love, and she says, 'What, after seven times last night?' You see, when you get old, your memory begins to slip a bit!" There ought to be a "Fond Memory" category for such humor.*

✳ The Ice Church

The story comes from Pulaski County [Kentucky] that years ago certain communicants of the Primitive Baptist Church once made a trip to Louisville; that they actually saw a man delivering *ice* from a truck on the street, although it was August. Returning home they spread the news. Everybody shakes his head; total disbelief. The church fathers consider the story and decide to "church" [excommunicate] the brethern who said they saw ice in August.

"God-Almighty, Himself, couldn't make ice in August," they said.

But the story gains credence, little by little. A committee of good brethern were appointed to go to Louisville and investigate. They came back and reported that they actually saw ice being made. They were in turn "churched." Their story gained favor, and finally the believers in August ice got together and organized a new church., called the "Ice Church."

Halpert, p. 57, notes that there were common humorous or derisive titles coming out of southern church splits. Sometimes there is inadvertent humor in the naming of churches. Once while driving along, I saw a church sign, "Little Hope Baptist Church," and I've heard of others with the same name (you can find one online). I surmise that this occurred because Baptists are humble and love the diminutive. The Indian Bottom Association of Old Regular Baptists in eastern Kentucky— they have a website—has nine churches with "Little" as part of their name.

✳ Too Much Surrendering

A mountain youth went off to college down in the Bluegrass. One Sunday morning he strolled downtown with another college student. Suddenly the words and music of a familiar hymn reached their ears from a choir in a church on the other side of the street:

> I surrender all.
> I surrender all;
> All to Jesus I surrender,
> I surrender all.

"Want to go in?" the young mountaineer was asked.
"Nope, too much surrenderin' goin' on over there."

In Loyal Jones and Billy Edd Wheeler, More Laughter in Appalachia: Southern Mountain Humor *(Little Rock, Ark.: August House, 1995), pp. 121–22, Peggy Davis of Pike County, Kentucky, tells the story of a church that was debating whether or not to excommunicate a man who had been caught one time too many with another man's wife, with one side arguing for churching him and the other reasoning that the church should forgive sinners and bring them back into the fold. Finally, an old lady rose to have her say: "I've been a member of this church for nigh onto forty years, and for forty years it's been 'Fornicate and forgive!' And I'm here to tell you, good brethren and good sistren, I'm gettin' tired of doing all the forgivin'!"*

✳ Double-Washing His Sins

A Primitive Baptist preacher was baptizing his neophytes, in the Kentucky River, at Jackson, Breathitt County. An erstwhile sinner was ready to be plunged beneath the waves. He had been a very wicked man. Just as he was ready to take the plunge, old man Hargis, standing on the bank of the stream, cried out: "Souse him twice, preacher, fer he's a damned sinner, and it'll take twice to wash his sins away."

Halpert, p. 58, wrote, "Humorous tales, both Negro and white, about baptizings are common in the South. . . . Cf. Williams, Master Book of Humorous Illustrations, *p. 37 ('one dip won't do him no good; you'll have to anchor him out in deep water overnight.') In an east Tennessee story printed by [Allan] Trout in his* Courier-Journal *column for Aug. 27, 1954, some ginger cakes float out of the apron pocket of a widow while she is being immersed. The steward on the bank yells to the preacher: 'Sock her again, Brother! Her sins are floating away in chunks.'" In my* Preacher Joke Book: Religious Anecdotes from the Oral Tradition *(Little Rock, Ark.: August House, 1989), p. 31, there's one about a backslider who has been rebaptized six times, on which occasion the preacher tells him, "You've been baptized so much the fish know you by your first name." One of my favorite baptizing stories is from the late Reverend Will D. Campbell, a notable Baptist, who said his Baptist father was asked if he believed in infant baptism, and replied, "Believe in it? I've actually seen it done!" Ibid., p. 41.*

❊ A Pastor and His Ewe Lambs

This is a real complaint filed with the committee of a Baptist church in Kentucky.

The complainant says that she is informed, believes, and charges the same to be true, that the defendant, the Rev. ____, was not in good standing with the church, since he was seen by various members of his church to be in a compromising position with one of the members thereof.

The charges were referred to a congregational committee of the church, a meeting was held, the defendant appeared in person before the committee, and to defend himself, filed a plea of confessions and avoidance, admitting the charges as alleged, but justifying them on the Scripture; saying that the Bible says that it is perfectly proper for the shepherd of the flock to hold in his arms the lamb thereof.

The plaintiff says that she is informed that the charges were referred to a special committee to act upon the charges; and having become very much perturbed by the evidence introduced, withdrew, and after a consultation lasting over two hours rendered a Scotch verdict [an inconclusive decision] in the shape of a resolution, which reads as follows: Whereas our beloved pastor has been seen by several of the observing members of his congregation holding in his arms one of the ewe lambs thereof, and, whereas, he has sought to justify his actions upon the Scriptures, saying that the Bible says that it is perfectly proper for the shepherd of the flock to hold the lamb thereof.

Now, therefore, be it resolved, in order to prompt the best interests of the congregation, and the best interests of all kinds whatever and whatsoever, the next time he feels constrained to grab a lamb, that he grab a ram lamb.

Plaintiff says that he did not observe the warnings of the congregation as to ewe and ram lambs, but that he is still affectionate with the ewe lambs, and has cast off the rams. Therefore plaintiff insists that the defendant be dismissed from the church.

"May It Please the Court" Stories

Combs's court-related manuscript of stories has never been published. Here is a sampling. They are located in the Combs Papers, series VI, box 3, folders 7–10.

✹ A Slight Disagreement

An aged, gray-haired and very wrinkled old woman, arrayed in calico costume, was summoned as a witness in the court, to tell what she knew about a fight in her house. She took the witness stand with evidences of a lack of sophistication. The judge addressed her in a kindly voice.

"Now, mother, don't be afraid. Just tell us in your own words what took place."

The old woman insisted that it did not amount to much. But the judge, by his persistence, got her to tell the story of the bloody fracas.

"Now, I tell ye Jedge, it didn't amount to nothin'. The fust thing I knowed about it was when Bill Saunders called Tom Smith a liar, an' Tom knocked him down with a stick of wood. One of Bill's friends cut Tom then with his knife, slicin' a big chunk out o' him. Then Tom bit off the feller's ear, an' then that feller got riled, an' went atter Tom. Sam Jones, who was a friend o' Tom's, shot the other feller, and two more shot him, an' three or four others got cut up right smart by somebody." Here, she hesitated.

"What happened then?" asked the judge.

"That nachly caused some excitement, Jedge, an' then they all went outside an' commenced fightin'."

Combs attributed this story to R. Lee Stewart of Morehead, Kentucky, and added, "I heard it when I was boy in the Kentucky mountains." Ironic understatement is an important element in Appalachian humor.

✳ Overruling the Statute

Judge Dave Calhoun was the first county judge in Knott County, in the 1880s. He was hearing a case, and made a decision contrary to all law and precedent. One of the lawyers protested vigorously, "Why, your Honor, such a verdict in this case is contrary to the Statutes."

"In that case I have seen fit to overrule the Statutes," replied his Honor on the bench.

✳ Outside of His Jurisdiction

A farmer was summoned to serve on the petit jury. At the moment he should have been present in court, he was buying a coat, having learned that he would not be permitted to appear in Federal court without one. The purchase having been completed, he rushed into the courtroom just after the jury had been empaneled. The judge, observing his confusion inquired,

"Are you on the petit jury?"

"Yes, your Honor."

"Then," said the judge, "hold up your right hand and be sworn."

The juror was a religious fanatic. "I would prefer to affirm."

Rather nettled by the juror's preference, the judge said, "All right then, affirm," and he administered the affirmation. Then he asked, "Are you a householder in the district, or a freeholder in the state?"

"May it please the court, your Honor," he replied, "I am a sojourner from this terrestrial sphere to the celestial city above, whose builder and maker is God."

The judge impatiently replied, "Stand aside. By God, that's outside my jurisdiction."

Combs gave credit for this story to Texas judge W. T. Andrews. The exchange supposedly took place in a federal court in East Texas.

✳ A Verdict on a Technicality

The most beloved old settler in a little Texas community had killed a worthless town character during the heat of a quarrel. Being an honest man, he pleaded guilty to the charge of first degree murder. It looked as if he would hang. But the jury, all friends of his for many years, determined to save him in spite of himself. They brought in a verdict of not guilty.

"How in the world," the judge demanded, "can you twelve men bring in an acquittal when the defendant has already admitted his guilt, is quite beyond me. Please explain your action."

"Well, your honor," offered the foreman, "the defendant is such a liar that we can't believe him."

✼ Honest and Upright, but Biased and Unchaste

A lawyer from the "Settlements" was representing a corporation at a session of the county court in Breathitt County, Kentucky. Judge Jim Hargis, of Hargis-Callahan feud fame, was in the chair. The county attorney was a bit wooly in the intricate mazes of jurisprudence and legal procedure, but he was not lacking in eloquence and poetic sentiments. When his turn came, he arose and unburdened himself to wit:

> May it please the court: the gentleman representing the corporation is a man who has pretensions at larnin'. He hails from the county of Henry, where the limpid waters ripple over limestone pebbles. From thar he hailed to the city of Louisville, where he rubbed his withers against college walls. From thar he hailed to the county of Lee, where the sarvice blossoms and the honeysuckle mingle, and from thar he hailed to this good county, where the lilies grow. But with all his larnin' he cain't change the mind of this Court; for your Honor on the bench is a man who knows the law, and is an honest, upright, biased, partial, and unchaste gentleman.

There is much humor about pretentious people who wander beyond knowledge of appropriate grammar and the law in trying to express themselves.

✼ Time to Milk

Two men were in jail, one of them for stealing a cow, the other for stealing a watch. The first day of their incarceration, along just before dark, the man that had stolen the cow grinned and said to the man that had stolen the watch, "What time is it?" The reply was forthcoming: "Time to milk."

This joke is pretty widely known.

❈ Defensive Action

Lawyer Stowers, of Pikeville, Kentucky, was a born diplomat and a suave gentleman. One day an elegant lady, accompanied by a poodle, met him on the street, and they began to chat. Soon the dog walked over and began to sniff Stowers' neatly pressed pants. Then it raised a hind leg to perform a common canine function. Stowers gave a mighty leap backward.

"Oh, Mr. Stowers, I'm so sorry," the lady exclaimed.

"Think nothing of it, Madam," the courtly lawyer replied. "I thought he was going to kick me."

❈ Swore the Child on Us

A very timid Tennessee mountaineer was accused of being the father of an illegitimate child. The child's mother had "laid" it to him, and he was summoned to the county seat to answer the charge. The same afternoon he arrived back home, and stood at the gate in front of the house with fear and trembling. His wife was standing in the doorway waiting for him.

Wife (sternly): "Well, out with it. What did they do about it?"

Husband (hesitating): "Why—er—don't you know, that nasty-stinking-thing went and swore the child on *us*."

❈ Bounds of Reason

When a mountaineer makes a show of trying to use correct grammar and syntax, soon the sobriquet "Proper" is tacked onto his name. "Proper" Jim Stacey lived on Troublesome Creek and was a magistrate. A case was being tried in his court. A lawyer or two from Hindman was there. The jury was ready to retire for consultation. "Proper" Jim looked very pensive, pretending to pore over the pages of a heavy law book as he thumbed through it. Then: "I thought I knew the law in this case, but I don't seem to find it here. Gentlemen, just retire and render a verdict within the bounds of reason."

❈ Judge Patton

Judge John S. Patton was circuit judge of the old twenty-fourth judicial circuit [in Kentucky], 1890–1896. This circuit lay deep in the heart of the old "pure feud belt," and comprised the counties of Martin (native county of Patton), Magoffin, Johnson, Floyd, Knott, and perhaps one or two more. Judge Patton was eccentric, tobacco-chewing, unorthodox in dress and speech, and liked his "hooch." But he was eloquent and humane, possessing a fine sense of the eternal verities, and withal a good judge. He was celebrated in his mountain district for his charges to juries. There were no stenographic reports of them at the time, and so we must rely upon oral tradition for its versions or variants.

Speaking of malefactors and lawbreakers, he once instructed his grand jury: "Gentlemen! when you see a young buck a-sittin' at the forks of the road with a banger strung across his breast, a-wearin' of a celluloid collar, a celluloid rose in his coat lapel, his breath a-smellin' of cinnamon oil, and a-pickin' of 'Sourwood Mountain,' indict that man, gentlemen, indict him, for if he ain't already done somethin', he's a-goin' to. Every time one of those characters comes into my community, I go straight home to my daughter."

"There is yet another circumstance, gentlemen of the jury, to which I invite your attention. There is a little country church by the roadside. Some good Christian mother has planted a little maple tree in the front to beautify and make comfortable the entrance to the church. It is yet a tender little tree. The good country folks on the inside of this little church are earnestly singing praises and uttering prayers to Almighty God.

"A young feller with a spur on each foot, his hat tilted to one side, a bandana handkerchief around his neck, rides up to the church on a mule. He dismounts, and instead of hitching his mule to a fencepost or the swinging limb of a beech tree, he hitches the mule to the tender little maple tree. And above the sound of the songs and prayers in the church the braying of the mule can be heard as he gnaws all the bark from this tree and destroys it.

"Gentlemen, that feller should be indicted and brought before me. A man like that would ride a jackass into the Garden of Eden, spit in the faces of Adam and Eve, and hitch the animal to the Tree of Life!"

Combs added that one version has "and banter Moses for a horse-swap." Different versions of these two stories, also credited to Combs, are in Jones and Wheeler, Curing the Cross-Eyed Mule, *pp. 105–6.*

Some Indecent Stag Yarns

These and others can be found in the Combs Papers, series V, box 2, folder 27.

Lincoln was in a field hospital visiting the sick and the wounded. Talkative lady: "Mr. Lincoln, where was this man hit?" "On the battlefield, Madam." "But I mean where did the ball hit him?" Lincoln, searching for the proper answer, and finally, "Madam, the bullet that hit him would have missed you."

Traveler stops at farmhouse. Very fond of soup beans for supper. Everybody slept in the same room. Grown girl's bed next to the traveler. She falls for him, and, late in the night, whispers, "Now's the time! Now's the time!" The traveler gets right up, goes in the kitchen and eats the rest of the beans.

Man shipwrecked on a lonely isle for ten years, beautiful, young naked woman washed ashore on a beer barrel. Revived, she said to him: "Now that you have been so good to me, I'm going to give you something you haven't had in ten years." He: "You mean to tell me that there's some beer left in that barrel?"

How low can a man sink? As low as whale shit, and everybody knows how low that is.

Lecture on ghosts. At close, lecturer asked if anyone had had a sexual experience with a ghost. A cowboy came forward. "You mean you have screwed a ghost?" asked the lecturer. "Oh, I thought you said a goat," replied the cowboy.

Circus comes to country town. One of the elephants gets loose, begins to pull up cabbage heads with his trunk in nearby garden and to eat them. Local boy runs to owner of the garden, Mrs. Jones, and says: "Mrs. Jones, a big strange animal is out here pullin' up your cabbage heads with his tail." Mrs. Jones: "What's he doing with them?" Boy: "I can't tell ye, Mrs. Jones, and ye wouldn't believe me, anyway."

Another, longer version of this story was told to me by Jesse James Bailey, who served as sheriff of both Madison and Buncombe counties in North Carolina, and was teller of many tales. He said once a circus came to Madison County, and an elephant escaped. He went to look for it and came to a cabin up a hollow where a distraught woman was looking over her demolished garden, and she began

*telling the sheriff about this "great big old ugly" animal that tore down her pal-
ing fence and began pulling up her cabbages with its "big old tail." Bailey asked
her, "What did he do with the cabbages?" She replied, "Sheriff, you wouldn't
believe it if I told you!"*

Woman to husband: "If it wasn't for two things I'd leave you." "Yes," said the
husband, "I know. I've got one of them and you've got the other."

Mountaineer had 8 children. He was blind. Charity committee of women
called on him at his cabin. One of the women said, "I see you have 8 children,
and you are blind." Quipped the mountaineer, "Madam, I just couldn't see
what I was doing."

Some Anal Caterwauling

*In this section, Combs shows his fondness for scatology, specifically here as he
lapses into autobiography honoring the Old English "arse." These are from the
Combs Papers, series V, box 2, folder 26.*

My master is inwardly proud of me, yet ashamed of me—for he will not
expose me in company, nor will he discourse on me in polite company.

Strange, that man should revile me and say all manner of indecency
about me, since I serve him so loyally and so constantly.

Sometimes, in their haste and anger men threaten to kick me. This is
the most common form of threatening resentment against my master.

They say that a one-legged man has no chance in a match at kicking me.
Would that all such participants could have but one leg each.

In the spirit of fine sportsmanship my master has asked certain men to
kiss me. I am kicked about shamelessly and repeatedly, but people rarely
accept an invitation to kiss me.

I have sunk so low that some people do not know me from a hole in the
ground.

There are times when even my master does not keep faith with me, for
when he has diarrhea he avers that he would not trust me with a fart.

Alas! my master has enemies. The other day I heard a man say he would
not pour water in me if my master's intestines were on fire.

My master sometimes rends me asunder with terrific ventosity; he gets
the laugh, while I bear the brunt.

St. Augustine says that my master was born between me and water. Considering the closeness of the affinity, I am entitled to more respect and affection.

Welladay! I am old, ever so old as a word, but I am no longer tolerated in polite speech. I am of Germanic ancestry, and I have been in the English language since very early times. I was once held in high respect, and the people used my name openly as the occasion demanded. Dean [Jonathan] Swift respected me so much that he wrote a famous essay on me. In English literature I go back as far as the fourteenth century. But I lived only on borrowed time, for the day of excommunication finally arrived, and I became a victim of prudery and false modesty.

Jonathan Swift's essay was "The Benefit of Farting Explain'd," published as a pamphlet in 1722. Benjamin Franklin was fond of fart jokes. While he was minister to France, he also wrote an essay aimed at the Royal Academy—never sent— suggesting that scientists should be about the task of making farts smell good.

Quips and Observations (1954–59)

Combs Papers, box 2, folders 17–21. His "Quips" ran to 147 pages with some 1,852 items. The following are selected.

In the belief that the average student's understanding of human nature— its foibles, inconsistencies and shortcomings—is of necessity restricted, I have written down these quips to read to my students (in French) from day to day. Considering the definition of a quip, I cheerfully admit that they are not all quips. Some of them are little pieces of advice, purely and simply; others touch on medicine, politics and religion. But I am no moralist, no political scientist, no theologian, only an humble observer of human nature.

Nor must it be hardly assumed that I am either a cynic or a pessimist. Unfortunately I am unable to defend the thesis that human nature is essentially good. But I do maintain that there is enough good in it to justify the hope that, in the centuries or the ages to come, society will be infinitely better. Here, human beings, themselves, will have to be arbiters, the master of their own fate. In such a happy, but hypothetical age I see no connection whatever between religious beliefs and the *summum bonum* [higher good].

I confess that all the quips are not my own brain-children. Indeed, the central ideas of a number of them are found or heard elsewhere; I merely set them down as they strike me. Finally, for obvious reasons I do not read all of the quips to my students. Nor do I seek to influence students in any way in their religious or political beliefs. I seek only to induce them to T H I N K, and to relieve the tension.

You are wondering what manner of man your professor is. He is two-legged, walks upright, puts on his socks one foot at a time, same as the rest of you, eats and drinks, is not infallible—and has no patience with bluffers.

You can marry more money in five minutes than you can earn in a lifetime.

Some strange specimens, including Puritans, came to Plymouth Rock in 1620 because the immigration laws at the time were far from satisfactory.

Education may be defined as the only commodity for which students insist on getting less than they pay for.

The automobile has divided society into two classes: the quick and the dead.

French is the irresistible force now in contact with an unmovable object, this class.

Some call it tact; others call it intuition. In the final analysis it is nothing but plain, common horse-sense.

Reform that prospective husband before you marry him, not afterward. Before you get him you can see wings sprouting on his shoulders; look out, later on, after the honeymoon, you may discover sprouting horns under his hair.

The word "student" is the biggest etymological misnomer in the dictionary.

Medicine is the noblest of professions, yet the great doctors have received less praise and credit than the conquering heroes and mass murderers. Pasteur and Lister will be known and honored long after Alexander the Great, Caesar and Napoleon are forgotten.

The Genesis version of the creation says that God created Adam first. This is sheer wisdom, as we may assume that He did not want a woman standing around telling Him how to do the job.

You can't digest chewing gum and a foreign language at the same time. Eject one or the other. Register another one for the cow; she chews her cud for a purpose.

Moderation in all things: never run when you can walk; never walk when you can sit; never sit when you can lie down.

I am a great believer in idleness—during which periods one should do some constructive thinking while he reposes.

The chief mark of a lady or a gentleman is not whether or not he or she drinks, but rather, whether or not he or she can hold his or her liquor.

I have always made it a point never to take a drink while asleep, never to refuse one while awake, and never to take two drinks at the same time.

Never ask a man why his nose is red. He may reply that it is glowing with pride because it is kept out of other people's business.

Stated in terms of mathematical proportion, French is to this class what water is to a duck's back.

"Existentialism" is just another fad in philosophy. Its author, himself, cannot explain it, nor can anybody else. In spite of theologians and philosophers and all the scientists, man will never be able to explain himself and the universe satisfactorily to rational minds.

The Daughters of the American Revolution will never forgive George Washington for dying without issue.

Lots of men are warned to give up "wine, women and song." Some of them solemnly promise never to sing another note.

The fine art of cussing has declined, especially among the English. Americans cuss more vigorously, but without refinement.

When I reflect upon the struggle of Woman down through the ages to reach her rightful place in society, and the painful trials she has undergone and is still undergoing, she gets my vote every time.

According to the Bible, woman is the author of original sin, she is penalized by child-bearing and manual labor, she is everywhere the root of all evil. Do you think she got a fair deal?

If human beings were blessed with only a fraction of the social organization, resourcefulness, energy and honesty of the lowly ant or honey bee, the race could dispense with jails, police systems, courts of law, relief and charitable organizations, economic depressions, divorce courts, armies and wars.

Nature has endowed the lower animals with instinct, or animal intuition, something that usually serves them better than intelligence, mind or will power serves human beings.

A short speech is like a short skirt; it should be short enough to be interesting, but long enough to cover the subject.

A smart man is one who always holds opinions similar to your own, and who occasionally seeks your advice.

It is of no concern to me as to whether it is a sitting hen or a setting hen. But when she cackles, my concern is whether she has laid, or whether she has lied.

Einstein's theory of relativity is easy to understand when compared with the Mother Church definition of the Trinity.

✺ Some Quips and Observations on Flatulence

Combs's work on flatulence amounted to some 186 pages. The following items are selected. Combs Papers, series V, box 2, folder 26.

A long-winded speech always reminds one of the long, dribbled poot which horses used to let back in the days of the horse-and-buggy when a fellow took his girl friend out driving: it seemed to never end.

There is a wild onion in Tibet which, when eaten, produces a nether stench so vile that a man must run away from his own farts. I prefer the species of the Western world: with it a man can at least remain stationary, maintain a poker face and palliate his guilt, if not the scent.

All persons of a goosey or ticklish disposition should avoid onions, and turnips and foods of high sulphuric content. Under certain conditions the *crepitus ventris* is no respecter of etiquette.

Social expediency long since tabooed the short four-letter words for wind-breaking—but no appendectomy can ever taboo the act itself.

Confucius say man that fart in church sit on *pew*. Woman that break wind in company break reputation.

A rose would smell as sweet by any other name. By the same token, a fart would smell as vile by any other name. Simple words, even when not accompanied by the object, or act, leave their imprint upon our sensibilities.

A man is well on his way to becoming a gentleman when his anal sphincter disports itself with decorum in the presence of the ladies.

A real gallant gentleman is one who, when a lady accidentally breaks wind in company, jumps to his feet at once and cries out, "Pardon me, ladies and gentlemen."

Why does an accidental volley from the Valley of Thunder always cause laughter—whereas, an eructation [belch], even a violent one, does no such thing. In the latter case the guilty party is slightly embarrassed, but he merely says "Excuse me," and that is an end to it. In the former case he is of course too abashed to speak. Now a poot-in-the-making travels downward, while an eructation travels upward. As to laughter or chagrin, why should mere direction legislate in the matter? Oh well, perhaps we should consider the point of *departure*.

We cannot fix with certainty the exact age in social history in which the Aeolean crepitation (vulgarly called the fart) was excommunicated. We know that a bouncing fart caused laughter among the ancient Greeks and Romans, as it does among the peoples of Europe and America today. . . . [W]e know only that in time it fell victim to social expediency, and was therefore ostracized. *Sed non requiescat in pace.*

When a man's anal sphincter plays him false and fails to head off an inadvertent Aeolian crepitation in company, he becomes the victim of a sudden and violent *contretemps*—and everybody laughs, or feels the urge to laugh; unless he can control his emotions and keep his at an even keel, in which case he may appear innocent and free from suspicion. If he blushes and openly betrays his embarrassment, it is useless to appeal to psychology for help.

Again: the lowly fart may have lost caste in the early stages of man's social development—not, however, from social or ethical [reasons], but from practical expediency, for example: as when our ponderous, hairy ancestor lay sleeping in his secret lair, pooting as he snored and snoring as he pooted—until his hefty spouse, annoyed by the noise and stench of his anal artillery, grabbed her mate's cudgel and bludgeoned him out of the cave, where the aroma of his farts could waste its sweetness on the desert air.

Farting is an art, as every experienced man knows. With experts, only the letter *f* separates art from fart.

❀ Lincoln at Gettysburg (1946)
In the vernacular of the Kentucky Mountains

Combs Papers, series IV, box 2, folder 4.

Away back yander, beyant the ricomembrance of our gran'sires, our forepappies went to straw and fotch on a free gineration of folks over here in this new world; 't were in our gum-and-sheepskin days, atter we'd jist fit a fair fight against that shoat-of-a-king and his redcoats that come from t'other side of the ocean. That generation had innard enlightenment, even a-bornin', and figgered ez how hit orter be ez free ez hell, and ez independent ez a hog on ice, an' sich an' sich; for hit war knowin' to all the sarcumstances; leastwise, hit strake a strong strike fer hit, and didn't come back from the hunt a-suckin' the gun-bar'l. Furdermore, them forepappies reckoned ez how the old Mortal above predestyned that one man is about ez good ez any other when he is borned. Now here we are slap-dab on the spot where a mighty fight was fit; we aim to fix up a hoop-and-a-holler of hit as ez a last restin' place and a moniment fer them ez fit so hard here to make this a fitten country to live in. And yit, ez the preacher-man sez, hit ain't prophesied that sich mortals ez me and you hev a call to dedicate and consecrate this fightin'-place; fer them fightin' men, fer them that's still a-fightin' and them that's been kilt off here has done so well that weuns cain't do much consecratin', one way or t'other. I reckon as how you and me was predestyned to be still amongst the livin' and we get to ricollect not to disremember that there's a lot o' fightin' to be done yit; furder, I feel to know that we don't aim to disremember what these dead men died a-fighten fer. What I'm a-sayin' here ain't a-goin' fer to retch from mountaintop, to mountaintop, and nobody's a-goin' to set much store by hit sich ez hit is; but what them fightin' men done here, that is goin' to be talked about ez long ez the Constitution stands; no dee-falcation about that. Right now we aim to make hit so's this country shall be borned agayn, seein' ez how God-'lmighty wills it; and ricollectin' that any government of the citizens, sot up by the citizens, and fer the citizens, ain't in for perishin' from this yearth. Anyways, not yit.

Language of the Southern Highlanders

The following excerpts are from Combs's "Language of the Southern Highland-ers," PMLA 46, no. 4 (1931): 1302–22. Used with permission.

Brevity is the soul of the highlander's language. He prefers it to clearness and to grammatical accuracy. In most of the rural schools over this "far country" the teaching of grammar exercises almost no influence upon everyday speech. The pupils are not taught to discard their dialect and their grammatical irregularities, because their teachers employ so much of it themselves. However, when a boy or girl goes away to school to be "taught up," he usually returns with a different manner of speech.

The highlander is slow to adopt anything foreign into his speech. English, with its early survivals, and a touch here and there of Irish and Scottish, are the predominant elements. Very few words related to French or German have been found, except in parts of Virginia and West Virginia. . . .

The following glib usage is expressive:

That cow has turned roguish, and is up to meanness. (A "roguish" cow is
   one that jumps fences, etc.)

. . .

The elements look threatenin. (It may rain, or snow.)
That gal of Zeke's is shorely dilitary.

. . .

Ole Shade's nearly blind, but he can discern the bulk of a person.

. . .

Samp's Bob got hisself cracked on the noggin (head) in the fray yistiddy.
Yer plum' bereft!

. . .

My nose informs me hit's time to stick my feet under the dinner table.

. . .

He tuk umbrage at what I said to him.

Highland speech is rich and expressive in figures. The following list is noted:

Steve ups and runs like a bat shot outn hell.
The dog tuk out after him, an' he lit a rag fer home.
I didn't know him from Adam's off-ox.
When the doctor looked at him he batted his eyes like a toad in a hail
   storm.

. . .

He wuz ez drunk as a biled owl, er a fiddler's bitch.

. . .

He's not exactly a damned fool. (Very shrewd, clever.)

. . .

Highland speech is rich in idioms . . . spicy and pungent, forming an even more interesting study than any word-lists. In his idiomatic usage the highlander often goes astray from his accustomed brevity.

That boy's got lots o' sand in his gizzard.
. . .
Ole Spence's head is a-blossomin' fer the grave.
. . .
I aim to foal that mare, come grass (in the spring).
. . .
Hell's broke loose in Georgy! (A fight has commenced.)
Hit's nary a thing but a tale-idle. (A false report.)
I know in reason he's right about it.
. . .
I had in head to plow to-day, but hit come on rain.
I've laid off an' laid off to dig that well.
. . .
Belly-to-the-ground, that hoss was a-flyin' offn the face o' th' yearth!
That feller don't know enough to come in outn the rain.
He couldn't pour water outn a boot an' the directions on the heel.

"Cuss-words," expressions of surprise and intense expressions are numerous, as one might expect. A few of them follow:

Hell's bangers!	Hell shot a buck rabbit!
I (by) God!	Gosh (A)lmighty!
By crackies!	By grab!
Lordy mercy! (Scot., Lord hae mercy!)	I (by) gonnies!
Dadburn it!	Jesus H. Christ!
Consarn it (or you)!	Confound it (or you)!
I niggle-double dare you!	A-law!
You're mighty right I'm a-goin'!	Gee-miny-crimminy!

. . .

There is considerable fondness for the Old English or Teutonic compound. . . . Some noun compounds . . . are offered:

biscuit-bread	flour-bread
sticking-stuff (mucilage,etc.)	rock-cliff
preacher-man	pot-vessel (any pot)
granny-woman (midwife)	gal-folks (girls)

store-teeth (false teeth)
beetle-bug (any sort of beetle)
hist'ry-book

tooth-dentist
reader-book
Bible-reader (preacher)

Pleonasm is often employed, for the sake of emphasis and terseness. Many of the compounds, the noun compounds in particular, are pleonastic. One hears for example:

During the while.
In this day and time.
He tuk a nap o' sleep.
That's a good meal o' victuals.

. . .

Hit wuz a small, little bitsy rabbit.
Ole Bringe was a tol'able big, large fleshy man.

. . .

Raleigh town, Richmond town, Lynchburg town, etc.

De-Standardized American English: A Study in Linguistic Pathology

Combs Papers, series IV, box 2, folder 8.

❁ Forewordwise

At the bottom of "Forewordwise" attached to this longer work, Combs typed "Josiah H. Combs, Fort Worth Texas, The ides of March, 1960," and the cover sheet indicates that the total work was sent to and dedicated to "George P. Wilson, Ex-PADster, scholarish, and eruditish Englewise and dialectwise, now a retiree and henpeckee, and piscatorish." Note that Combs died on June 28, 1960, and so this may well have been the last piece he wrote.

I reckon ez how they ain't no excuse fer writin' of all of this stuff touchin' on an' pertainin' to what a feller reads and hears around hisself every day. But seein' es how this nightmare's done been a-dancin' about on my bosom by day an' by night hand-goin' fer sich a long spell o' the years, I jist had a hankerin' to git it off'n my chest. I ain't had no call, neither from hither nor from yon, ceptin' this-un. Now I feel plum' good an' relieved, a-knowin' that I can sleep better'n ever hereinafter.

I feel to know that them as loves the outlandish language doin's of this day an' time will take a sight of umbrage at what I'm a-sayin about them an' their didoes; I know in reason they will 'cuse me of sparcy learnin' an' 'timidation, seein' ez how sich people ain't a-gwine to change their way of talkin'. I ain't a-gwine to git down on my bendified knees to make no excuse to them people. Closin' of my twaddle, I hope sich people go right on a-gobblin' but so loud an' long that they won't have time to look: in sich a manner, they may come back to their senses, same ez the rest uv us.

❋ Preliminary Caterwaul

I am now on the outer fringes of the period of senile dementia, or at least on its periphery. The fact is a daily, doleful reminder that I may shove off from this Vale of Tears at any time. Yet even at this late date of my departure could be possibly a bit premature, in that I might unintentionally allow it to circumvent what is doubtless my final fling at some of the stupidities of the English language as written and spoken in this country today. Further delay in the undertaking, with the subsequent danger of further exposure to the aforesaid stupidities could well hasten my exit. The load gets heavier daily, and the call for quick action is obvious. . . .

Like the swan of ancient tradition. I hereby propose to sing my swan song. I shall sing as I damned please, where fancy leads me, in tones high and low, now shrill, now subdued, as I kick up the dust of controversy; for here I am not courting the good graces of any publisher, nor do I expect to pronounce this diatribe before any club, society or organization. . . . The linguistic anomalies, irregularities, and other monstrosities of spoken and written English have come to me from various and widely differing sources during the past thirty years by way of the electro-magnetic waves, or radio beams, and the speech of my fellow Americans heard *tete-a-tete*—as it all bombarded my helpless tympani at close range; and from the printed pages of the press, magazines, periodicals, commercial advertising garbage, etc., etc., bringing upon me accelerated and aggravated astigmatism.

I am not sanguine enough to claim that what my ears and eyes have las-soed during these long years is complete, or comprehensive. The Augean stables are cluttered up with it, and there seems to be no tendency on the part of any constituted authority to summon Hercules and the River Alpheus. As a result, our fine old mother English tongue is suffering increas-ing and more violent mayhem from year to year, until she is a sick old lady.

I am merely kicking the crust off of the foul dunghill, leaving the main body of it, perhaps, to the work of other investigators; for my olfactories might weaken and break down completely under the strain of further research on my part.

My strictures against the usage I propose to attack must not in any way argue me a bigoted purist. On the other hand I do not choose to be labeled a complete free-wheeling non-conformist. It is blazing no new trail—it is axiomatic—to say that language, like many other things, does not remain static; it is in a state of flux and change, as it has always been, and the law of semantics still operates. But there is such a thing as a middle ground, of sweet reasonableness, which dictates that we should lean neither toward excessive purism nor toward unbridled license.

My thesis is that in America we are rapidly becoming free-wheeling and non-conformist in the matter of language. The reasons for this are not far to seek; we are a new nation, as history goes, a nation of dissidents, never satisfied with the *status quo* (and we are not entirely in error here); always out for something "new," something "different," which will catch the fancy of the eye or the ear. Thus have we become rebels, defiant of discipline and authority, and of standardization. . . .

Our general discontent, then, our itching restlessness, has been allowed to spread out and invade the field of language. In this respect the present era has much in common with the Elizabethan age, when our English forefathers spoke and wrote to suit themselves—before the language was standardized. Much that was Shakespearian is now difficult to read and understand; and, were the whole truth known, much of the pronunciation of that period could not be grasped by us moderns. The language has gone from "non-standardization" to standardization, from standardization to "de-standardization," and, let us fondly hope, that it will again arrive at an age of standardization—when the present standardization (?) will be considered "non-standard," "de-activated," and "de-vitalized."

While I pause to prime my guns for further attacks upon a recalcitrant enemy, and to allow the perhaps now none-too-gentle reader to regurgitate my unsavory remarks, let me inject a little humor to ease the tense situation. On the very front cover of a certain screen or movie magazine of March 1960 some words of doubtful meaning appeared in bold, screaming type, causing this bad man's eyes to blink and take a second, longer look: "REVEALED! LIZ' [Elizabeth Taylor] SECRET SPLIT WITH EDDIE [Eddie Fisher, one of Liz's several husbands]." What a wonderful opportunity, this, for hair-splitting, punning and interpretation: Is "secret" a noun or an adjective, and is "split" a verb or a noun? What-er-er- if "secret" were a noun!—it would follow that "split" is a verb—and the normal and natural thing for Liz to do would be to "reveal" her "secret" to her husband, who would then "split"—but let's just let the matter stand. Shucks and tut! tut!! is not a woman the split infinitive in the grammar of life? Q.E.D.

❋ Word-List

I have selected these words with Josiah's comments on them from a much longer list of words and terms that he disdained to supplement the essay above. Combs Papers, series IV, box 2, folder 8.

- *activate, activation.* Good Bafflegab, or Pentagonese words, too well known to require comment. Everything is activated, de-activated, or re-activated.
- *allergy.* Widely and loosely used, in spite of its scientific or medical connotation. The boy ate a green apple, it gave him a bellyache, and he is therefore allergic to green apples. Every time I smell feces I have an aversion to it, and I am allergic to it. I am allergic to all of these or-dures, languagewise.
- *an.* Replaces *a* even before aspirate *h*: "an historical fact." This is incor-rect, even though it is the second syllable of "historical" that carries the stress. One might as well say "an history." I say, old chap, quite British.
- *atom bomb.* Atomic bomb. One of the seemingly never-ending examples of the wide-spread tendency to humiliate nouns by making adjectives of them.
- *audition.* Bad enough meaning a trial test of an actor or singer—but ludicrous as a verb, "They are going to audition her."
- *aunt.* It ain't ant. but ah, it's ahnt—and quite British (and Virginian) too.
- *author.* Did you know that authors have almost quit writing books? They simply author them. Publishers, book reviewers and the literary gentry may be responsible for this stuff. Here and there, an author, himself will fall for this garbage.
- *bifurcate.* A high-falutin' word beloved of the high brass. To you and me, it means to fork or divide into two branches.
- *bosomy.* Very expressive, Hollywoodwise.
- *brackets.* An overworked term. Nowadays, one is always either in the up-per, middle, or lower brackets, financially, economically and otherwise.

- *chair.* Can you believe it—that this word is now also a verb? As such it means simply to act as a chairman.
- *commercial.* A radio advertisement, even though it is an adjective.
- *date.*, v. and n. Yes, he dates the sweet little thing; and if he dates her regularly, she is his date, or he is her date.
- *debut.* "Borrowed" from the French, disgraced by its use as a verb: "She debuted along with her cousin."
- *different than.* Hard to believe, but a lot of educated folks now affecting it, for "different *from.*"
- *double-header.* As a baseball term, without sense or authority.
- *envelope.* Look upward a little, at *envoy.*
- *envoy.* My word! it is not envoy, which every American grew up saying,—but ahn-voy. It sounds so polished and proper. Radio and television folks dote on it.
- *eye-ther.* Either. This pronunciation was hardly known in America before the turn of the twentieth century. All too many Americans have heard the English pronounce it that way, and have spread it among others. Quite elite; it sets you aside from the proletariat. Same with *nyether* for neither.
- *fact-finding.* All committees these days . . . are "fact-finding." What the—? What's a committee for, anyway?
- *Foodarama.* My goodness, yes, nothing but an ice box, or refrigerator.
- *ghost.* This is a spooky word, having actually become a verb, as to ghost write; but an expert can go that one better, by omitting the word "write" . . . "He has ghosted several volumes."
- *happenstance.* A portmanteau word that would have tickled the fancy of Lewis Carroll.
- *indisposed.* Unpretentious people say simply sick, or unwell.
- *IN-quiry.* An affected pronunciation.
- *judgment.* Widely but incorrectly used for opinion, view, idea, estimate, etc. "In my opinion" is the correct usage; for there one is not sitting as a judge, to make a decision.
- *Lez-lie.* Leslie, that's all. Hands across the sea stuff.
- *love.* v. Overworked these days to the point of ridicule. Listen and you will hear any day, "I'd just love to" for "I'd like to." In most cases "love" and "like" are synonymous terms.
- *luggage.* I say, quite British for baggage, even for stuff too heavy to "lug." Trunks are not luggage.
- *Ohia.* Nothing but Ohio.
- *pass away.* Stupid euphemism has been carried so far it is now ignominious to die; one passes away. Christian Science, or *The Christian Science*

Monitor is said to have originated this bunk. Anyway, a corpse is too dead to worry about the difference.

- *personally.* Rank tautology, totally unnecessary, in such an expression as "I personally believe."
- *powder room.* Only a ladies toilet in a gas station, restaurant, etc. Also, presently "rest room." I have never seen such prudery anywhere else but in stalwart America. Once in Czechoslovakia I observed the door with the simple word "SDE!" (HERE). I believe it was in Germany that I saw "AHA!" and again, simply "!" (Quick, James, three more corn cobs!)[32]
- *presently.* Misused daily, by nearly everybody, for now, at present, at this time.—and if I have to say it, "currently." It means soon, at once, in the very near future, etc.
- *reaction.* I do not have a vocabulary strong enough to express my reaction to the excessive use of this word. In daily usage it is almost always incorrectly employed. "What's your reaction to that?" and no end to examples where the meaning is simply "What do you think of that?" The word has a specific meaning, which is simply discarded or overlooked.
- *sabbatical.* It's no longer a sabbatical leave, just sabbatical. College hokum.
- *stool.* Euphemistic term for plain old sh—t, or excrement. Even the word "bowels" has become inelegant. A doctor never would ask milady if her bowels had moved, or if she had had a bowel movement. She is asked if she has had a stool—and the nature of said stool.
- *unique.* The word means singular, only one of a kind, having nothing like or equal, never modified as "very," or "somewhat."
- *university.* The American woods are full of little jerkwater schools and colleges calling themselves universities. The process of evolutionary nomenclature, for example, might run like this: Groun' Hog Flat Institute; Groun' Hog Flat Normal School; Groun' Hog Flat Teachers College; Groun' Hog Flat State College; then the final, grand sweep— Groun' Hog Flat University, or better The University of Groun' Hog Flat.

Final Note: A certain genus of thrush was supposed to defecate itself to death. . . . Let us hope that the unhealthy stuff in the American language today may in time imitate that thrush.

Combs Papers, series IV, box 2, folder 8.

Ballads and Songs

❀ Barbara Allen

Child 84, Roud 54, Combs 24

Combs got this ballad from Newton Gaines in Fort Worth, Texas, in 1933, who learned it from his mother, born in Mississippi about 1875. Gaines had recorded it for Victor in 1930 (V-40243). This tune and most of the text are from John and Ruby Lomax's recording of Combs for the Library of Congress: John and Ruby Lomax 1940 Southern States Recordings Collection, AFC 1940/003. However, since their recording equipment could record only shorter pieces, Combs dropped several verses. I have restored some stanzas from Combs's printed texts in the Wilgus Folklore Collection, box 1, to make the narrative clear. "Barbara Allen" is said to be the most collected ballad in the world.

2. As she was walking through the street,
   She heard the death bells ringin';
   She thought she heard her true love say,
   "Come here, oh, Barbary Allen."

3. They sent a message to her house,
   They sent it to her dwelling;
   "Young Jemmy's sick and sends for you,
   If your name be Barbary Allen."

4. When she came to his bedside,
   She said, "Young man, you're dying ."
   "Yes, I am low, and low indeed,
   For the love of Barbary Allen."

5. "Oh, do you remember in yonder's town,
   In yonder's town a-drinking;
   You drank a health to the ladies all,
   And you slighted Barbary Allen?"

6. "Yes, I remember in yonder's town,
In yonder's town a-drinking;
I gave a health to the ladies all,
But my love to Barbary Allen."

7. The more she looked, the more she grieved,
She bursted out a-crying';
"Take away, take away this fair young man,
For I think that he's a-dyin'."

8. He turned his pale face to the wall,
And death was in him dwellin';
"Adieu, adieu to my friends all,
Adieu to Barbary Allen."

9. "Oh, Mother, oh, Mother, go fix my bed,
Go fix it soft and narrow;
My true love, he has died for me,
I'll die for him tomorrow."

10. They took them to the new churchyard,
And there they did bury them;
They buried his true love by his side,
Her name was Barbary Allen.

11. Out of his grave, there grew a rose,
And out of hers, a briar;
They lapped and tied in a true lover's knot,
The rose outgrew the briar.

Lord Thomas and Fair Ellender

Child 73, Roud 4, Combs 18

Combs commented only that his version of the ballad came from a "lost manuscript." It is also known as "The Brown Girl," and the story indicates that "fair" was synonymous with "beautiful" in Old England, with light-skinned blondes favored over dark-skinned brunettes. Combs also truncated this ballad because of the limitations of the recording system. I have restored verses from Combs's text from the Wilgus Folklore Collection, box 1.

"Oh Moth-er, oh Moth-er come rid-dle my score, Come rid-dle it all as one;

Must I mar-ry Fair Ell-en-der, Or bring the Brown Girl home?" "The

Brown Girl she has hous-es and land, Fair Ell-end-der she has none; There-

fore I warn you of a bless-ing, To bring the Brown girl home."

2. "Go saddle up my milk-white steed,
   Go saddle him up for me;
   I'll go and invite Fair Ellender
   All to my wedding day."

   I rode and I rode till I came to the hall,
   And jingled all on the ring;
   No one was so ready as Fair Ellender herself
   To arise and let me in.

3. "What news, what news?" Fair Ellender cried,
   "What news have you brought to me?"
   "I've come to invite you to my wedding.
   Is that sad news to thee?"

   "Sad news, sad news," Fair Ellender cried,
   "Sad news you've brought to me;
   I once did think I'd be your bride,
   And you my bridegroom be."

4. "Oh, Mother, oh, mother, go roll a song
   Go roll it all as one.
   Must I go to Lord Thomas' wedding,
   Or tarry with you at home?"

"It's enemies, enemies you have there,
The Brown girl she has none;
Therefore I warn you of a blessing,
To tarry this day at home."

5. "There may be many of my friends there,
And many more at home,
But if I never return again,
To Thomas' wedding I'll go."

She dressed herself in scarlet red,
Her waiting maid in green;
And every station that she rode through,
They took her to be some queen.

6. She rode and rode till she came to the hall,
And she jingled all on the ring;
No one was so ready as Lord Thomas himself
To arise and let her in.

He took her by her lily-white hand,
And led her through the hall;
And sat her down at the head of the table
Among the merry maids all.

7. "Is that your bride," Fair Ellender cried,
"That looks so wonderful brown?
Ye once could have got just as fair a lady
As ever the sun shone around."

"Despise her not, Fair Ellender," he said,
"Despise her not to me;
For I love the end of your little finger,
Much better than her whole body."

8. The Brown Girl had a little pen-knife,
It was both keen and sharp;
Between the long ribs and the short,
She entered Fair Ellender's heart.

"What is the matter?" Lord Thomas he cried,
"You look so pale to me."
"Oh, don't you see my own heart's blood
Come trickling down by thee?"

9. He took his new bride by the hand,
   He led her down the hall;
   He drew a bright sword and cut her head off,
   And threw it against the wall.

   He put the butt against the wall,
   The point against his breast,
   Said, "Here's the end of three lovers,
   God sent their souls to rest."

❀ Frog Went A-Courting
Roud 16, Combs 136

Combs got this song from H. R. Power, Hampshire County, West Virginia, in 1924. It is an English nursery rhyme and song first published in 1548. It has been recorded by many artists, including Bradley Kincaid (Silvertone 5188) in 1927, Judy Canova (Brunswick 264) and Chubby Parker (Columbia 15296D) in 1928, Tex Ritter (on the album An American Legend) *in 1973, and Suzy Bogguss (on the album* American Folk Songbook) *in 2011.*

2. He rode right up to Miss Mouse's door, uh-huh,
   He rode right up to Miss Mouse's door
   And said, "Miss Mouse, are you in?" uh-huh.

3. "Yes, kind sir, I sit and spin . . .
   Lift the latch and walk right in," uh-huh.

4. He took Miss Mousie on his knee . . .
   And he said, "Miss Mouse, will you marry me?" uh-huh.

5. "Not without Uncle Rat's consent . . .
   I would not marry the President," uh-huh.

6. Old Uncle Rat he grinned and smiled . . .
   To think his niece would be a bride, uh-huh . . .

7. Old Uncle Rat he went to town . . .
   To buy his niece a wedding gown, uh-huh.

8. And while he was walking the streets around . . .
   He stumped his toe and fell to the ground, uh-huh.

9. Where will the wedding supper be? . . . .
   Away down yonder in the old holler tree, uh-huh.

10. O what will the wedding supper be? . . .
    Two blue beans and a black-eyed pea, uh-huh.

11. The first to come in was a big blacksnake . . .
    With his custard and his cake, uh-huh.

12. The next to come in was Mr. Flea . . .
    With his fiddle on his knee, uh-huh.

❋ Cluck Old Hen

Roud 4235, Combs 234

Combs wrote: "A song common among highland fiddlers, sung by Tom Kelley and Dan Gibson, Hindman, Kentucky, 1915." The tune is from the 1940 Lomax recording. The first transcription of this tune was in 1886. Ralph Peer, with OKeh Records, first recorded it from Fiddlin' John Carson in 1923. Other artists soon followed: Fiddlin' Powers and Family in 1927 (Edison 52083) and Grayson and Whitter in 1928 (Gennett 6656).

3. Cluck, old hen, cluck and sing,
   I ain't seen an egg since away last spring.

4. Cluck, old hen, cluck and squall,
   I ain't seen an egg since away last fall.

5. Sometimes three, sometimes four,
   Sometimes she lays behind the door.

6. Cluck, old hen, cluck along,
   Cluck, old hen, your chickens all gone.

7. Some in the garden, some in the barn,
   Some in the new ground, scratchin' out the corn.

❀ The Little Black Mustache

Combs 154

Combs indicated that he got this comic song from "an old manuscript." Written by James M. Dow in 1881, it entered the oral tradition and was performed widely, with several recordings, including Henry Whitter in 1925 (OKeh 40395) and Vernon Dalhart in 1926 (OKeh 74151). It can be found in Vance Randolph, Ozark Folksongs *(Columbia: State Historical Society of Missouri, 1946–50), vol. 3:* Humorous and Play-Party Songs, *no. 404; and in* The Frank C. Brown Collection of North Carolina Folklore, *vol. 2:* Folk Ballads from North Carolina *(Durham, NC: Duke University Press, 1952), no. 202.*

It's once I had a charm-ing beau, I loved him dear as life; I longed and longed some fu-ture day To be his charm-ing wife.

2. His pockets they were filled with gold,
   And he could cut a dash,
   With a diamond ring and a watch and chain,
   And a darling, black mustache.

3. He came to see me last Sunday night,
   And stayed till almost three;
   He said he never loved a girl
   As well as he loved me.

4. He said we'd live in grandest style,
   For he had lots of cash;
   And then he pressed upon my lips
   That darling, black mustache.

5. And then there came a sour old maid,
   She's worth her weight in gold;
   She had false teeth, and wore false hair,
   She's forty-five years old.

6. So cruel he deserted me
   For this old maid and her cash;
   And now I know I've lost my beau
   With a darling, black mustache.

7. Then take my advice, ye thoughtless girls,
   And do not be too rash;
   But leave alone those stylish chaps
   That wear the black mustache.

✳ Jacob's Ladder
Roud 2286, Combs 320

Combs got this song from his mother, Clementine Combs. He called it a Negro spiritual in his doctoral thesis and an example of "group improvisation." Roud listed it as a "White, Negro Folk-Song" in his index, and gives fifty-eight results from the main collections. Bascom Lunsford titled his version "Hide Thou Me," as in "We're climbin' up Jacob's ladder, hide thou, hide thou me." This tune varies from the slow-moving spiritual to a sprightly song that I heard recently played as a banjo-fiddle tune.

1. I'm a-climbin' up Jacob's ladder,
   And I won't be troubled anymore;
   I'm a-climbing up Jacob's ladder, Lord,
   And I won't be troubled anymore.

   Chorus: And I won't be troubled anymore,
   And I won't be troubled anymore.
   I'm a-climbin' up Jacob's ladder, Lord,
   And I won't be troubled anymore.

2. Gonna meet my father in the Kingdom,
   And I won't be troubled anymore;
   Gonna meet my father in the Kingdom, Lord,
   And I won't be troubled anymore.

   Chorus

3. Gonna meet my mother in the kingdom . . .

   Chorus

4. Gonna meet my brother in the kingdom . . .

   Chorus

5. Gonna meet my sister in the kingdom . . .

   Chorus

❊ Decretum Est (1936)

The essay that follows, written on Texas Christian University stationery in 1936, is a shorter version of a forty-four-page essay with the same title written in 1933. Combs had scribbled on the title page, "To be re-arranged—re-written." Combs Papers, series VI, box 3, folder 4. This Latin title means "It is a decree."

At the age of forty-six I do not feel the heavy hand of the years. I have never felt better, physically or mentally. Certainly, at this age of life, I am not thinking of that mysterious journey which all of us, owing to the infirmities of the flesh, must take. But this human flesh falls heir to various ills, and is also subject to countless accidents and mishaps. Now, one of these fine days I shall have to answer to the inevitable summons, whether I will it or not, whether I am ready or not; the history of the race in the past proves to me beyond a reasonable doubt that I cannot evade the call. If I may be fortunate enough to attain to a reasonable age before the Grim Reaper stands before me (and I am enjoying life so much not to express this desire), the infirmities of the flesh, incident to senility, will not tempt me to want to live longer. My chief regret at passing out still will not be the traditional, superstitious fear of death; rather will it be the regret at leaving Charlotte (if she survives me), my relatives, and my friends.

As to the disposition of my earthly remains, when the *vital élan* has left them, I am but little concerned, no matter where I pass out. When that time comes, I shall, of course, be unable to protest. Thus shall I quit the world as I came into it, without my knowledge or consent. Yet I may make a not immodest little request as to disposition of said remains. Since I am shackled neither by the chains of the Christian faith nor by the fatuous worship of superstition and tradition, my simple request is that I be buried totally and completely without ceremony ordinarily attendant upon such occasions: to wit—the undertaker, the expensive coffin (which could not in time prevent the worms from boring into my flesh!), the religious services at church or at the graveside. A plain box—for a plain man. No tears, no flowers. Tears could never bring me back, and I should be unconscious of the fragrance of the flowers. If, on that occasion, I should bolt into the Elysian Fields, I should thank you for complying with my simple request; if there are no Elysian Fields I shall never know the difference, and it would not matter.

To my friends and relations my blunt "statement of faith" may come as a shock. But I have no faith; that is the basis of all religions, and is therefore illogical, unreasonable, unscientific, unbelievable. If there had been one iota of tangible evidence of an Almighty and a hereafter during these more than nineteen hundred years, I should indeed be among the first to embrace the faith that preaches them. I have a dead mother, father, and brother. Now, common sense dictates a desire on the part of most human beings to see and greet again, their deceased relations and friends. I could conjure up no fonder wish than this, myself. If I could bring myself to the point of subscribing to belief in the immortality of the soul, this fond wish would be something to live for, to die for. But alas! there is no convincing proof that the soul is immortal. During these many years no voice from my dead mother has pierced the thick veil that separates her from me, no voice to encourage or to assure me as to a hereafter. The gentle voice of my dead mother would constitute more powerful of the immortality of the soul than all the vacuous preachments of the priesthood during all these many centuries. "Faith" is the keynote of most religions. The various religions have worked wonders with this little word of five letters. Naturally so; since all religions have nothing substantial nor logical upon which to base their claims, they have resorted to rank superstition as the foundation of their flimsy, theological structures. "Now, faith is the substance of things hoped for, the evidence of things unseen," cries one of the New Testament crusaders. No ranker hypothesis, no more fatuous flapdoodle has ever been palmed off on human beings since the beginning of society.

All religions are man-made, man-nourished, man-propagated. I cannot conceive of any segment of the human race, from the South Seas aborigines to the highly civilized Western European nations, that would do without a religion or a god. The undercurrent of superstition and tradition still mightily inherent in even the most civilized beings is the basic cause of these man-made institutions; that is to say, most of them. Some of them may have had their inception as moral codes—and in this instance, in fact, in either instance, they have probably made mankind better. But this is no argument for the immortality of the soul, for a hereafter. The average human being whenever he is intelligent, could live as well, as honestly, without any religion whatsoever.

The incorrigible zealot attempts to prove his beliefs, his faith, by his Bible, his Koran, or whatever handbook may be—too blind to the fact that his "handbook" is impossible of proof. It is strange that you may differ with a man about his politics, his philosophy of life, his views of various topics, and still remain his friend; while, if you express no belief in any religion nor a hereafter, you are usually consigned to the damned, hopelessly lost, an irrational being. Many religions would have us believe that they were "revealed," to certain prophets; of course, they had to come from some-where, and this has been a shrewd little subterfuge for the faithful. If they had been revealed to these old-timers, they should also be in the process of revelation, today, to all of us in order that the faith might not falter! A little visible, outward, tangible evidence today, let us say such as the appear-ance of an angel, or Jesus Christ himself, at a great public gathering, would settle the question once and for all, and the inane gibberish and loquacious fulminations of the priesthood would no longer be necessary, either for the faithful or the rest of us. All recorded revelation has been the result of either the hallucinations of an over-emotional mind, or of the desire of some charlatan or mountebank to lord it over his fellow man.

Religion is, then, the result of tradition, superstition, and not of intelligent, rational thinking. No follower or communicant of any religion can give you a sensible reason for his beliefs; he does not, in reality, *believe*; he thinks he believes because he wants to believe—and because he thinks he believes, he *knows* he believes, and because he *knows* he believes, and he *knows* he is right. Gentlemen of the cloth are especially guilty of this false logic and refuse to be unhorsed. Many of them, along with certain of their parishioners, have seen Jehovah face to face, and have communed with him; insane asylums are full of them.

FIGURE 6. Josiah Combs's family. *First row, L–R*: brothers Ira and Denny; sister Dora; father, John; mother, Clementine; and Josiah. *Back row*: sister Allie and brothers French and Burnam. Another brother, Monroe, is missing. Courtesy of the Josiah Combs Papers, SAA 71, Southern Appalachian Archives, Hutchins Library, Berea College, Berea, Kentucky.

FIGURE 7. Josiah at age eighteen with the dulcimer made by local craftsman Edward Thomas that was presented to him by Katherine Pettit, co-director of Hindman Settlement School, when he left to enroll at Transylvania University. Courtesy of Hindman Settlement School.

Josiah H. Combs, about 1913

FIGURE 8. Josiah at age forty-seven with his beloved dulcimer, which he played in ballad recitals all of his active life. Courtesy of the Josiah Combs Papers, SAA 71, Southern Appalachian Archives, Hutchins Library, Berea College, Berea, Kentucky.

FIGURE 9. Josiah in his Sorbonne (University of Paris) doctoral regalia. Courtesy of the Josiah Combs Papers, SAA 71, Southern Appalachian Archives, Hutchins Library, Berea College, Berea, Kentucky.

FIGURE 10. Josiah and Charlotte Combs at their Fort Worth, Texas, home. Courtesy of the Josiah Combs Papers, SAA 71, Southern Appalachian Archives, Hutchins Library, Berea College, Berea, Kentucky.

Cratis D. Williams

I first met Cratis Williams at an educational meeting in Louisville in 1958. He introduced himself and asked if I would deliver a copy of the typescript of his New York University dissertation, "The Southern Mountaineer in Fact and Fiction," to Dr. Willis D. Weatherford Sr. at Berea College, a mover and shaker who was then interested in getting works published about the region. In addition to serving as the chairman of the Berea College Board of Trustees, Weatherford was the director of Southern Appalachian Studies, a Ford Foundation–sponsored regional survey project. As we were hauling the typescript out of the trunk of Williams's car, I thought, "This thing must weigh half as much as he does," for Cratis was a slight man. In fact, the printed copies of this three-volume study ran to more than 1,600 pages.[1]

I later ordered the dissertation from University Microfilms and read it with great interest, because I was then employed by the Council of the Southern Mountains, an organization that had evolved out of an annual conference, established in 1913, of workers in educational, religious, and social service institutions in Appalachia. Williams's work examined almost everything written about the Southern Mountains and its people, from colonial times until the middle of the twentieth century. It was a tremendous gift to me, as I also sought to understand my own people and myself. Although Williams thought that he was laying the Appalachian culture and its literature to rest, his work was to become a major foundation for the field of Appalachian studies, which burgeoned during the rest of his lifetime.

Williams was born on Caines Creek, near Blaine, in Lawrence County, Kentucky, on April 5, 1911. He was the oldest of the five children of Curtis and Mona Whitt Williams. He liked to say that his forebears included "Indian fighters, long hunters, veterans of the American Revolution, Tories escaped to the backwoods, refugees from the Whiskey Rebellion, Kentucky mountain feudists, and religious dissenters."[2] He grew up among this pioneer stock, who still remembered the earliest happenings in the Big Sandy River country of Kentucky. The first post office on Caines Creek was called Sacred Wind. Cratis later wrote of its naming, giving us an example of the robust and ribald nature of his people. The scene is the home of Uncle Dave Sturgill, a farmer and United Baptist preacher. Uncle Dave is sitting with his son Dick, who has just received word that his application for a post office has been approved. Cratis wrote:

> Dick, a fiddler, dancer, and great hunter and trapper, wanted an imaginative name for his office. One day, during the rest hour from labor in the fields, Uncle Dave and Dick sat in the porch following dinner. . . . Dick, thumbing through a list of Kentucky post offices, said that he couldn't decide what to call his new post office. Uncle Dave lifted up his leg and broke wind vigorously, like tearing new bedticking, and said, "Call it that!" Dick named the post office Sacred Wind in honor of the occasion.[3]

Williams went from a one-room school, to the county-seat high school, to a B.A. and M.A. at the University of Kentucky, to a Ph.D. from New York University. He started his career as a school teacher and principal, and that led to a professorship, deanship, and chancellorship. But his achievements went beyond and were more fundamental than degrees and titles and offices. He radiated a rare spate of qualities that drew people to him and caused them to speak his name in a way that exalted his status. His parents chose "Darrell" as his middle name, but in the Eastern Kentucky dialect it came out as Dearl and was written down as such on his birth certificate. Later on, he liked the sound so much that he never corrected this spelling. Cratis Williams, like his first and middle names, was different.

Williams lived through times of tumultuous change, in lifestyle, economy, and fad and fancy, but he weathered time and place with equanimity because he knew who he was. He came face to face with persons of varied

ideology and temper, treating them all with benign and respectful attention, and nearly all of them expressed their affection and appreciation for
him. That is rare in a time of opinionated assertiveness and harsh judgment of those who do not embrace one's own views. Cratis himself was
rare in that he had his world in his head and made his own agenda. His
native culture was of great interest to him, and he gained strength from
it. Educational institutions supplied the humane and profound ideas that
had not penetrated his narrow valley. Yet to Cratis, university humanism
was no more important than the rich veins of his family and community
culture. He embodied both worlds as few others did. He also bridged a
span of time that gave vantage to the ever-changing history and events of
the region and the world. The people he knew in the waning days of the
frontier were as interesting to him as Chaucer's companions, and his own
quest to understand them employed the fruits of his formal education. It
was an intellectual and spiritual search, although Cratis did not boast of
religious faith. Underneath the jocularity, the bawdy stories in the night,
the enlightened and attentive ear, the reasoned and kindly advice, and his
achievements in academia, he was a loner. It was not that he craved solitude;
he loved convivial company. However, he saw so much more in this world
than most of us do, and his purpose was so different that he had to go his
own way. The loneliness of solitary knowledge and being different, even in
esteemed ways, was bittersweet in his early days because there were few
with whom to discuss and evaluate what he knew. Cratis once said that the
Appalachian mountaineer was schizoid in that he had the ability of standing
outside himself to assess his own situation and abilities. In writing about
his first educational venture outside his valley, where he was shamed by
his teachers and fellow students for his perceived backwardness, he commented, "I felt unreal. The real me stood within the shadows to monitor as
I asked myself from time to time, 'How am I doing?'" Cratis was a shrewd
judge of himself, as he was of his associates, and with the same grace and
forgiveness he showed toward them, he guided himself into becoming one
of my ideal persons.

He sometimes called himself "a complete mountaineer." He was an early
student of the traditions of his people, whom he viewed as nineteenth-century people. He loved their music, tales, dances, songs, and hymns and was
aware of their distinctive religious attitudes, practices, manners, customs,
folkways, and speech. He described himself as being mostly Scotch-Irish,

although a trip to Wales in his retirement years reminded him that the name Williams was Welsh in origin, and he resembled the popular image of the Welsh more than the Scots. Ever in his mind, though, his people were the fierce, strong, tall, florid, red- or tow-haired Scotch-Irish, although he himself was short, dark, kindly, and gentle. Cratis held on to the term "Scotch-Irish" rather than "Scots-Irish," explaining that this was the designation this ethnic group itself had logically coined. They were Scots who had settled with the encouragement of the English Crown in northern Ireland and later migrated in large numbers to the American colonies.

Cratis's grandfather, David Williams, strong-jawed and burly, was one of the last legal whiskey distillers in eastern Kentucky, although his distilling did not entirely end with the Volstead Act, and his son Curtis continued the craft surreptitiously. Cratis later acknowledged that he paid for his years at the University of Kentucky by bringing quantities of moonshine his father had distilled to sell to willing purchasers on and around campus.

He had a grudging admiration for his grandfather's vivid rhetoric, especially his "cussing." In later years he still remembered a time when his grandfather was underneath a mowing machine on a hot day trying to unscrew a rusted and reluctant nut. At last, flushed and sweaty, he threw down his wrench and declared, "By god, I wish this damnable thang wuz in the fur fork of hell with its back broke!"[4]

Many years later, faculty colleagues told of traveling with Cratis to a conference. When they got there, they couldn't get the trunk of the car to open. After each of his companions had tried the key and banged on the lid, Cratis stepped forward and said, "What this thing needs is a good Kentucky cussing!" He braced himself, threw back his shoulders, and delivered a blistering stream of invective. To the astonishment of his companions, so they said, the trunk popped open.[5]

Cratis commented that the people of his community were noted for lawlessness and bloodshed and other misdeeds. His great-grandfather had participated in a feud. A cousin, his third-grade teacher, was shot to death. His grandfather Jeff (Jefferson Davis) Whitt was "churched" for adultery when he was in his eighties. Cratis's people were lusty and interesting to him, and he told their stories, good and bad, with great humor and satisfaction.

The Williamses attended the Calvinistic United Baptist Church, with its once-a-month services, its lined-out hymnody, and its mostly genial view of human frailty. He learned the old hymns and studied the rhythm and tuneful preaching style of the ministers, and years later he would perform the hymns and imitate the preachers. But he had another vision for his life, one at variance with the religion he learned there. In his later years, he joined the intellectually oriented Unitarian Church. He related the exploits and frailties and excesses of his people in seeming conflict with his role as a gentleman-scholar. He performed the ballads, the folktales, the bawdy jokes, and even the "cussing" along with other folk practices as he lectured. Although he embraced the humanistic ideals of the scholars of Western civilization, the folklore of his own kin was part of the mixture.

Cratis's father was a tenant farmer on the land of his own father. When Cratis was eight, Curtis moved his family to Ohio to another tenant farm. There, Cratis saw for the first time the land and people beyond the narrow hills of eastern Kentucky—the great Ohio River with its mighty steamboats and barges, trains, level land, and people who looked different and talked differently from those back home. However, this was a brief view of the outer world. The family soon moved back to Blaine.[6]

In July 1917, Cratis began school in the Blaine United Baptist Church House. There were seventy-five students enrolled in eight grades, ranging in age from six to eighteen. He had a string of short-term teachers, none of whom had finished high school, but they had attended teacher institutes or normal schools to learn enough to pass the teacher exams. One of his teachers, Ulysses Williams, a cousin, was killed by a drunken man for unknown reasons. This tragic event was a powerful impetus for Cratis to further his own education. He heard his father say to his mother that Ulysses was the only Big Sandy Williams who had ever sought to get an education, but that if any of his own children wanted an education, he "would work on his hands and knees for a dime a day, if need be, to see that they had a chance to get it." Hearing this at the age of eleven, Cratis was determined to get that education.[7]

Cratis was a diligent student, and when he was eleven, he advanced from the third grade to the sixth. At twelve, he passed an examination to gain admittance to the high school in the county seat of Louisa. His family was worried that he was too young to go away from home, even though he would be boarding with relatives. In the end, his mother convinced his father that he should go, but not before she warned the boy against worldly temptations and instructed him on how to behave. His father took him to Louisa by mule wagon, but when they attempted to enroll him, the superintendent and principal decided that he was too young to go to high school and sent him to the seventh grade. He already knew the material taught in the class, and he excelled, so his teacher nominated him for the "best-student prize." However, the principal ruled that he was not eligible because he had enrolled late in the year. Instead the prize went to the son of a school board member.[8]

Cratis looked forward with great anticipation to high school, but the next fall, on the morning he was to enroll, his father informed him that he had changed his mind about letting him go. Cratis fled the house and did his usual chores while weeping bitterly, but when he returned, his mother told him that she had talked to his father and that he had changed his mind again and had gone to get his brother to take them to town in his car. When Cratis showed up at the high school that day, he weighed only sixty-five pounds, and when Principal Godby spotted him, he asked some senior boys standing with him, "What's that little cricket doing here?" Cricket became his nickname.[9]

His first four classes were algebra, English, general science, and Latin. He found that all of his teachers were from outside the mountain counties, but in study hall he met William H. Vaughan, a local man just out of college who was soon to become the principal of Louisa High School. He was also to become an academic father figure to Cratis.

Cratis was aware of some condescension toward him for his back-country ways from the outlander teachers and even the county-seat students, and this must have pained him deeply, but perhaps it had a positive effect in that it made him acutely aware of the differences between the people in even small Appalachian towns and those from the country. William Vaughan was the only person in the school who took an interest in Cratis's background and what life was like, historically and presently, on Caines Creek. Cratis soon learned that Vaughan loved a good story and was skilled at telling jokes. He often invited Cratis into his office and encouraged him to share the family stories that he remembered and what he knew about his family's history. No doubt Vaughan's interest in his background influenced Cratis to publish "Why a Mountain Boy Should Be Proud" in the school paper, the *Louisian*, which he also edited during his senior year. Vaughan filled a role that Cratis's own parents could not, for they knew little of the educational world beyond the one-room school. At his high school graduation, Cratis received the honor student award. "While returning to my seat," he remembered, "I felt that Mr. Vaughan's regard for me was deeper than that of a teacher for his student, that he loved me as a father loves a son."[10]

And yet, though Vaughan obviously liked Cratis—he had advocated that he be selected as the graduating honor student and secured for him a scholarship at Cumberland College and a job to earn extra money—and though Vaughan served as a model of the educated person, Cratis sensed that his principal viewed him as someone from an undesirable class whose objective should be preparation for a successful life in middle- or upper-class society. The two men carried on a lifelong correspondence and friendship, but running through it are clues to the profound differences between them, and the feeling on Cratis's part that while his intellectual parent always thought him remarkable for having risen above his beginnings, he nevertheless believed that there were limits to his achievements. For example, as a teacher, Vaughan never gave Cratis a grade above a B and never gave him the slightest encouragement to apply for a teaching job at Morehead after Cratis had earned his master's degree from the University of Kentucky and was desperate for a job during the Great Depression. There is no question but that this relationship caused Cratis unhappiness, but it nevertheless helped him shape his ideas, values, and humanistic understanding of life.

Many years later, Cratis published a small book for Morehead State University entitled *William H. Vaughan: A Better Man Than I Ever Wanted to Be*. Vaughan had gone on to become dean and president of that institution when it was still known as Morehead State College. In the book, Cratis described Vaughan as a humane gentleman who had taken a special interest in him. However, he also described a man who "did not use tobacco, drink alcoholic beverages, or speak profanely," concluding that Vaughan was "a better man than I ever wanted to be."

After a year at Cumberland College in Williamsburg, Kentucky, Cratis began teaching in the one-room school at Blaine in 1929. He continued his education at the University of Kentucky by attending during spring semesters and summer school. He received his A.B. degree in English in 1933. He was hired as a science teacher at Blaine High School, then switched to English, and was both teacher and principal there from 1934 to 1938. He continued his studies at the university at the same time and received his M.A. in English in 1937.

Williams's thesis was on the ballads and folksongs of eastern Kentucky, and it has been referenced by folklore scholars.[11] It contains 171 ballads and songs. In the first hundred pages he discusses the history of ballads, with theories of their origin and survival in the oral tradition, their structure and motifs. He also discusses American ballads about dramatic and tragic events and other types of songs, such as love lyrics and play-party dance songs. He included and commented on the songs that were popular in Lawrence County. Since there were no musical notations for the ballads and songs in his thesis, many years later, when Cratis taught in summer workshops at Berea College, I persuaded him to sing the tune and at least one verse of each song and chorus that he could remember in his collection. That recording is in the Southern Appalachian Archives at Berea College, where there is also a printed copy of his thesis.[12]

In 1938, he became the principal of Louisa High School. There he developed one of the first comprehensive testing, guidance, and counseling programs in the state. He also initiated a college-preparation class, as well as a class in vocational agriculture. However, the superintendent and the school board did not favor his innovations. He was by this time married to Sylvia Ruth Graham from the Lawrence County community of Cherokee, who had graduated from the Berea Academy and Morehead State College. She was a poet, and they had many common interests. Sylvia was a teacher at the school, and the board now voted not to rehire her, leaving the Williamses in a precarious situation. When the school board elections came up, supporters of Cratis asked whether he would serve as superintendent if a favorable board were elected. He reluctantly agreed, but the favorable candidates were defeated, and he saw that he would have to leave his county to find another job.[13]

Blacklisted as a troublemaker, Cratis faced his darkest days. The Great Depression still sat heavily on eastern Kentucky in 1941, and he could find no other job as a teacher or principal. With Cratis out of a job, he and Sylvia had to give up their house in Louisa and move in with her parents. He and three other unemployed teachers went to Dayton, Ohio, in search of work, but he had to settle for a common labor job at forty cents an hour at a cardboard box company. He graduated to clerk in the parts department and continued to apply for teaching jobs in Kentucky and Ohio.

Back home at Christmastime and having failed to find another job, he and Sylvia could not afford to exchange gifts, and he had to borrow money from his mother-in-law to look for work. The poet and novelist Jesse Stuart, then superintendent of Greenup County Schools, offered him a position, but the salary of $65 a month was so low he kept looking. Then the International

Nickel Corporation of Huntington invited him to interview for the job of assistant to the director of their apprentice school. "My wife and I were so excited that we wept," Cratis wrote.[14] The job was primarily a secretarial one, but he was shortly asked to begin teaching an evening class. This was in addition to his regular job, and with preparation time, plus teaching, he got only a few hours' sleep each night. His pay at this point was $170 a month.

Fearing the draft, he tried to volunteer for the navy but was turned down for physical reasons. Then Sylvia came down with an illness that was diagnosed as tuberculosis of the throat, and it was necessary for her to go to a sanitarium. In the meantime, Cratis had applied to the University of Illinois for an assistantship in English. He was accepted but was unable to go because of Sylvia's condition. He visited her on weekends and kept up with his arduous schedule. His weight dropped to 135 pounds.[15]

In August 1942, he received a telephone call from Chapell Wilson, director of campus schools at Appalachian State Teachers College, offering him a job as critic teacher in their demonstration high school, where he would teach English and also supervise student teachers who were learning to be teachers. He was offered less money than he was already making, but he accepted the job when a rent-free apartment was thrown in. He visited Sylvia on his way to Boone, and I was told by someone that he was a forlorn and disheveled person when he arrived there early one morning by bus to begin his duties.

Although he was warned by his mentor Vaughan that Appalachian State Teachers College was a poor school and that Wilson was a "slippery horse trader" in salary negotiations, Cratis immediately fell in love with what he called "the quaint little town, the people I met, the poverty stricken school with mostly handmade and pitifully inadequate equipment."[16] There was much work to do, and he went at it with energy and imagination. It was the beginning of his professional life as a college English teacher, administrator, linguist, balladeer, literary scholar, sage, and advisor.

Just when he was getting settled in his new job and feeling comfortable with the college, Sylvia's condition worsened, and she died in December of 1942. Since she was a graduate of the Berea Academy, Cratis later placed her considerable body of poems in the archives at Berea College.

Cratis's fortunes rose with those of Appalachian State, which benefited from generous appropriations from the legislature that enabled it to expand and increase enrollment, eventually leading to its transformation into Appalachian State University in 1967. Cratis became a leader in this academic battalion. For four years he was English critic teacher in the demonstration high school, as well as assistant principal and college dramatics teacher. In addition, he created and directed one of the first guidance and counseling programs in the state. He then joined the English Department and taught there for twelve years—literature, speech, folklore, and dramatics. He directed the Playcrafters in their productions, advised the student newspaper, directed the artist and lecture program, and served on numerous faculty committees.[17]

Cratis remarked that while he was a graduate student at the University of Kentucky, he had been discouraged from pursuing a study of American and southern literature, but at Appalachian State, while teaching American literature, a subject the senior faculty passed on to the junior ones, he began a reading program on American literature and criticism, and he researched whatever he could find on the Appalachian region and its people. He spent the summers of 1948 and 1949 studying at the New York Public Library. In New York, he kept company with Elizabeth "Libby" Lingerfelt of Athens, Tennessee, whom he had met briefly in Boone when she visited a friend there. She was a 1947 graduate of East Tennessee State College and had followed a sister to New York, where she was a receptionist for Brooke Cadwallader, a designer of expensive women's silk scarves.

Cratis's summers at the New York Public Library led him to enter New York University to begin studies for a Ph.D. in literature. He and Libby were married in 1949 in Levittown, Long Island. Cratis then took classes toward his Ph.D. He had made a decision about the subject of his dissertation—the southern mountaineer in fiction—and it was approved by his advisors. When Libby and Cratis returned to Boone, Cratis resumed his full load of teaching, except for the summer of 1954, which he spent in the Duke University library on an Angier B. Duke Scholarship researching his dissertation topic.

A daughter, Sophie, was born to Libby and Cratis in 1953, and a son, David Cratis, in 1955. The family moved into a house of their own in 1954, high on a hill overlooking the university. Libby pursued a course in teacher preparation in English but eventually went to work in the university's Belk Library. Both Sophie and David remembered their father spending long hours in his study with his many writing projects, but he always insisted on a dinner hour together, when they discussed topics of the day, told stories, and played word games. Best remembered were the making of bad puns. Both children remembered hearing their father sing the ancient ballads in the morning as he shaved and dressed. At bedtime he told them stories and encouraged them to make up stories to tell him.[18]

Cratis delivered his dissertation to NYU in 1959, but because of its massive size, his advisors decided to give themselves a two-year reading period so that all of them could fully read it. So it was 1961 before it was accepted and his degree was granted. "The Southern Mountaineer in Fact and Fiction" was a study of the social and cultural history of Appalachian mountaineers and of the vast body of fiction and nonfiction written about them. It is the definitive work on Appalachian literature up to that time, and it established Cratis as the foremost spokesman for the region. At 1,661 pages, it is said to be the longest dissertation ever accepted by an American university. The bibliography alone runs to 56 pages. In 1962, the Board of Regents at NYU awarded Cratis its Founders' Day Certificate for excellence in scholarship.[19]

Although Cratis was encouraged by Dr. Weatherford of Southern Appalachian Studies to edit his dissertation for publication, he never complied, probably because he was too busy with other tasks. However, Martha H. Pipes edited the work down to about five hundred typed pages, and the *Appalachian Journal* ran this edition in four installments in 1975–76.[20]

In his dissertation, Cratis came to the conclusion that the mountaineer "turns out to be a rather complex individual when we examine him closely." He dealt with this complexity perhaps better than most others, who often generalized. He described the main groups who made up the Appalachian population—the English, Scotch-Irish, and Germans—and their diverse religious beliefs, and noted the fact that many were Tories at the time of the Revolution. He also showed, through early travel accounts, that Appalachia until the time of the Civil War was not distinctly different from other rural areas in the rest of the country. In the end, however, he too generalized, portraying the culture as a Scotch-Irish culture even though he earlier had shown that the English were the largest single group in the mountains and that the Germans, Welsh, and others were a significant factor. To him, the colorful Scotch-Irish were overwhelmingly influential, and he greatly admired their positive qualities while also expressing interest in and even enthusiasm for some of their less desirable traits.

Cratis wrote about books and authors that many have not heard of and will never read, but he carefully and sympathetically critiqued both major and minor writers. In his last years, he made a list of eleven authors and their works that he recommended to anyone who wished seriously to study the region through fiction. They are Charles Egbert Craddock (Mary Noailles Murfree), *In the Tennessee Mountains* (1884) and *The Prophet of the Great Smoky Mountains* (1885); Sarah Barnwell Elliott, *The Durket Sperret* (1898); John Fox Jr., *The Cumberland Vendetta* (1900) and *The Little Shepherd of Kingdom Come* (1903); Charles Neville Buck, *The Code of the Mountains* (1915); Anne W. Armstrong, *This Day and Time* (1930); Grace Lumpkin, *To Make My Bread* (1932); James Still, *River of Earth* (1940); Jesse Stuart, *Foretaste of Glory* (1946); Harriette Simpson Arnow, *The Dollmaker* (1954); Wilma Dykeman, *The Tall Woman* (1962), *The Far Family* (1966), and *Return the Innocent Earth* (1973); and Gurney Norman, *Kinfolks: The Wilgus Stories* (1977).[21]

Cratis's memoirs in the W. L. Eury Appalachian Collection at Appalachian State University contain stories and other extensive materials, some of which were edited and published posthumously. He himself never got around to editing them for publication. Once when I was looking over his memoirs, he selected two or three items and asked me to read them. One began as a charming story about a rooster. I paused halfway through to comment that it would make a good children's story. He looked up with a twinkle and said, "Better read on to the end." I did, and found material that definitely would not be recommended for children. His remembrance of W. D. Weatherford Sr. was so interesting that I paused in my reading to suggest that Dr. Willis D. Weatherford Jr., then president of Berea College, would appreciate a copy. Cratis again suggested that I read on to the end, because there were some negative comments. Cratis's scholarly honesty required that he include some of those critical comments as he reviewed the life and accomplishments of Weatherford Sr. at one of the annual Weatherford Literary Award ceremonies. Weatherford Jr. rose at the end of his presentation to compliment him on his attention to detail and honesty. There was a kindness and compassion in Cratis's critical comments that disarmed those who otherwise might have taken offense. While he never wished to offend, he nevertheless was compelled to be tactfully honest and thorough in his presentations.

Appalachian speech was another interest that consumed much of Cratis's time. Between 1961 and 1967, he wrote a series of eleven articles on the subject for *Mountain Life and Work*, published by the now-defunct Council of the Southern Mountains, where I worked for a dozen years. (It was a casualty of the War on Poverty.) These articles addressed different aspects of mountain speech, such as the heavy emphasis on the "r" and the use of vowels and diphthongs, rhythm and melody, verbs, manners, metaphors, prepositions, and subtlety. He published a more general article in the *North Carolina Historical Review* in 1976, which is included at the end of this essay. Three of his articles were reprinted in *Language and Culture*, edited by Patrick Gleeson and Nancy Wakefield (Columbus, Ohio: Charles E. Merrill, 1968). Cratis had worked on a glossary of Appalachian speech to go with a collection of these articles, but he never completed it. I have heard that linguists who read the articles were critical of the "unscientific" approach taken by Cratis, and his son, David, verified this information.[22] While these readers no doubt had valid points, they perhaps failed to appreciate that as a native, Cratis was an exquisitely sophisticated listener who had an astonishing recall of what went on around him in his early years and a rare ability to reproduce nuances of sound in both speech and song. Thus, I think, his comments on regional dialect and usage are important. Eventually, Jim Wayne Miller and I edited these articles and added a preface and introduction as well as a glossary of words and phrases and published them as *Southern Mountain Speech* (Berea, Ky.: Berea College Press, 1992).

Cratis was a major source on southern mountain speech in the Emmy Award–winning nine-part television series *The Story of English*, which aired in 1986, produced jointly by MacNeil/Lehrer Productions and the BBC. He is also quoted in the companion book, *The Story of English*, by Robert McCrum, William Cran, and Robert MacNeil (New York: Elisabeth Sifton/ Viking, 1986).

Of the folklore of the region, Cratis had the greatest love for the ballads. He was also an entertaining tale-teller, especially of "Muts Mag," an Old World traditional tale about a gifted woman, which had come down through his family. He also told other tales in mountain dialect, such as "The Three Little Pigs," when he lectured on mountain speech. He was not an entertainer such as most people may think of when they hear the word "folksinger" or "storyteller." He was a sharer, a presenter of gems from his collection. His love and respect for ballads and those who had perpetuated them shined through his presentations and comments. Cratis did not play musical instruments, though he owned a dulcimer and a banjo, the latter of which he was photographed with, leading the folklorist Ray M. Lawless to list him as a banjo picker in his *Folksingers and Folksongs in*

America (New York: Meredith Press, 1965). Cratis was one of many who had become hooked on ballads and who treasured them as literature and as a key to the aesthetic of a people who have been accused of being without a literature. His comments on the ballads were scholarly but reflected a deep personal appreciation. His renditions were traditional in tune but refined in delivery. He inspired a love of these musical forms of story in his students, and he encouraged those who had a talent to render the ballads. Bobby McMillon, the well-known North Carolina balladeer and tale-teller, said to me in appreciation of Cratis, "He first showed me the light of day about my family and friends, love songs, and tales. I probably would never have gotten up in front of people to sing or talk without his encouragement."[23] He was a "teacher, advisor, mentor and friend," said Grace Toney Edwards, director of the Appalachian Studies Program in the English Department at Radford University, "who when asked for help and advice responded promptly, fully, generously, not always waiting to be asked, but through letters that came, unexpectedly, like treasures themselves."[24] Williams himself wrote:

> As a humanistic interpreter of my culture and as a teacher, speaker, enter-
> tainer, and writer, I feel that I have helped hundreds of other Appalachians
> toward self-acceptance and pride in who they are. I am most gratified that
> my sustained effort over many years helped to mount burgeoning Appa-
> lachian studies in school and college curricula throughout the region and
> inspired sincere scholarly reevaluation of American's most easily identified
> and possibly most significant subculture.[25]

In assessing William Vaughan's influence on him as a teacher, Cratis revealed his own values and purposes, which made it possible for him in turn to become an intellectual father to scores of students at Appalachian State University, and to others wherever he taught or spoke.

He was a natural-born administrator who did not need a course in management. Those who were led by him talk of his quiet, reassuring manner, his stately tones, his lack of irritation, and his reluctance to say negative things about those with whom he differed. Clues to his philosophy of administration are also found throughout the memoir where he discussed his relationship with Vaughan:

> As a teacher, principal, university professor, administrator, I found that I
> could honestly tolerate without feeling compelled to attack social agencies
> and institutions and that I could work with students, fellow teachers, and

administrators with backgrounds much different from my own without "putting anybody down." My good will and spirit of tolerance were the foundation stones of my "educational statesmanship." My acceptance of people as they themselves saw themselves stood me in good stead.

My ability to listen, consider, ask questions without condemning or rejecting appealed to those whose fate it was to work with me. It has seemed to me that such success as I might have enjoyed as a "public person" is owing largely to my having accepted myself with confidence, and without significant loss of self-esteem, as an Appalachian. I never feel the need to apologize for who I am or try to obscure my identity. I find it enormously comfortable to be myself.[26]

His leadership went far beyond Appalachian State University. When community colleges began to spring up in the region, he foresaw that there would be a shortage of qualified teachers for higher education and wrote a proposal for preparing teachers for these new institutions. He was also a nationally recognized authority on graduate programs in education. For ten years he was a member of a three-person consulting team that evaluated graduate study for the American Association of State Colleges and Universities. He took the ASU graduate school, which is now named for him, from fewer than a hundred to nearly a thousand students, and in 1974 he noted that the university had awarded over six thousand master's degrees. Since many of those who received higher degrees were teachers and leaders, his influence was felt throughout western North Carolina and elsewhere in the region. He developed a folk festival and courses in Appalachian literature and folklore that grew into the first Appalachian studies program in the region. Anthropologist Dr. Patricia Beaver, one of Cratis's disciples, developed a master's degree program in Appalachian studies at ASU, which she headed for many years until her recent retirement. The program continues under new leadership.

Cratis first saw the need for the Appalachian Consortium of colleges and other institutions and worked to see it formed. The Appalachian Consortium Press has published numerous books that have been vital in Appalachian studies. He was also one of the founders of the Appalachian Studies Association. For his work in education, he received the prestigious O. Max Gardner Award in 1973 from the Board of Governors of the University of North Carolina. Though he made numerous speeches at colleges and universities throughout the region, however, there is no evidence that he was ever invited to speak at the premier institution at Chapel Hill.

In recognition of his total body of work, he was honored widely. Over the years of his work in Appalachian studies, he came to be known as "Mr. Appalachia." On his retirement from Appalachian State in 1976, the university held a three-day Appalachian Symposium, at which twenty-one scholars from across the region and the nation read papers. They were subsequently published as *An Appalachian Symposium: Essays in Honor of Cratis D. Williams*, edited by J. W. Williamson and published by the university in 1977. This symposium was the primary inspiration for the creation of the Appalachian Studies Association and its annual Appalachian Studies Conference, which has grown in numbers and influence in the region.

Cratis's major awards were the Outstanding Alumnus Award from Cumberland College (now University); the Brown-Hudson Award from the North Carolina Folklore Society, which named him the "Master Folklorist of Appalachia"; the Weatherford Award from Berea College; and the Appalachian Consortium's Laurel Leaves Award for Distinguished Service. The Appalachian Studies Association established the Cratis D. Williams Service Award in his honor (later the Cratis D. Williams/James S. Brown Service Award). He also received honorary degrees from Berea College, Cumberland College, the College of Idaho, Morehead State University, Marshall University, and Appalachian State University.

Cratis Williams died on May 11, 1985. He is buried in the Williams cemetery on Caines Creek in Lawrence County, Kentucky. His wife, Libby, and his two children survive him. Sophie attended Antioch College and then studied botany at North Carolina State University. After working as a governmental research botanist, she earned a nursing degree, then qualified as a nurse-practitioner and worked at several locations before returning home to care for her mother, who had suffered a stroke. David earned degrees in English at the University of North Carolina at Chapel Hill and a Ph.D. in speech, communication and human relations at Kansas State University. He is associate professor of communications studies at Florida Atlantic University. He and Patricia Beaver coedited two volumes of his father's memoirs, *The Cratis Williams Chronicles: I Come to Boone* (Boone, N.C.: Appalachian Consortium Press, 1999) and *Tales from Sacred Wind: Coming of Age in Appalachia* (Jefferson, N.C.: McFarland & Company, 1999).

Following his death, the Appalachian Consortium held a Cratis Williams Symposium at Appalachia State University in 1989 to honor Williams and also expand understanding of Appalachian studies and the subdisciplines of

Appalachian music, folklore, history, and literature. Major regional scholars spoke in support of these aims to a large appreciative audience.

"Unique" is the word that truly fits Cratis Williams. He had rare gifts of intellect, personality, and character. He understood himself and his native region, and was a pioneer scholar of his place. He was a lecturer without peer, and he freely shared his knowledge and himself. He saw humor in most of human activity and had a vast storehouse of jokes, tales, and observations that he told with enthusiasm. I shall miss him as long as I live and will regret all of those questions that I didn't know enough to ask him. I chuckle often in remembrance of one of his rare stories, and I shall never hear them told so well again.

A Sampling of the Scholarship, Wit, and Humor of Cratis Williams

✺ Appalachian Speech

"Appalachian Speech" was originally published in the North Carolina Historical Review *55, no. 2 (1978): 174–79. It is reproduced here with permission.*

Appalachian speech was determined by the predominance of the Scotch-Irish in the settlement of the Mountain region prior to and after the American Revolution. Recently arrived from Northern Ireland and not yet assimilated into the older colonial culture, the Scotch-Irish who moved into the mountains brought with them an old-fashioned northern English dialect that had changed but little during the stay of their ancestors for four or five generations in Northern Ireland. Isolated in the rugged terrain of Appalachia, their descendants continued until recent times to speak essentially the dialect of their remote Lowland Scots and northern English ancestors. In the meantime the speech of their cousins along the Scottish Border and in Ireland was becoming modern. Thus the sixteenth-century dialect of the Appalachian people is the oldest living English dialect, older than the speech of Shakespeare, closer to the speech of Chaucer.

Of the 9 million people living in Southern Appalachia, 94 percent of them descended from pre-Revolutionary American ancestors, between a half million and a million of them, mostly older people living in isolated rural areas, continue to speak the old dialect, essentially the same from West Virginia to the mountains of North Georgia and Alabama. However, almost all people of native stock, regardless of economic, social, or educational status, have traces of the older dialect in their speech. Most persistent are traditional pitch, intonation, melody patterns, inflection, and rhythms.

Prototypical Appalachian speech overlaps extensively with the folk speech of other American rural groups of colonial British stock, particularly with reference to the use of archaic strong past tense forms, old-fashioned words and idioms, case forms, and certain vowel sounds that are generally considered dialectical. "He *skun* the 'possum"; "Aye *gonnies*, I'll try it"; "*Me and him* both *heared* it"; "I *growed* up about *haaif* way between *Gaaistonia and Gaaaaifney*"; and the vowelization of the long *i* into something that approaches *ah* may be heard throughout the South as well as in Appalachia.

Many aspects of speech in the mountains differentiate it from other dialects. First, there is the traditional manner of speaking. Appalachia folk appear to speak with fixed chins and half-closed mouths. Both front and back vowels and diphthongs are pulled toward the middle of the mouth as if all were being reduced to schwa, or the light "uh" that often clutters up the speech of educated people. This tendency leads to a fracturing of all of the short vowels except ŏ in Appalachian speech. "Bat" becomes "ba-it"; "bet," "be-it"; "hit," "hi-ut"; "cup," "cu-up"; "where," "whu'ur." Back vowels except ō slide forward toward schwa: "what," "wha-ut"; "brush," "bresh"; "shut," "shet"; "nice," "nahce." The long *u* sound in Appalachian speech, like short and long *o*, is singularly pure. Mountain folk consistently use the long *u* in such words as "roof," "root," "school," and "stool," but "put" and "soot" rhyme with "nut."

Appalachian speech, like the speech along the Scottish Border, is heavily oriented toward *r*. Mountain folk use a strong *r*, but it is never trilled as in Scottish speech. The mountaineer loves *r* so well that he rarely passes up an opportunity to pronounce it. In fact, he loves it so well that he will attach it to certain words with open endings: "narrow," "narrer"; "window," "winder"; "widow," "widder"; "tobacco," "backer"; "potato," "'tater." Unlike the New Englander, he does not attach *r* to words like "Cuba" or "idea." Instead, he says "Cuby" and "idy."

The sound of *r* is also inserted in many words in mountain speech: "woman," "womern"; "breakfast," "breakferst"; "ruin," "rurn"; "onion," "ingern"; and sometimes "bursh" for "bush."

The mountaineer, his mouth fixed comfortably for schwa and *r*, begins to blend *r* with the preceding vowel or diphthong as soon as he can. In "bear," for example, as soon as *b* is articulated, blending begins. The result is a diphthong peculiar to mountain speech which outsiders spell and pronounce "bar." However, it is not "bar," which, for the mountaineer, is a castrated pig [barrow]. Instead of a broad *a*, as the outsider would have it, the diphthong becomes vowelized in a glide from schwa to *r*, a kind of twisted sound which outsiders, even those trained as actors, find difficult to master.

The average American accepts without question four pronunciations of "bear": bĕ-er, bĕ-uh, bă-er, bă-uh. But when he hears the persistent "barr" of the mountaineer, he laughs. Including those who have migrated elsewhere, nearly 13 million Appalachians use this sound, a larger number, it is believed, than those who say "bĕ-uh" or "bă-uh." With history on their side, are 13 million people wrong?

The mountaineer's blending of vowels and and diphthongs with following *r*'s leads also to a different quality for a long *i* preceding *r*: *fire* and *wire* become *far* and *war*.

The diphthong *ou* is a triphthong in mountain speech, a sound particular to Appalachians. This sound, which had not yet stabilized in English speech in colonial times, is sounded differently among Americans of colonial ancestry. In parts of Virginia, North Carolina, and South Carolina one hears "abā-ot the hā-os." Perhaps 3½ million persons use this sound, but they do it with pride. However, the preponderance of mountain folk, who say "ab ă u uht the hă u uhs," become self-conscious and hang their heads in shame when attention is called to their way of saying *ou*.

Mountain folk, along with other Americans with colonial ancestry, do not sound *g* in -*ing* endings. We cannot say that they leave off the *g*; they never did get around to adding it, which appears to have been an unfortunate accident in the development of our language anyway, for final *g* is very definitely a brake on the movement of speech and does damage to melody. But the Appalachian, who has retained the Middle English preposition *a* as a prefix to -*ing* verbals, pronounces -*in'* in his own way. In Coastal Carolina one hears *wri-tin'*, *fly-in'*, *speak-in'*, with a slight stress on the short *i* in -*in'*. The mountaineer says *a-writ-un*, *a-fly-un*, and *a-speak-un*, with the vowel in the -*ing* ending a very slight schwa that might best be understood if the words were spelled *a-writ'n*, *a fly'n*, *a-speak'n*.

Mountain folk also indicate cultural values in some of their idiomatic expressions. With a traditional respect for the integrity of the individual and the sacredness of private property, the mountaineer says *you'ns* (you ones) rather than the illogical *you all* heard throughout the South. "This hyur book is *his'n* (his own, his one), an' that thair'n is *her'n* (her own, her one)" reflects the emphasis upon ownership and a desire for preciseness in identification.

Outsiders note readily numerous obsolete strong past tense forms in Appalachian speech: *holp* or *hope* for *helped, skun* or *skunt* for *skinned, axt* for *asked*. Mountain speech, if differentiated at all in this regard from folk speech of other people with colonial ancestors, is differentiated only by the frequency of the occurrence of these forms rather than the quality.

Past tense forms of strong verbs in which *a* occurs are generally not used: past tense forms of verbs like *come, run, swim, begin* are *come, run, swum, begin* or *begun*. Transitive and intransitive differentiations are not made for *sit-set, lie-lay, rise-raise*, the mountaineer preferring *set, lay,* and *raise* both transitively and intransitively.

A few preferences that are almost prejudices also obtain in mountain speech. *Those* is a hifalutin' word. *Them* both as pronoun and demonstrative adjective is preferred. Such contractions as *isn't, doesn't, aren't* rarely occur. *Wasn't*, which is both singular and plural, is pronounced *wŭdn't.*

The following is a folktale in the prototypical dialect of Appalachia. It is the kind of tale a seventy-five-year-old grandmother who either did not go to school at all or did not get to go long enough for her teachers to do damage to her speech might tell her four-year-old grandson.

THE FOX AND THE BUM'LEBEE

This folktale is part of the preceding article. The meanings of some potentially obscure words have been added within square brackets.

Oncet thay uz a fox 'at tuck a notion one mornin' he'd walk daown to the store in the settle*mints* at the maouth of the creek. He had to have 'im some lampawl [*lamp oil, kerosene*] an' a plug o' chawin' 'backer, an' 'laowed, by Jacks, he might buy 'im a can o' sammons [*salmon*], ef the price uz right. Wul, sar, whilest he uz a-sankerin' [*sauntering*] along, a-thankin' abaout first one thang an' then t'other, he jist happened to spy a survagerse [*vigorous,* *active*] big yaller-stripedy-bellied bum'lebee a-smaoulin' over a blossom 'at uz a-growin' on a mornin' glory vine on one of the post-es thair by the side o' the big road. So's an' he snuck up, right cyurful like, an' recht aout an' snabbed 'im, an' popped 'im into a poke he had with 'im . . . an' didn't git stung nary time . . . an' then he went on.

D'reckly, he come to this hyur haouse 'at uz a-standin' acrosst the bra-a-anch. So's an' he walked right daown ferninst [*corruption of* fornent, *opposite to, facing, alongside*] the gate an' hollered, "Hello!"

A womern come an' stuck her head aout at the door an' said, "Haowd-do? What'd ye have, mister?" The fox says, "Haow abaout me a-leavin' this hyur poke hyur whilest I go daown to the maouth o' the creek to the store? I aim to git me some lampawl, an' a plug o' chawin' 'backer, an' I 'laow, by Jacks, I might buy me a can o' sammons, ef the price is right."

"W'y, come right in, ef ye can git in fer all the clutter*mint*. I've been a-layin' off fer might-nigh a week to redden [*tidy*] up this hyur ol' place, but a body jist cain't never git araound to doin' nothin', don't 'pyur like. Jist putt it daown hyan side o' the farplace, ef ye can find room fer it."

Wul, the fox he walks over and putts the poke daown, an' then he looks at the womern, right straight like, an' says, "Naow, don't ye be a-openin' that thair poke whilest I'm gone." An' then he went on.

Agin he uz aout o' sight an' saound o' the haouse, that thair womern says, "Naow, I wonder jist what's in that thair poke. Aye gonnies, I'll see!"

So's an' she walks over an' picks up the poke an' onties the strang. The bum'lebee, a course, flies aout. Wul, her ol' rooster 'at jist happened to be a-standin' thair tuck aout atter it, but the danged thang got away.

She tied the strang back, jist like it wuz, best she c'd ricollect, an' putt the poke back daown, and hooved it up in the middle jist like it wuz so's an' hit'd look like nobody had teched it.

Then she grabbed her snuff-box daown from upon the farboard whur it stayed at an' set daown in the rockin' chur fer a little rub whilest she commenced to begin to a-thinkin' abaout a-startin' to redden up the haouse, an' that thair ol' fox come back.

He walks over an' picks up the poke an' onties the strang. The bum'lebee, a course, hain't thair. He looks at the womern, right mad like, an' says, "Whur's my bum'lebee?"

The womern says, "W'y, I jist ontied the strang an' peeped in the poke and' the bum'lebee flew aout. My ol' rooster 'at jist happened to be a-standin' thair tuck aout atter it, but the danged thang got away."

"Wul, then," says the fox, "the rooster's mine."

So's an' he cotch the rooster an' popped *him* into the poke. An' then he went on.

Atter a bit he come to another haouse 'at uz a-standin' by the side o' the road. Thay uz a ol' womern a-settin' on th porchstep a-peelin' Arsh 'taters an' a-throwin' the peelin's to her pet pig. The fox walked right up ferninst her an' says, "Hello!"

The womern says "Haowd-do? What'd ye have, mister?"

The fox says, "Haow abaout me a-leavin' this hyur poke hyur whilest I'm gone daown to the maouth o' the creek to the store? I haf to have me a quart o' lampawl, an' a plug o' chawin' 'backer, an' I 'laow, by Jacks, I might buy me a can o' sammons, ef the price is right."

"W'y, jist putt it daown thair agin the wall sommers. Jist anywhurs'll do, I reckon."

The fox walks over an' puts the poke daown. Then, he looks at the womern, right straight like, an' says, "Naow, don't ye be a-openin' that thair poke whilest I'm gone." Then he went on.

The womern went on -a-peelin' her Arsh 'taters. When she uz done, she riz up to go in the haouse an' noticed that sompin' in that thair poke was a-movin' araound. She says to herse'f, "Naow, I bet you the yurs offen my head that that 'air ol' fox is the very varmint that made off with my choice turkey tom. I thinks to myse'f yistid'y when the turkey tom didn't come to be fed that I seed his ol' crookedy track in the sa-a-nd along the bra-a-anch. I aimed to ax my ol' man to set a trap fer the lowdown varmint an' clean fergot it. Aye, gonnies, I'm a-goin' to see what's in that thair poke! Hit jist maought be my turkey tom."

So's an' she hitched her apern up, an' went over an' picked up the poke an' ontied the strang. The rooster, o' course, flew aout. She grabbed at it but missed it. She called her little boy 'at uz araound behin' the haouse a-playin' in the bra-a-anch. He come a-runnin' an' chased that thair roster all over the yard, an' clean daown the haul road to-wardge the barn, an' plum' around the barn, an' through the entry of the corncrib, but the dang thang got away.

So's an' she wropped the strang back araound the poke an' tied it back jist like it wuz, best she c'd ricollect, an' putt it back agin' the wall, an' hoooved it up so's an' hit'd look jist like hit hadn't been teched. Then she went on in the haouse an' put her Arsh 'taters on to fry. An' she she come back to the porch an' set daown in her rockin' chur to rest a spell, an' that thair ol' fox come back agin.

He walked over an' picked up the poke from agin the wall whur he'd putt it at an' ontied the strang. The rooster, o' course, wudent thair. Then he looked at the old womern, right mad like, an' says, "Whur's my rooster?"

"W'y, I seed sompin' a-movin' araound in it, an' so's an' I jist ontied the strang an' peeped in, an' the rooster come a-floppin' aout. I grabbed at it, but the dang thang got away an' went a-squawkin' acrosst the yard. I called my little boy 'at 'uz back araound the haouse a-playin' an' he come a-runnin' an' tried to ketch it. That pore li'l younguen run that ol' rooster all over this hyur yard, an' clean daown the haul road to-wardge the barn, an' all over the barn lot, an' clur through the entry of the corncrib, but the dang thang got away. When that thair chil' got back to the haouse agin, hit 'uz a-pa-aintin' sn' a-blowin' and hits tongue 'uz a-hangin' aout, hit 'uz so-o-o tard!"

"Wul, then, the younguen's mine," says the fox. An' so's an' he ketched that 'air li'l boy an putt him in the poke. Then he went on.

Hit uz a-gitten' way up in the day when he come to a haouse 'at uz a-standin' on a little ba-a-nk above the big road. Thay 'uz a womern a-settin' on the porch an' a-strangin' beans. She 'uz a-sangin' a song-ballet an' ditn't pay the fox no mind, pyeerd like, whilest he's a-waggin' the poke with the little boy in it up the pa-a-th that led out from the ind of the porch. When he got right up ferninst the porch he says, "Hello!"

The womern stopped her song-ballet and says, "Haowd-do? What'd ye have, mister?"

The fox says, "Haow abaout me a-leavin' this hyur poke hyur whilest I'm gone daown to the maouth of the creek to the store? I'm a-layin' off to buy me a quart o' lampawl, an' a plug o' chawin' 'backer, an' I 'laow, by Jacks, I might buy me a can o' sammons, ef the price is right."

"W'y, jist put it daown thair on the ind o' the porch sommers. Jist anywhurs'll do, I reckon."

So's an' the fox he putt the poke daown agin the wall. Then he looked at the womern, right straight like, an' says, "Naow, don't ye be a-openin' that thair poke whilest I'm gone." An' then he went on.

Naow, this hyur ol' womern wuz awful busy. She hatent got a soon-a-nough start with her work, an' she had workhands to fix dinner fur that day besides. So's an' she started her song-ballet another gin an' begun to strang her beans like the devil a-beatin' tanbark an' fergot all abaout the poke.

Atter a while she thought she heared sompin'. She hushed her song an' stretched her neck aout to listen, but she ditent hear nothin' no more. Then she begun to a-strangin' her beans an' heisted her tune agin an' hatent more'n got it aouten 'er nose when she 'uz dead shore she heared sompin' agin. She stopped a-sangin', an' gethered up the tail o' her apern, an' riz aouten her chur, an' walked to the fur ind o' the porch, an' listened. She ditent hear nothin' no more. So's an' she went back an' set daown an' begun to a-strangin' her beans another gin, an' uz jist a-gittin' her maouth all waound up fer to heist her tune agin when she heared somebody a-sayin', "Let me aout o' hyur! Let me aout o' hyur!" She'd plime-blank fergot all abaout the poke. Hit 'uz that thair little boy a-wantin' aout!

So's an' she hitched up her apern an' went over an' ontied the strang an' the little boy stepped aouten the poke. He told 'er haow come he happent to be in it. So's an' she called the haouse dog an' put him in the poke an' wropped the strang araound it an' tied it back jist like it wuz, best she c'd ricollect, an' putt it back daown in the same place whur it wuz at.

She hatent hardly more'n got set back daown in 'er chur agin when that ol' fox come back. He walked over an' picked up the poke. Seein' as haow hit hatent been pestered with none, as fur as he c'd tell, he swung it over his shoulder and went on.

Hit uz a-gittin' way up to-wardge noon an' the sun uz brilin' hot. 'Twarn't long afore that thair ol' fox begun to pa-a-nt an' huff an' he uz a-gittin' awful hongry. A-finally he seed a maple tree 'at flung a dark cool shade on a little gra-a-ssy patch on a knoll acrosst a fence. So's an' he clumb over the fence an' started to a-waggin' his load up the hill, a-thankin' abaout what a good dinner that fat juicy little boy uz -a-goin' to be everwhen he got hisse'f up thair agin that maple tree.

Wul, he set daown an' leaned hisse'f back agin the tree an' pulled the poke up a-twixt his knees, a-thankin' the live-long time 'at he uz a-goin' to have him a larrupin' fine dinner of little boy any minit naow. He got hisse'f all fixed fer to eat his dinner.

So's an' he ontied the strang . . . an' aout baounced that haouse dog an' caught ol' Mr. Fox by the nose!

That dog had him a good dinner, 'baout that time.

Cratis's Jokes and Stories

Williams collected the following stories and apparently rewrote them to his satisfaction. Some of them are reproduced here courtesy of the Cratis D. Williams

Papers in the W. L. Eury Appalachian Collection, Appalachian State University, box 107, folder 6, and used with permission.

❀ Grandma's Whorehouse

Adapted from a story told around 1970 by Bob Allen, Boone, North Carolina.

A traveling salesman was driving through the beautiful Blue Ridge Mountain country of western Virginia one lovely day in June when he was startled by a sign with bright red lettering nailed to a fence post by the side of the road. The sign said "Grandma's Whorehouse, 3 miles." Hardly believing his eyes, he touched his brake to make sure.

He drove along for another few minutes and saw another sign that said "Grandma's Whorehouse, one mile." Having decided that the first sign was somebody's prank, his curiosity was aroused by the second.

Just about that time he had forgotten the sign while considering the approach he would take in attempting to make a big sale to the merchant he was to call on in the next town, and as he was maneuvering a bend in the road before it was to cross a green hill, he saw a third sign with an arrow painted on it pointing down a side road. The sign read "Grandma's Whorehouse, 1/4 mile."

Popping his foot on the brake, he slowed the car down and turned on to the side road, which dipped down into a shady vale and continued between lush rolling pastures in which fat cattle were grazing. The road ended against a white picket fence that enclosed the beautifully landscaped yard of a neat, freshly painted white cottage with green shutters. In an old-fashioned rocking chair on the porch sat a little blue-haired lady. She had on glasses with lavender rims and earpieces and wore a bunch of lavender at her throat She was knitting. A clean soft-haired blue kitten was playing with a ball of yarn lying on the slate-colored floor of the porch.

The salesman got out of his car, and the little lady rose from the rocking chair.

"Good afternoon, ma'am."

"How do you do, sir?"

"Is this, uh, is this . . . Grandma's Whorehouse?" he blurted.

"Yes, it is," the lady said, matter-of-factly. "Won't you come in?'

"I saw your signs along the road and thought I would just stop by," the salesman hesitated, "for service," he concluded, feeling embarrassed as he stepped up on the porch.

"That will be $10.00," the woman said.

The salesman took out his billfold, selected a crisp $10.00 bill from among the worn and tattered ones he observed in his pocketbook, and handed it to her, noting that the kitten was hopelessly tangling the yarn.

The little lady opened the door to the cottage and said, "Just go through the door at the end of the hallway and you will get what you came for."

The salesman noted that the hallway was newly papered. A polished hat rack and hall tree must have been antiques. A slender-legged table with a family Bible resting on it stood under a lighted picture in color of Jesus wearing a crown of thorns. On the wall opposite the table hung in a gilt frame a piece of elaborate needlework asking that "God bless our happy home."

The salesman opened the door and was amazed to find himself in the backyard. But it was a beautiful and well-kept yard. He followed a cobblestone walk, edged with English ivy, past shrubs and banks of flowers. Bird baths stood in sunny spots. Neatly clipped boxwoods surrounded a freshly painted gazebo with brightly colored furniture. The cobblestone walk led to an arbor of rosebushes in full bloom. On either side of the arbor was a low stone bench, and on the other end of it was an elaborately worked iron gate.

As the salesman approached the arbor he noticed an arched sign over the walk and reaching from one side of the arbor to the other. In gold and red Old English lettering the sign read:

"YOU HAVE JUST BEEN SCREWED — GRANDMA."

✸ A New Republican

Learned from Jay Aldridge, Boone North Carolina.

Just after the presidential election, a graduate student at Appalachian State was hitchhiking on U.S. 421 towards Winston-Salem late on a Friday afternoon. He was just east of Boone when he thumbed a woman driving a fine new car for a ride. She stopped shortly after passing the young man. He rushed up beside the car and was about to climb in.

The attractive driver asked, "Are you a democrat or a republican?"

He paused for a moment and responded, "Why, I'm a democrat."

The woman slammed the car door and drove on.

Soon another car approached, a small new red car driven by a young woman, perhaps a graduate student at the University. The graduate student flung out his thumb. She stopped the car and rolled down the glass.

"Are you a democrat or a republican?" she asked.

"I'm a democrat," he replied.

She hurriedly rolled up the glass and drove on.

The graduate student concluded that he was affiliated with the wrong political party. If he wanted a ride, he would have to switch parties, he decided. Just then, he saw a clean big Oldsmobile approaching. He flung out his thumb.

The car came to a stop beside him and the door opened. The driver, a finely dressed older woman, asked, "Young man, are you a democrat or a republican?"

"Republican," the young man responded aggressively.

"Get right in," the woman said, as she patted the seat beside her. He climbed in and the car moved on.

After a brief conversation about the fine autumn weather, the woman said, "Young man, would you like to be with me a little while? We can stop at the rest area and picnic site at the Parkway School."

"Of course," the graduate student responded.

She turned off at the Parkway School and drove to the upper side of the picnic area. They got out and prepared the seat for lovemaking.

In the midst of lovemaking, the young man considered his situation.

"Here I am," he thought. "I haven't been a republican for more than ten minutes and I'm screwing someone already."

✸ A Bull's Pedigree

One of the farmers in my valley took his cow to a neighbor's farm to be serviced by a young registered bull. The neighbor was not at home, but his wife went along with the farmer to the lot in which the bull was kept. To make conversation while the bull was preparing to mount the cow, the farmer asked, "How far back does your beast's pedigree go?" The wife, puzzled for for a moment, looked at the pawing bull and responded, "Well, I don't know how far back it goes, but you can see for yourself how far down it comes."

An observation we would make in response to an illogical statement was, "Well, you can see for yourself how far down it comes."

❃ Scare Me Again, John Blythe

As told by Bernard Whitt, Morgan County, Kentucky, about 1960.

A story was told in the valley of how John Blythe and his wife became engaged and married. John had called on the young woman only a few times when he "popped the question." Confused and frightened, the young woman did not respond.

Realizing that his proposal had scared the young woman, John did not ask the question again the next time he met with her. In the meantime, though, she had been thinking the matter over and was prepared to say yes when he got around to asking it again. On the third date, a logical time for John to ask the question again arrived, but he did not ask it. Instead, he looked at her hungrily and remained silent. At length, she said to him, "Scare me again, John Blythe." He did, she accepted, and they were married.

It became customary for one who was willing to comply, to encourage a person who was finding it difficult to ask a favor by saying, "Scare me again, John Blythe."

❃ His Operation

As told by Glen Wallace, Mountain City, Tennessee, in 1980.

Two bulls found themselves in adjoining pens at a livestock market. They became acquainted. The market was poor that year, so their owners took the bulls back to their farms with the hope that the market might improve.

A year after, the bulls again found themselves in adjoining pens at the market. One was fat, sleek, and bright. The other was thin. His hair was dead and dull-looking, and his eyes were weak and rheumy.

The sleek bull said, "Don't I know you? It seems to me that we must have met some time in the past."

"Yes," said the thin one. "We met at the market last year. What kind of year have you had?"

"It couldn't have been better," said the sleek one. "My master took me back home and fed me well and strawed me down every night in a clean stall. I had plenty of sweet water to drink every day. When spring came, he turned me into a pasture of lush grass up to my knees and with three bold springs of cool sweet water and spreading shade trees here and there. I had as my companions seven young heifers that had never yet calved. Now that I think about it, it was the best year of my life.

"How was your year?"

"Miserable," replied the thin bull, glancing at the dry horny hooves on his front feet. "My master took me back home and turned me into a rocky field that had nothing growing in it except broom sedge, sawbriers, and scrubby bushes. There was only one little spring of muddy water that almost dried up when summer came, and there was not a tree big enough to make a shade in the whole field. Last winter I had to pick straw from a rack that the farmer filled every now and then, and during the spring and summer, I spent all of my waking hours finding enough grass and weeds in that old clay field to stay alive. It was the hardest year of my life.

"Worst of all, my only companion was a bedraggled old steer with watering eyes, an ugly distemper, and peeling hooves who stayed right beside me day in and day out, week after week, and month after month. And all that steer could talk about that livelong year was his operation."

✻ Bible Religion

As told by Joe Logan, north Georgia, about 1970.

A traveling salesman's car broke down one Friday afternoon in a little town in North Georgia. The mechanic in the local garage found that it would be necessary to order a part from Atlanta before the car could be repaired. The part would arrive on the bus on Monday morning and the car could be ready by noon. The salesman went to the little hotel, engaged a room for the weekend, and called his family to report his situation.

About the middle of Sunday afternoon the salesman decided to take a walking tour of the town. Beyond the business district he turned on an unpaved street leading toward a pasture.

At the end of the street, which dead-ended against a fence, he found two Baptist churches, directly across the street from each other. While he was reading the bulletin board of one of the churches, a man with a sun-tanned face and wearing a a dark suit emerged.

"Good afternoon," he greeted the salesman in the sepulchral voice of an undertaker. "A stranger in town?"

"Good afternoon. I am a weekend guest at the hotel out for a Sunday stroll. Are you the preacher at this church?"

"Yes, I am. You would be welcome to attend the evening service. We preach the word as it is written in the Holy Bible."

"Thank you. Could you tell me why in such a small town there are two Baptist churches located directly across the street from each other? It looks as if it might be better if you were to come together as one body."

"Oh, no, we could never do that. Our doctrines are entirely different."

"What do you mean? You are both Baptist churches, aren't you?"

"Yes, but we don't believe the same way. In *this* church we believe in the word as it is written. The plain Bible way is the only way, we hold. God don't play games with his saints. He says straight out in the holy writ what he means. Now, you take them people across the street. They say you've got to interpret the word. F'r instance, we believe that when the Bible says Pharaoh's daughter found Moses in the bullrushes, that's exactly how it was, but them thaire folks across the street say 'That's just what *she* said.'"

❊ A Spring for the Screen Door

As told by Glen Wallace, Mountain City, Tennessee, in 1980.

A man's wife over here in Ashe County decided suddenly one Saturday morning that she needed to ride to West Jefferson with her husband to buy a spring to replace a worn out one on the screen door to her kitchen. She dressed herself hurriedly and climbed into the half-ton truck beside her husband, who was in a great hurry to get to the bank in West Jefferson and back home by the time the dew had dried in his meadow, which he planned to mow that day.

The wife got out at the hardware store while her husband went on to the bank. She was the first customer. The clerk met her at the door with, "Good mornin', ma'am. What can I do for you?"

She explained that she wanted a screen-door spring to replace one that had worn out. He took her to a shelf on which springs were stored. Finding one that was just like the spring that had worn out, she said, "I will take this one."

"The price for that is 85 cents," the clerk said.

On the way to the cash register the clerk turned suddenly toward the farmwife and said, "Oh, don't you want a screw for it?"

She was stunned for a moment. "No-o-o," she said, while surveying the contents of the store rapidly, "but I would for that pop-up toaster over there on the shelf."

✺ Bedridden

As told by Stafford Hartley, Blackberry, near Blowing Rock, North Carolina, about 1975.

My old aunt, who had moved from the country into Lenoir to live with her granddaughter, was getting ready to celebrate her 100th birthday. One of the young reporters from the *News-Topic* came to interview her for a story.

My aunt, chipper and bright-eyed, was sitting in her rocking chair by the fireplace. The reporter sat near her.

"I hear that you will be 100 tomorrow," the reporter said. "You've lived a long life. To what do you attribute such a long life?"

"Well," began the old woman thoughtfully, "I've worked hard all my life, eaten good country grub, took things as they come, not worried over what I couldn't do nothin' about, and gone to bed early and got up with the birds."

"Did you have any bad habits?"

"What do you mean?"

"Well, have you ever used tobacco, for example?"

"Oh, yes, I've chewed and dipped and smoked. I enjoyed smokin' best."

"What did you smoke, a pipe, cigars, or cigarettes?"

"All of 'em at one time or another. I've rolled 'em from home grown ter-baccer in pieces of brown paper pokes, I've rolled 'em from Bull Durham and Duke's Mixter in cigarette paper, and I've smoked ready-made ones from packages that we could buy at the store. I liked the roll-yer-owns best."

"What about alcoholic beverages. Have you ever drunk?"

"All my life. We made wine and home brew at home, and I drunk hard liquor when I could get it, both moonshine and fotched-on. I allus liked good moonshine whiskey better than anything, though, 'specially the kind that was doubled and twisted in a copper still by a man 'at knowed what he was a-doin'!"

"Then you've always enjoyed good health in spite of your bad habits. Tell me, have you ever been bedridden?"

"Bedridden? Lord, yes, honey, a thousand times."

❊ New and Improved Privies

This story with its punch line is a play on an organization formed in 1958 called the John Birch Society, a conservative group promoting anti-Communism, limited government, and individual freedom.

Back in the Depression agricultural extension agents, public health officers, and WPA supervisors in mountain counties cooperated to mount programs to help farmers improve the appearance and sanitation of their outdoor privies.

Now, in the valley in which I grew up water birches grew in profusion along the banks of the creeks and branches. When the water birch grows to a diameter of about three inches, its bark begins to color various shades and becomes pied with stripes and spots ranging in color from mother of pearl to deep rich brown. The thin, paper-like bark also peels away from the trunk of the tree in colorful flags.

Some of the families had new WPA privies moved out back, but those who already had good privies were content simply to improve them and spruce up their appearance. Someone got the notion of decorating his privy with split trunks of small birch trees with the bark left on.

The idea caught on. Soon families that thought of themselves as proud, respectable, and progressive were all competing in the elaborateness and artistic touches that they could give their privies by decorating them with the beautiful paper birch trunks.

The more common sort of people, however, did not respond to the innovation and change going on in the valley. Many continued to live without the convenience of a privy of any kind and did their business behind the barn or out in the woods anywhere. Others were content to use unadorned WPA privies or the old privies they had.

Those of us with the birch-decorated privies considered ourselves the social elite of the valley. To distinguish ourselves from the unprogressive and trifling folk in the community, we gathered ourselves into an organization with officers and a constitution which we proudly called the Birch John Society.

❋ Ma's Been A-Eatin' Wild Ingerns Agin

As told about 1936 by David Bishop, Laurel County, Kentucky.

When I was a high school student my parents sent me back one summer to work on my grandfather's farm in Laurel County, Kentucky. One Sunday all of us went to the monthly meeting of the local hardshell Baptist church.

There was a bench full of preachers, and the members of the faith and order occupied the front of the one-room church, the women seated parallel to the preacher's platform on one side and the men on the other. In front of the preacher's stand there was a small table with a bucket of water on it and a dipper floating on top. Sinners and spectators sat on benches in front of the preachers.

The day was hot and the church house was filled. The preachers were fired by the spirit and each was preaching a long time, paying no attention to the coming and going of the members of the congregation, the children romping in the aisles, the dogs lying on the floor, the babies crying in their mothers' arms.

After about two hours a boy about six years old appeared in the aisle and waddled his way toward the women's amen corner. He was barefoot and tousle-headed but dressed for the meetin' in his blue short pants, hickory shirt, and wide suspenders crossing in the middle of his broad flat back.

He found his mother, who lifted him onto her lap, unbuttoned the front of her dress, and produced a breast for her son to nurse. The boy nursed for a minute or two and then leapt off his mother's lap and ran to the water bucket. He hurriedly lifted the dipper to his mouth, took a long draught, and washed his mouth loudly, spurting the water on the floor as he made a wry face.

Then he rushed over to his father in the men's amen corner and took a position directly in front of him. The father, whose attention was being directed at the preacher, gave the appearance of not knowing that his son was standing in front of him.

His head tilted back and as if he were talking to a man on a tall horse, the boy called out above the preacher's chant, "Hey, Pa! Gimme a chaw o' 'baccer. Ma's been a-eatin them wild ingerns [onions] agin."

✺ Strawberries

This is one I remembered from Cratis's telling.

This farmer was up in one of those nice neighborhoods in Asheville going from house to house selling baskets of strawberries. He was down to his last basket when he went up the front walk to a fine house and knocked on the door. Presently a good-looking woman opened the door.

"Would you like to buy some strawberries, ma'am?" he asked.

Looking him over carefully, she said, "Come around to the back door."

He trudged around to the back door and waited. When the door opened, there stood the woman with ne'er a stitch on. He stared at her momentarily, and then began to sniffle and then to weep.

She asked in an irritated voice, "What in the world is the matter with you. Why are you crying?"

He wiped his eyes on his shirt sleeve, and hesitatingly replied, "Well, you see, ma'am, it's been a bad year. Last fall, my wife run off with a traveling salesman, my barn burned down last winter, my mule died this spring so that I couldn't put out a crop, my daughter is goin' to have a baby, and we don't know where the daddy is, and now . . . and now . . . I see that I'm about to get screwed out of my strawberries!"

I remember Cratis pausing thoughtfully after telling this joke, always conscious of how words sound, and saying, "You know, that joke would not be half so funny if he were selling something other than strawberries."

✺ Hell or Texas

A quote from Cratis: "If you messed around with a mountain man's womenfolk in the old days, and he found out about it, you had two choices, Hell or Texas."

"Hell or Texas" was a well-worn phrase in early America, meaning the choice one had if he grievously offended someone.

✺ A Feller in a Tree

As remembered and told by Dr. James Gifford, Ashland, Kentucky, who heard it from Williams.

This man in eastern Kentucky went off to Ohio to get a job, leaving his wife at home. Times were hard and they were short on money, and so he was gone for several weeks. In the meantime, a preacher from over the mountain started calling on his wife, and they developed a passionate relationship. Her husband finally got a few days off and wrote that he would be home for a visit. She told the preacher, and they both were concerned that they couldn't get together while he was home. The preacher said, "I'll tell you what to do. Tell him you've planned a picnic, and you've invited your new preacher to come, and we'll go into the woods and have a picnic. That way you and I can be together while he's here."

So the husband came home, and she said that they were going on a a picnic and that she'd invited the preacher from her new church. The preacher came, was introduced, and they went into the woods until they came to this tall sycamore tree. The wife spread out a blanket, took out the fried chicken, ham, and biscuits, and two kinds of pie. They started eating, but the preacher had been sizing up the situation, and he said, "I'm going to climb that tree and look around." So, he climbed up to the top of the tree, looked all around, and then yelled, "What are you two doing down there?"

The husband yelled back up at him and said, "Why, we're just eating our picnic dinner."

The preacher said, "It looks to me like you two are making love down there."

The husband said, "No, we're just eating."

The preacher said, "I'm going to come down, and I want you to climb up here and look."

So he climbed down, and the husband climbed to the top of the tree. The preacher and the wife got onto the blanket and started making love. The husband looked down and yelled, "Hit sorta do look that-a-way to a feller in a tree!"

❀ At the Hair Stylist

Another Cratis story as remembered and told by Jim Gifford.

A native strip-mine operator from one of the eastern Kentucky counties became wealthy, and he and his wife decided to move to Lexington, where they could live in style while enjoying what their money could buy.

The mountain man found it easy to get into clubs and societies in the Bluegrass City, for other coal-rich operators from the mountains had prefaced the way for him. He soon learned how he was expected to dress, where one bought his clothing, and the kind of cars that rich people drove, but it had not occurred to him that his crew cut was not appropriate for the new social circle in which he was moving.

One day a new friend complimented him on his attire and suggested that he might look more like a millionaire if he should get his hair styled. The mountain man, eager to fit in, asked his friend to recommend a stylist for him.

"Well," his friend said, "a hair stylist is not just a barber. You can't just drop in and wait for a styling. Instead, you call ahead, as you would for a doctor or a dentist, and make an appointment. When you get there, you might find that only you, or not more than one or two other customers will be there. The stylist takes plenty of time. He studies your face and your head and figures out a hair arrangement just for you." He then recommended his own stylist as one who was patronized by particular people who counted for something in this world.

The mountaineer made an appointment and reported for his styling. There was only one other customer in the shop besides himself. Another stylist was working on his hair.

Noticing an especially pretty young woman on a stool beside the other customer and playing with his hand, he asked, "Who is she?"

"Oh, she's a manicurist."

The mountaineer thought a moment and responded, "Uh-huh!" his voice sliding upward significantly.

Soon the manicurist moved her stool beside the mountain man and began working with his hand. He could not see precisely what she was doing, but her hands were soft, and she smelled good.

She leaned forward and asked in low voice, "Would you like for me to push your cuticle back for you?"

After considering the question, the mountaineer responded, "No, you don't need to. It'll go back by itself after you quit playing with my hand."

❋ Cratis's "Peer" Story

As remembered and told by Gurney Norman, Lexington, Kentucky.

During a break from a cabinet meeting, President Woodrow Wilson and six of his cabinet members approached the urinals in the men's room. Seeing that there were only six urinals for the seven men, the cabinet members were quick to defer to the president. Standing aside, they said, "After you, Mr. President. After you."

"No, gentlemen," said the president. "Please go ahead. After all, here we are all peers."

❋ Equality

This is another story that I remember Cratis telling.

One summer a Florida tourist was driving down a back road along a river in the Blue Ridge Mountains, and he saw a swinging bridge hung across the river. He slowed down and peered through the trees and saw a picturesque log cabin with an old man sitting on the front porch. He pulled over to the side of the road, got out and climbed onto the swinging bridge, and began inching across the river, with the bridge swaying precariously. Halfway across, he called to the old man, and asked, "Do you mind if I come over and visit with you?"

"No," the old man said. "Come on over and set a spell."

So he got across the bridge, went up on the porch, shook hands with the old man, and explained that he was a "ferriner" from Florida and wanted to learn all he could about the mountain way of life. The old man pointed to a nearby rocking chair. The stranger sat down, looked around, and saw that the man had an abundant garden and had a couple of milch cows grazing in a nearby pasture. He said, "You've really got a nice place here. It's pretty as a picture."

"Much obliged," the old man said. "Me and Sarie like it here."

The stranger said, "You don't seem to have many neighbors nearby. Do you have television?" The old man said they did not.

"Well, what do you do for recreation or amusement?"

The old man though a minute and said, "Wal, when we git up, we have a little breakferst, and then we set out here and watch the sun come up and listen to the birds. Later we might go hoe a little bit in the garden, or in the evenin' we might jes' dig us a can of worms and go down to the river and ketch a fish or two. Atter supper, I might play the fiddle a little bit, or Sarie might sing one of them old love ballads. But some days, we might just set here and fart."

The stranger, somewhat, startled, said, "You mean before your wife?"

The old man said, "Oh, no, sometimes she farts before I do."

Stories in Dialect

Cratis had an abiding interest in mountain speech and often told his stories in dialect, with careful attention to how every word or syllable was pronounced. In his papers are numerous stories that he grew up with or that he had heard from others and usually had carefully rewritten, some with dialectical spelling in order to pass on some sense of the dialect in which they were told. Some require effort by the reader to discern their meaning. I offer a few of these stories here.

✴ Grandma's Pie

This is folklorist William Lightfoot's remembrance of a story Cratis told about stealing a pie that his grandmother had set on the windowsill to cool, and taking it under the dining table, where he proceeded to eat it, hidden from sight by a low-hanging table cloth. It illustrates her prolific and precise use of prepositions.

"Cratis remembered hearing his grandmother's footsteps approaching the table when she discovered that the pie was missing and her command, 'Cratis, you come on up from out back down in under there, or I'll wear ever' inch of hide from off of yore back!'"

✴ Coldest Day I Ever Saw

I could find no source for this tale. I surmise that Cratis had put two stories together to illustrate mountain speech as well as to to entertain.

Back hyur a few days ago I uz a-settin by the stove in Galloway's Grocery store one night after work. Hit'd been a tolleble cold day with a right smart of wind. Some of the fellers got to tellin about the coldest day they had ever seed. I kep' a-eyin a feller a-settin thaire. His face looked familiar to me, like I'd knowed him sommers sometime, but I couldn't place him. Pyeared like he uz a-takin a lively interest in the lies them thaire fellers wuz a-tellin an' wuz a-aigin on one of the members.

Dreckly I told about the coldest day I ever seed.

"Boys," I sez, "the coldest day I ever recollect wuz right hyur in Boone back in the winter of 1937. Hit was so cold that aour fangers froze to metal if we happent to tech it when we ditn't have aour gloves on. I uz a-wearin thri er four pa'rs of wool sox an' heavy overshoes but my toes got so cold I thought they uz a-goin to drop off. We kep a far a-goin all day an' 'ud come a-runnin to it ever ten or fifteen minutes to warm aour hands and feet. The wind wuzn't a-blowin much that day, as luck 'ud have it. Hit uz one of them quiet clur days with the snow froze on a layer of ice.

"Wull, that evenin wen I got home I set down by the stove to thaw aout an' listen to the radio whils't the old womern finished gittin supper.

"In a little bit she sez 'Supper's on the table. Come on.'

"I thought I'd step outside a minute before I warshed up fer supper. I walked aout to the edge of the bank in the yard an' unbuttoned my britches to take a leak. Wul, the moon had jest clured the top of the ridge acrosst from my haouse an' wuz as big as a punkin an' as yaller as one of them thaire Floridy oranges. The snow wuz a-glistenin like gold. I got through an' started to button my britches, an' I jest happent to glance down an' thaire all rared up to me like a rattlesnake a-dancin on the end of its tail was that stream froze hard an a-glistenin like gold. I stepped back an' kicked it jest as hard as I could. Hit broke into a thousant pieces that went a-scooten an' a-crackin along on the face of the ice. Boys, that wuz the coldest 'at ever I seed in my life."

Ever'body laughed.

Then the stranger says, "Fellers, has any of ye ever been to North Dakota in the winter time?" Nobody had.

"Wul," he sez, "I uz out thaire a few years back at one of my cousin's 'at had moved aout thaire. One afternoon we wuz a-settin at home and a-listenin to the radio when the news come through 'at a blizzard wuz a-blowin in from the northwest an' 'at farmers 'at had stock in the fields 'd better straw 'em daown in their shelters an' git feed ready for 'em, fer the storm 'ud be a-movin in in thri er four haours.

"My cousin jumped up and sez 'Let's git dressed an' git aout to the back field as quick as we can. Put on everthang you've got an' these here leather britches and this old leather coat overtop of all that, fer if we git caught in the blizzard we'll freeze to death if we ain't dressed warm enough.' Sosun I put on two union suits over the one I already had on, three pa'rs of wool sox, three pa'rs of wool shirts, two pa'rs of my own britches an' then the leather britches over top of that. An' I pulled on boots an' laced 'em up, an' put on the leather coat. Then I hunted my gloves an' my leather cap with wool yeaur warmers an' a scarf to wrep around my neck. We hopped into his truck an' went roarin over to the back field. Hit uz still warm whur we wuz an' I could feel the sweat runnin' down the trough of my back.

"We scattered straw in the shelter, forked daoun enough hay to last a week, an wuz a-drivin the cattle into the shelter when the blizzard hit. The caow's eyelashers wuz froze stiff with ice in three er four minutes. We couldn't hartly see what we wuz a-doin for the blindin snow that hit aour hard leather coats and rattled pime blank like gravels throwed agin a winder. But we finally got all the cattle in the shelter an' got in the truck an' headed back. The snow was blowin so that we wuz a-feared we mought get lost, but we didn't.

"Atter we got back home his old womern sez, 'Wal, peel off some of them duds an' warsh up. Supper's at the pint of bein served.'

"I stepped into the room where I slep at an' begin to take thangs off, the leather coat and britches, the shirt and britches, the boots and sox, an' the extry suits of underwear. When I got daoun to the last suit of underwear I hyerd sompin strike the floor an' bounce an' roll like a marble.

"Wal, I got to lookin around an' I found it. Hit wuz jest abaout the size of a marble, but hit looked a right smart like one of these hyur moth balls. I uz puzzled abaout it because I hatn't noticed nothing like that whilst I was a-puttin them union suits on.

"I picked the little ball up and wuz a-holdin it between my fanger an' thumb next to the light so I could see what it wuz.

"All of a suddent, hit went 'Pf-f-f-ft!' right in my face. 'Phew!' I hain't never seed as cold a day as that'n an' I hope I never do agin."

✳ A-Hoppin' over the Benches like Flyin' Squirrels

As told by Joe Logan, north Georgia, about 1970.

When I was a boy, my parents would sometimes send me up to North Georgia to spend the summer on my grandfather's farm.

One day after crops were caught up with, my grandfather invited me to go walking with him down the road. Grandfather, interested in the progress of his neighbors' work, stopped to talk with them as we met them on the road or saw them in their fields close by. As we passed the somewhat neglected farm of a preacher-farmer, we saw him sitting on his porch. Grandpa stopped at the gate to exchange greetings and pleasantries with him.

"Well, haow ar yer crops a-coming along?"

"They'uz a-doin fine till I begin to fall behind with 'em. I didn't git to work at 'em atter Tuesday of last week."

"What happened? Have ye been sick?"

"No. I went acrosst the mountain to hep aout in the revival meetin' they've been a-havin over thaire at the Holiness Church. I hat'n meant to go because I wanted to git caught up with my work."

"Well, why did ye go?"

"Brother Starnes started the revival la-a-ast Sunday. But ditn't seem to be able to git it offen the groaund. So a Tuesday some of the brethren come over to see me to ast would *I* come over an' he'p 'em aout an' see could *I* put some far in hit," sliding his voice upward with self-congratulation as he said I.

"Haow did ye git along with it?"

"Me? Jist fine. The sparrit wuz with me. Attendance picked up and thangs livened up considerable. W'y, by Friday night I had them sons-a-bitches a-hoppin over the benches like flyin' squirrels."

Songs and Ballads

✸ I Came Home the Other Night
(Our Good Man)
Child 274, Roud 114, Williams 57

Williams learned this ballad from his father, Curtis Williams, and included it in his master's thesis, "Ballads and Songs of Eastern Kentucky." It was published as a broadside in London in the 1760s and collected in Scotland in the 1770s. It later spread over much of Europe and was a popular song in America with both white and black singers. Olive Dame Campbell and Cecil Sharp have two variants in their book English Folk Songs from the Southern Appalachians *(New York: G. P. Putnam's Sons, 1917), collected from Jane Gentry, Hot Springs,*

North Carolina, and Mrs. Tom Rice, Big Laurel, North Carolina, both in 1916 (No. 32, pp. 134–36). Many singers have performed it, including Earl Johnson in 1927 (Document 8005), Blind Lemon Jefferson in 1929 (JSP Records 7705), Gid Tanner and the Skillet Lickers in 1934 (JSP Records 7780), Ed McCurdy in 1956 (Elektra 108), and Sheila Kay Adams in 1998 (at the Berea College Celebration of Traditional Music). With the exception of "Vance's Death Song," these ballads and songs are from Williams's master's thesis, and the tunes are from his singing of the tunes that he remembered in the Southern Appalachian Archives at Hutchins Library at Berea College.)

3. I came home the other night just as drunk as I could be,
   Found a coat a-hanging on the rack where my coat ort to be.
   "What's this now, my little wife? Explain this thing to me,
   How come a coat's a-hangin' on the rack where my coat ort to be?"

4. "You fool, you fool, you durned old fool! O can't you never see?
   'Taint nothin' but a bed-quilt your granny sent to me."
   "I've traveled this wide world over a thousand miles or more,
   But a pocket on a bed-quilt I never did see before."

5. I came home the other night just as drunk as I could be,
Found a head a-laying on the pillow where my head ort to be.
"What's this now, my little wife? Explain this thing to me,
How come this head's a-laying on the pillow where my head ort to be?"

6. "You fool, you fool, you durned old fool! O can't you never see?
'Taint nothin' but a cabbage head your granny sent to me."
"I've traveled this wide world over a thousand miles or more,
But a mustache on a cabbage I never did see before."

✼ The Farmer's Curst Wife

Child 278, Roud 160, Williams 58

Cratis learned this ballad from Georgia Graham, Cherokee, Lawrence County, Kentucky. Miss Graham had taken it down from the singing of her father, Lem Graham. It was listed in the London Stationers' Register in 1630. Variants are in the major American printed collections. Virginia singers Horton Barker and Estill Ball each recorded it for the Library of Congress in 1939. You can hear Pete Seeger sing it on his American Favorite Ballads *(Smithsonian/Folkways SFW40155, 2009), disc 2.*

2 The devil came to the old man one day . . .
Fa-la-la-la-la-la;
Sayin' "There's one of your family I'm for now . . ."

Refrain: Sing tiro addle, sing fal dal diddle,
Sing tiro addle, sing day. (after all verses).

3. "It's not your oldest son that I do crave . . .
It's your old scoldin' jade* and her I will have . . ."

4. "You may have her with all my heart . . .
   Hopin' you and her will never part . . ."

5. He picked her up on his old hull of a back . . .
   An' like an old peddler he carried his pack. . . .

6. He took her down to the forks of the road . . .
   Saying, "Old lady, you're a helluva load! . . ."

7. He took her down to the gates of Hell . . .
   Saying, "Now old jade, I'll roast you well . . ."

8. Three little devils came rattlin' their chains . . .
   With a chunk of cudgel she beat out their brains . . .

9. Three more little devils peeped over the wall . . .
   Said, "Take her outta Hell, Poppy, or she'll kill us all . . ."

10. "Well, old devil, I'll match you at that . . .
    You fetched me here, you shall carry me back . . .

11. He picked her up all on his old hull of a back . . .
    And like an old peddler, he carried her back . . .

12. She's seven years goin' and more a-getting' back . . .
    She called for the cornbread she left in the crack . . .

13. She found her old man all wrapped up in bed . . .
    With her old pewter pipe she walloped his head . . .

14. "Well, well, old man! This's what old jades can do . . .
    They can wallop their husbands and kill devils too . . ."

   *Jade: a headstrong or disreputable woman.

✺ Vance's Death Song
Laws F17, Roud 2216, Combs 67

Cratis was fond of this ballad and sang it in recitals, although it was not among the ballads in his master's thesis. However, the text is in John Harrington Cox's Folk-Songs of the South *(Cambridge, Mass.: Harvard University Press, 1925), pp. 207–11, and in Combs's Folk-Songs of the Southern United States, p. 163.*

It can also be found online. The basic story that Cratis told before singing the ballad was that Abner Vance, an Old Regular Baptist preacher and hunter, and his wife, Susannah, had a daughter, Elizabeth, who was seduced by a neighbor, Lewis Horton, who kept her away from home for several days. He brought her back across the Clinch River behind him on his horse and set her down in front of her parents. As Cratis put it, he said, "I brought your heifer home." The old couple pleaded for him to marry her, but he turned his horse back to ford the river. The old preacher went inside for his hunting rifle and shot Horton while he was in the middle of the river. Vance was tried for murder in Russell County, Virginia, but the jury tied for conviction. He was tried again in Washington County, was convicted, and was hanged on July 16, 1819. Legend has it that he wrote this ballad with its remarkable stanzas while he was awaiting execution, and sang it on the gallows before he was hanged. Roud has only one listing, and it is from the Virginia Folklore Society Collection at the University of Virginia, collected by E. J. Sutherland from William Skeen in 1931. Several other variants have been collected in Kentucky and Virginia. See also John A. Lomax and Alan Lomax, Our Singing Country: Folk Songs and Ballads *(Mineola, N.Y.: Dover, 2000), pp. 322–23. This is the text and tune that I remember from Cratis.*

Bright shines the sun on Clinch's Hill, So soft the west wind blows; The woods are cov-ered with blooms so fair, Per-fumed with the wild rose.

2. Green are the woods where Sandy flows,
   The wild beasts dwelleth there;
   The bear is secure in the laurel grove,
   And the red buck roves the hill.

3. But Vance shall no more the Sandy behold,
   Or drink of its crystal wave;
   The partial judge has pronounced his doom
   The hunter has found his grave.

4. There is Daniel, Bill, and Lewis,
   A lie against me swore;
   That they might take my life away,
   So that I may be no more.

5. But they and I together will meet,
   When Immanuel's trumpet blows;
   While I'm at rest on Abraham's breast,
   They will rove in the gulf below.

6. Farewell to my true and loving wife,
   Your face I'll see no more;
   But I'll meet you in the land above,
   Where parting is no more.

7. I come, I come, ye angels of God,
   To the realms of joy above;
   A Christian hope cheers my hours of death,
   Dear Jesus, receive me home.

❊ The Jealous Lover

Roud 500, Williams 10, Combs 63

See Cox, Folk-Songs of the South, pp. 197–98, for an account of the confusion of this song with "Pearl Bryan" and similarities between the two songs. "Pearl Bryan" is based on the actual murder of a girl of that name in 1896 in northern Kentucky by two Cincinnati dental students, much covered by newspapers. However, "The Jealous Lover" is an older ballad, as are the parodies "Ellen," "Florella," and "Florilla." It appears that "Pearl Bryan" was based on "The Jealous Lover." Most of the major collections have variants of these ballads. Burnett and Rutherford recorded it on Champion 15113-D in 1928, and they can be heard online.

Down in yon lone-ly mead-ow Where the vio-lets fade and bloom; There lies my own Flo-ril-la, In a cold and si-lent tomb. She died not bro-ken-heart-ed, Nor from dis-ease she fell; But in one mo-ment part-ing From the home she loved so well.

2. One night as the moon shone brightly,
   The stars were shining too;
   Up to her cottage window

A jealous lover drew.
He said, "Love, let us wander
Down in yon meadow gay;
While wandering we'll ponder,
And name our wedding day."

3. So deep into the forest
   He led his love so dear;
   She said, "It's for thee only
   That I am wandering here;
   For the night is dark and dreary
   And I am afraid to stay;
   For I am growing weary—would like to retrace my way."

4. "Retrace your steps? No, never!
   No more this earth you'll roam;
   So bid adieu to parents,
   And to your friends and home;
   For here in the wilds I have you,
   From me you cannot fly!
   No mortal hand can save you,
   Florilla, you must die!"

5. Down on her knees before him
   She begged him for her life;
   When into her fair bosom,
   He plunged the fatal knife.
   She said, "Dear Ed, what have I done
   That you should take my life?
   I always have been faithful,
   And would have been your wife."

6. "'Tis adieu, kind friends and parents,
   You'll never see me more;
   Long, long you'll wait my coming
   At the little cottage door.
   But dear Edward, I'll forgive you,
   'Tis my last and dying breath;
   I never have deceived you—"
   And she closed her eyes in death.

7. The birds sang in the morning,
   But mournful was their song.
   A stranger found her body,
   A cold and lifeless form.
   Come all ye fair young maidens
   That choose to look this way:
   Don't put your trust in young men
   For they will lead you astray.

❈ Come All Ye Fair and Handsome Girls

Roud 3606, Williams 16

Williams got this song from his mother, Mona Whitt Williams, who learned it from local sources in about 1900. He indicated that it is similar to "Little Sparrow," Williams 38. Another variant is "Come All Ye Fair and Tender Ladies," which is widely known. Olive Dame Campbell collected it from Mrs. Sarah Concle in Perry County, Kentucky, in 1908, and it is in the Campbell and Sharp book, English Folk Songs from the Southern Appalachians, *no. 103, p. 289. Green Maggard sang it at Jean Thomas's American Folk Song Festival in 1934, and he can be heard on* Kentucky Mountain Music *(Yazoo 2200, 2003), disc 6.*

Come all ye fair _____ and hand-some girls, _____ Take warn-ing from a friend; To learn the ways ____ of this wide world, ____ And on my words de-pend. The minds of girls ____ are weak you know, ____ The minds of boys are strong; And if you lis-ten to __ what they say, ____ They'll tell you some-thing wrong.

2. They'll tell you that they love you dear,
   And wish you no harm;
   That before they would betray your trust,
   They'd give up their right arm.

When I was in my sixteenth year,
Sweet Willie courted me;
He said if I'd run away with him,
His lawful wife I'd be.

3. My mind was so confined to him,
I could not well say no;
I thought I knew he was my friend,
And away with him did go.

Now I am away from home,
Enjoying a happy life;
Says he, "Dear girl, you must go home,
You cannot be my wife."

4. "My papa he was kind to me,
My mama loved me dear;
You have persuaded me from home,
How can you leave me here?"

"O, Nature, Nature, my kind girl,
I found no fault to you;
My mind is on a-ramblin' around,
So, I'll bid you adieu."

❋ I Am a Man of Constant Sorrow
Roud 499, Williams 43

Contributed by Miss Esta Riggs, Caines Creek, Lawrence County, Kentucky. Cratis noted that this song was not in the standard collections. Dick Burnett had it in his 1913 songbook Songs Sung by R. D. Burnett—The Blind Man— Monticello, Kentucky, *under the title "Farewell Song," and it is usually credited to him. Emry Arthur recorded it on Vocalion in 1928 (Vo 5208), and the Stanley Brothers also sang it. It became a hit when Dan Tyminski sang it in the movie and on the CD* O Brother, Where Art Thou *(2000).*

I am a man of con - stant sor - row, I've been in trou____ ble all my days; I bid fare - well to old Ken - tuck - y. The place where I____ was borned and raised.

2. O, for six long years I've been in trouble,
   My pleasures here on earth are done;
   For in this world I have to ramble,
   I have no parents to help me now.

3. O, it's fare thee well, my old true lover,
   I fear I'll never see you again;
   For I'm bound to ride a northern railroad,
   Perhaps I'll die upon the train.

4. O, you may bury me in some deep valley,
   For many a year there I may lay;
   Then you may learn to love another,
   While I'm sleeping in the clay.

5. O, it's fare thee well, my native country,
   A place that I have loved so well;
   For I have seen all kinds of trouble,
   In this vain world no tongue can tell.

6. My friends may take me to be a stranger,
   My face you'll never see no more;
   But there's one promise that is given,
   I'll meet you on that beautiful shore.

FIGURE 11. Cratis Williams
as a young man. Courtesy of
the Cratis Williams Papers,
SAA 56, Southern Appalachian
Archives, Hutchins Library,
Berea College, Berea, Kentucky.

FIGURE 12. Libby and
Cratis in their younger
years. Courtesy of the
Cratis Williams Papers,
SAA 56, Southern
Appalachian Archives,
Hutchins Library, Berea
College, Berea, Kentucky.

FIGURE 13. Cratis in the library. Courtesy of the Cratis Williams Papers, SAA 56, Southern Appalachian Archives, Hutchins Library, Berea College, Berea, Kentucky.

FIGURE 14. Loyal Jones, Cratis D. Williams, and President Willis D. Weatherford Jr. when Williams received an honorary doctorate in humane letters from Berea College in 1977. Courtesy of Berea College Public Relations Department, Berea, Kentucky.

FIGURE 15. Cratis sings a ballad. Courtesy of Dr. James Gifford, the Jesse Stuart Foundation.

Leonard Ward Roberts

When Leonard Roberts told a story, you could see that he enjoyed it as much as his audience. Every now and then, he would be overcome by the humor or absurdity of his tale and pause to laugh outright and slap his leg. Roberts was a master storyteller, but beyond that, he was a noted scholar of the Old World folktales that had been brought to eastern Kentucky by the ancestors of his kinfolk and neighbors and passed down through the generations. He collected and published several volumes of these tales, and through them he showed the world that these wonderful old stories were still being told in the Cumberland Mountains.

Leonard was born in a weatherboarded log house at the head of Toler Creek in Floyd County, Kentucky, on January 28, 1912. His parents were Lewis Jackson Roberts and Rhoda Jane Osborn Roberts. Leonard was the seventh of eleven children, and the sixth son. His siblings were William Vernon, Edward Virgil, Mary Bayard, Samuel Jesse, Teddy Adrian, Alonzo Dale, Elmer Wall, Arminta Helen, Carl Foch, and Faustina Fern. The Roberts, Osborn/Osborne, and Sturgell/Sturgill families began intermarrying in Virginia in the late 1700s, before they moved to Floyd County at the end of the eighteenth century. There they intermarried with the Barnettes, Kings, Monroes, Rices, Comptons, Ratliffs, Keatherleys, Martins, Iricks, and others.[1]

Lewis Roberts, Leonard's father, was a farmer who also floated log rafts on the Big Sandy to sawmills at Catlettsburg and later operated his own sawmills. About 1920, he also became a preacher in the Church of Christ, which outnumbered the Baptist churches seven to one on Toler Creek. Leonard's mother, Rhoda Jane, was hard pressed to feed and clothe her large family, but she also ran the Osborn post office, which had been established and named by her brother, Edward Leonard "Dick" Osborn, for whom Leonard was named.

Leonard entered the first grade in a one-room log schoolhouse when he was only five, having already learned to read. His teacher was Rachel Roberts, no doubt a relative. According to an autobiographical account he wrote later, entitled "My Life," all the schools in the county were closed in 1918 because of the influenza epidemic, so he missed that year. During his elementary school years, he was taught by several other teachers, including his brother Sam. For parts of three years, he lived with and did chores for his grandmother Arminta Sturgill Osborn, a widow. From 1921 to 1926, he lived back with his family and helped to work the farm and garden and care for livestock. He finished the sixth grade in a new white-framed school, still with only one room.[2]

Eventually, Lewis's sawmills, the farm, and his preaching brought in enough money for him to put some aside, and in 1926 he moved the family to Pikeville, where he had bought two houses, one for the family and one to rent. He also purchased one of the first automobiles in the town, but he demolished the shed he was using for a garage while learning to drive it. The children were enrolled in the Pikeville schools, but they were all set back a year because of assumed poor schooling on Toler. Lewis wanted all of his children to get an education, so he set up an account for their books and school supplies and encouraged them in their learning.

According to Leonard's biographical account, after eighteen months Lewis bought a boundary of timber that was nearer to Toler than to Pikeville, and he moved his family back to Toler. Another family version is that Rhoda learned that Lewis had begun an affair with a woman in Pikeville, and *she* moved the family back to the farm. Later, the story goes, when Rhoda found out that Lewis had bought a hotel in Pikeville and set the woman and her husband and child up in it to manage, she put the sidesaddle on their mule, Old Stafford, and rode to Pikeville. There, Leonard wrote, "She made a bee-line for the hotel and went in. She asked for ___ ___, and she came to the office waiting room. Ma asked her two or three questions, slapped her face half off, and turned back over the mountains for home. The story was told far and near, about the lady who rode twelve miles through mud and water to do nothing but slap hell out of a bitch. We felt right inwardly proud of Ma."[3]

Lewis wanted Leonard to continue his education, so he arranged for him to board with a family living in one of the houses he had bought in Pikeville until he finished the eighth grade in 1929. Leonard later wrote that the Pikeville years changed him; he was introduced to poetry and literary stories, and he greatly enjoyed the mostly western picture shows at the movie theater, as well as other forms of entertainment. He was converted and baptized there in a tent revival run by a Church of Christ preacher. He confessed that thereafter, he had a conflict over his desire to be both a cowboy *and* a Christian.

The summer after Leonard graduated from the eighth grade, he and two cousins got jobs in a coal mine. In the meantime, Lewis declared bankruptcy, owing some $8,000, and ran off with his mistress. Rhoda struggled with the help of the children to keep the farm and household going.

That fall, Leonard was invited by his aunt Columbia Roberts to come live with her in Harold, where he could enroll in the Betsy Layne High School. In return, he was required to help her run the telephone system that she owned. That required maintaining miles of wire strung on trees, houses, outbuildings, fence posts, and poles. He figured out how the boxes for each house and business were wired so that he could install and repair them, and he sometimes worked the switchboard. In addition, he fed the cattle and chickens, milked the cows, split cook-stove wood, and carried in coal to heat the house. He had to get up early to do his chores and then walked two miles to the high school, taking his pole-climbing spikes and tools with him. He frequently had to skip classes to make repairs to the telephone system.

Leonard praised his teachers at the school, especially Jesse Elliott, the director of the band, who taught him to play the trombone and found an old one for him to buy. In the school, Leonard was known to tell funny stories, and one about bathing a dirty tomcat earned him the nickname "Old Souser." Even with his missed classes, he earned seven A's and a B+ that year, while also playing in the band and on the basketball team.

He went home the following summer and helped put out a crop, but he wrote that he had rambling on his mind. He yearned to see the big cities, so he went to Lexington and then on to Ashland and Huntington, West

Virginia, hoboing on freight trains. In Ashland he visited an army recruiting station and found that he could join up and be sent to Hawaii. He passed the entrance exam, but he needed a parent's signature because of his age. He returned home with his papers, but his mother refused to sign them because he was needed at home. He was adamant, however, and remembered a day he worked in the cornfield. "I stepped along behind the mule, watching the dusty ground slide away from the plow point. But all the time, I was thinking of cities and their million lights and of the sea. I was going down to the sea in ships."[4]

His mother eventually signed the papers, and he was sworn into the army in Columbus, Ohio, then shipped through the Panama Canal to Schofield Barracks in Hawaii. Because he knew how to play the trombone, he was sent to army music schools and learned to play all of the band instruments. He served three years as a member of the 21st Infantry Regiment Band.

Leonard came home to Kentucky in 1933 and went back to Pikeville to finish high school. He also joined a dance band that played for dances on weekends. The high school had a dormitory on the school grounds, Wright Hall, that allowed students from remote areas in the large county to attend high school. Leonard's sister Arminta was a dorm student, and her roommate was Edith Reynolds; Edith and Leonard began to date there. They both graduated in the spring of 1933. Leonard had visited Edith often at her home on Grapevine Creek. That fall, she entered Pikeville College, which was supported by the Presbyterian Church.

Leonard found out about Berea College through an advertisement in a Montgomery Ward catalogue. Apparently, applicants were encouraged to recommend other students who might apply. He decided to go to Berea, and he took along five others: his brother and sister Carl and Faustina; his cousins Rell and Lydia Roberts; and his friend Frank Akers. Leonard was accepted into the college, and the others entered its Foundation School.

I heard a story during my years at the college that Leonard once showed up at Berea's athletic field, where they were having low-hurdle races, and asked, "What are those fellers in their underwear doing?" After inquiring about the rules, the story goes, he entered the next event in his regular clothing and set a new record! This is probably an early example of his trickster nature. Actually, Leonard, who was tall and well-formed, succeeded in most of the field sports at Berea—javelin throw, shot put, pole vault, and broad jump. He majored in both English and music. He gained attention by winning a music competition, demonstrating on the stage of the college auditorium that he could play all fifteen instruments in the college band.

In the meantime, Edith Reynolds had transferred from Pikeville College to Eastern Kentucky State Teachers College in Richmond, just twelve miles from Berea. Her roommate was Myrtle Mae Dotson, a relative who had a crush on Leonard's Berea roommate, Gether Irick, his distant cousin from Floyd County. Myrtle arranged a double date with Leonard and Gether. Thus Edith and Leonard resumed their courtship, and they were married in 1939, the summer after he graduated from Berea. For two years he taught English and organized and directed a band at the City School in Jackson, Kentucky. A daughter, Sue, was born to Leonard and Edith in 1940.

During this time, he and Lawrence Bowling, a fellow Berea graduate who had earned an M.A. in English at Vanderbilt, got together at a Berea College reunion, and since they both admired Jesse Stuart, the celebrated Kentucky novelist, poet, and educator, they made plans to visit him at his remodeled log home in W-Hollow in Greenup County. They arrived unannounced, but Jesse and his wife, Naomi Deane, received them graciously and fed them dinner, and they spent an exciting evening talking with Stuart about his writing. Stuart offered them a cigar and a glass of wine, but, heavily influenced by Berea's abstemious values, both refused. Jesse called to Naomi Deane and said, "Here are two young men, graduates of Berea College, and they neither drink nor smoke! Isn't that wonderful!" (It was rumored that Jesse's brother James had been kicked out of Berea for smoking, but that is another story.) Bowling took along a couple of his unpublished manuscripts to show to Stuart, but Leonard said that he never mentioned his own desire to become a writer at this meeting. However, he was so inspired that he wrote in the guest book, "Time of my life!"[5] He later published a fictional account of this visit, "A Night with Jesse Stuart," and he and Stuart corresponded over the years.[6] Stuart was complimentary of Leonard's writing and would later write letters to publishers promoting a novel that Roberts had written.

In 1942, Leonard taught English at Brevard Junior College in North Carolina. He had harbored a strong desire to be a writer and felt that he ought to do further study toward that end. He was influenced by his friend Lawrence Bowling to apply to the premier creative writing program at the University of Iowa, where Bowling was studying toward a doctorate in the English Department. He was accepted, and as part of his studies he wrote "A Personal History of Eastern Kentucky" and, as his master's thesis, "Home in the Rock: A Novel of Eastern Kentucky," which earned him a Master of Arts degree. In the summer of 1943, Professor Hardin Craig, a native Kentuckian and distinguished Shakespearean scholar, came to the university to lecture, and both Bowling and Roberts attended. Craig, who was a visiting professor at the University of North Carolina at Chapel Hill, offered Bowling a fellowship at UNC for further study in Shakespeare, but Bowling decided to complete his doctorate at Iowa, and he recommended Leonard, who received the fellowship.

Enrolled as a doctoral student at UNC, Leonard moved his family to Chapel Hill. In December 1943, his second daughter, Margaret, was born. During 1944–45, Leonard taught for the U.S. military: the V-12 program for future naval officers at Chapel Hill and a similar program for future army officers at North Carolina State College in Raleigh. He took graduate courses in English and studied folklore under Dr. Arthur Palmer Hudson.

From 1945 to 1948, he taught English at the Berea College Foundation School, where a third daughter, Rita, was born in 1946. His students were mostly from eastern Kentucky and elsewhere in Appalachia, and they were homesick away from their own people. Leonard had acquired a copy of Richard Chase's *The Jack Tales* (Boston: Houghton Mifflin, 1943), folktales about a boy named Jack that Chase and others had collected in the mountains of North Carolina and Virginia, and he read them to his students. Jack in these tales lived in the same kinds of places his students had grown up in, and he triumphed over all sorts of troubles through cunning or magic. Leonard's students perked up and let him know that they had heard these tales before, back home from relatives and neighbors.

Folklorist Carl Lindahl, the Martha Gano Houston Research Professor at the University of Houston and the premier scholar of Leonard Roberts's work, saw this as a transformational time in Roberts's life, changing him from English teacher to folklorist. He quotes Roberts from an interview:

> I never could get the students to write more than about a half a page of some sort of narrative about something like their favorite pet or their vacation time. . . . By this time the book *Jack Tales* was out. And I began to read those to the students and noticed an immediate change in attitude, change in attention. . . . I would read one of these stories and ask them . . . , "Now, can you write that story?" And I was very surprised to find that they could write and recapture that story almost word for word. . . . And that would make a page or two of writing. . . . And they hadn't done [that] before. . . . So they learned how to feel, think and handle the language.

. . . I sampled the students for stories they had heard and realised that many of them, maybe half a class of twenty, had been hearing oral folktales at home. I began to ask them to write for their exercises, write a story they had heard. And again three or four more pages. . . . And I began to realise that each family in the mountains had some store or stock of stories that they passed along at various times in the seasons—day and night and so forth, holidays and so forth . . . and carried on a kind of a cultural pattern that we were not too aware of until we began to find it and began to ask for it.[7]

His students revealed to him that tales about characters like Jack, Nippy, and Mutsmeg were still being told in the mountains of eastern Kentucky. This led him to go home with them on weekends to begin putting on paper, and later on primitive recording equipment, tales, jokes, riddles, and also songs and ballads from their kinfolk and neighbors.

These excursions included the small schools of eastern Kentucky as well, where he found students who knew the old tales. The best of all his informants was Jane Muncy, an eleven-year-old girl in a remote one-room school in Leslie County, who in 1949 told him more tales than any of the other students, leading off with her favorite, "Merrywise." She had learned these tales from her grandmother, Sidney Farmer Muncy, with whom she had lived as a child while her father served in the army. Dr. Lindahl heard this actual recording of Jane in 1997 and wrote about her:

[H]er performances outshone the others to a degree that astonished me when I first heard the recordings. . . . I immediately resolved to find out more about this child who, though very much a little girl in voice, seemed to be vocalizing a maturity and wisdom beyond her years. . . . When Leonard Roberts first found her, Jane had been unknowingly rehearsing for him for more than seven years, coached by her grandmother in a nightly ritual [of tale telling].[8]

There are no recordings of Jane's grandmother. However, her aunt Nora Morgan Lewis (who was never recorded either) left several notebooks containing "forty tales with forty-six variants" that she had heard, which Lindahl called "the largest märchen repertoire reported for a single teller anywhere in Kentucky."[9] More will be said later about Carl Lindahl, Jane Muncy, and the lore that Jane's interlocking families possessed.

Leonard also inquired about tales in his own family and found that his aunt Columbia Roberts, with whom he had lived and whose telephone company he had helped maintain, knew a tale about the character Jack, a magic horse, and a magical girl, but by the time Leonard got around to interviewing her, her memory was shaky. However, her daughters, to whom she had told the tale as children, were there to prompt her. Thus, it was from his aunt that Leonard learned his favorite tale, which he often told: "Raglif Jaglif Tetartlif Pole."

After he had taken down numerous tales, Leonard felt the need to begin classifying them, and he went to the Indiana University Department of Folklore during the summer of 1948 to study with Professors Stith Thompson, William Hugh Jansen, and W. Edson Richmond, authorities on folktales and their classification. He had probably learned about these scholars while he was a graduate student at UNC with Arthur Palmer Hudson. Thompson was the best-known American authority on the classification of folktales. Not only did he and his associates teach Roberts what he needed to know, but Thompson loaned Leonard "a big old tape recorder" and taught him how to use it, gave him "twenty reels of tape," and sent him back to Kentucky with great encouragement.[10]

He was still teaching at the Berea College Foundation School, and called on President Francis S. Hutchins, who had succeeded his father, William J. Hutchins, as president of the college. He stated his desire to pursue a doctorate in English and folklore and to return to Berea to teach in the English Department. Both Hutchinses were educated at Oberlin and Yale, and the younger was director of Yale in China when he was called to Berea. Leonard told me that he said, "I don't believe there would be a place for you there." Berea was famous for educating and thus uplifting "poor but bright" Appalachian young people, and although there had been teachers there, such as James Watt Raine, John F. Smith, and Gladys Jameson, and even former president William Goodell Frost, who were interested in folklore and other aspects of Appalachian culture, folklore apparently was not seen by President Hutchins as a plausible vehicle for intellectual uplift in Berea's curriculum. This rejection was a hard blow to Leonard's self-esteem, but he went on to become one of the most-published graduates of the college, and his papers and recordings are now among Berea's huge research collections on Appalachia.

Roberts entered the doctoral program in English at the University of Kentucky in 1950, where he again studied under William Hugh Jansen, who had moved from Bloomington to Lexington to establish a curriculum in folklore at the university. After finishing his coursework, Leonard moved his family to Pine Mountain Settlement School in Harlan County, where he and Edith taught, and he continued his collecting trips and worked on his dissertation, a collection of folktales from eastern Kentucky that was accepted for his doctorate in English and folklore in 1953. This collection is meticulously annotated to show parallel variants in other cultures, particularly from the British Isles and Germany.

Leonard's and Edith's last child, Lynneda (a combination of her parents' first names), was born in 1952. In 1953, Leonard served as head of the English Department at Piedmont College in Demorest, Georgia. From 1954 to 1958, he was chair of the Division of Languages and head of the English Department at Union College in Barbourville, Kentucky, where he continued his collecting in the southern part of the state.

In 1958, the president of Morehead State College recruited Leonard to the position of head of the Division of Languages and Literature, Speech, and Drama with the rank of full professor. However, he soon ran into conflict with the president and dean over the hiring of faculty and the grading of students. Roberts wrote that in his interview, the college dean told him that he would need to teach more on the high school than the college level because the students from eastern Kentucky were not really prepared for college work. Also, Henry P. Scalf, a friend of Leonard's and a respected eastern Kentucky historian and newspaper editor, had described Morehead in a 1960 *Floyd County Times* article as an "Educational Haven for Those from Other States." Scalf questioned the large number of out-of-state students (25 percent) and alleged that some were unable to get into colleges in their own states but were actively recruited for Morehead because they paid a higher tuition than Kentucky students. He wrote that these out-of-state students were placed in the limited number of dormitory rooms, while eastern Kentucky students had to find housing in town.[11]

When some students, including those from out of state, got low or failing grades in Leonard's department, the president and dean came down hard on him and ordered him to go easier on grading in his division so as not to lose students. A solution suggested to remedy the problem of teaching and grading was to hire English teachers out of the local high schools, who presumably would better understand the students' needs, instead of perhaps better-trained teachers from elsewhere. The president even ordered Leonard to tell one of his Ph.D. English professors to quit teaching Jonathan Swift's famous 1729 satirical essay "A Modest Proposal for Preventing the Children of Poor People from Being a Burthen to Their Parents or Country and for Making Them Beneficial to the Publick" because a young mother taking the class had complained to the president that the professor was advocating eating babies.

The culminating event was a meeting of members of the faculty to vote on a resolution (rumored to have been written by the president and dean) giving strong support to the administration for making Morehead State College into a well-run example of higher education. Three faculty members voted against the resolution. Leonard was one of them, and he soon got a letter from the president notifying him that his employment would be terminated at the end of his current yearly contract (1961). Leonard later wrote a novel, *Sheepskin Carnival*, about his Morehead experience, but it was never published.

From 1961 to 1968, he held a similar position teaching language and literature at West Virginia Wesleyan College. There he taught folklore classes as well as English. He also started and edited the *Laurel Review*, a literary magazine. In 1968, he was invited to return to Kentucky by Pikeville College to head its Languages and Literature Department. He was delighted to be back in his home neighborhood. There he developed an Appalachian studies program; edited a magazine, *Twigs* (later retitled *Cumberlands*); and established the Pikeville College Press to publish historical and literary works by regional writers and to republish some of his own out-of-print books. He also worked with the Pike County Historical Society to research and publish numerous books and articles on Pike County history and the Hatfield and McCoy families. He enlisted other members of the faculty and students to participate in plays, folk dances, and musical concerts reflecting Appalachian culture. During these years, he was frequently invited to many places in the region to lecture and tell the wonderful magical tales that he had collected.

Roberts was involved in the Kentucky Place Name Survey, initiated in 1971, and he personally interviewed, and enlisted Pikeville College students in interviewing, residents of obscure places to be added to the survey. This material was included in the late Robert M. Rennick's important work *Kentucky Place Names* (Lexington: University Press of Kentucky, 1984).

Leonard's greatest achievement was the documentation of the Couch family of eastern Kentucky and their vast lore. He describes his discovery of this family:

[A]cross the long ridge of Pine Mountain to the northwest lie the most isolated acres of the state—on the headwaters of the Kentucky River. Here are such picturesque branches and valleys as Cutshin, Greasy, and Big Leath-erwood. Here I have explored for a decade, discovering many strange and lingering folkways, primitive farming and folk handicrafts, lumbering and hunting, funeralizing and moonshining. The most valuable treasure that I have found, however, has been an old-fashioned family tradition of Old World folktale telling and ancient ballad singing. On a small branch of Cut-shin Creek I met Mandy Couch Hendrix, who directed me back across Pine ridge to Putney on the Cumberland, a stringtown lumber camp some eight miles above Harlan, to her brothers Jim and Dave Couch, who recorded for me the family store of folklore—sixty old tales and one hundred folksongs and hymns.[12]

Most of the tales and songs, riddles, and jokes came from Jim and Dave Couch, who had learned them from their father and mother, Tom and Mary Ann Couch. Additional material came from other Couches. The material was collected in ten sometimes lengthy sessions from 1951 to 1955, while Leonard taught at Pine Mountain Settlement School, Wallins High School, Piedmont College, and Union College. After he had filled thirty reels of tape, Leonard commented that even though he had finished up "the collecting phase of my work" with the family, he had done so "with their lore still unexhausted."[13] He shaped the material into a seven-hundred-page manu-script containing one hundred folksongs and sixty-one folktales, riddles, and jokes, with copious notes and annotations. The entire body of the col-lection was too large for a single book, but the University of Kentucky Press released it on microcard in 1959. Leonard then decided to break the material into two parts, family narrative and family story and song. The first part was published as *Up Cutshin and Down Greasy: Folkways of a Kentucky Mountain Family* by the University of Kentucky Press in 1959, with a few illustrative stories and songs included. Then in 1974, the University of Texas Press published the entire work for the American Folklore Society's Memoir Series as *Sang Branch Settlers: Folksongs and Tales of a Kentucky Mountain Family*, with musical notations by one of Roberts's West Virginia Wesleyan colleagues, music professor Buell Agey. With this book, the society paid homage to one of its most distinguished members. When the book went out of press, Roberts secured the copyright and reissued it through Pikeville College Press in 1980. In his interviewing and his arrangement of this mate-rial, Leonard had little interest in the new trend in folklore of theoretical analysis, but he was in the vanguard of another trend, that of placing the performance of folklore in the context of the lives of the performers.

At the time Leonard found Jim Couch, Jim and Dave's father, Tom, was ninety-two, living in a nearby house. He was unable to sing or relate the tales, but he reminded his sons of items from time to time. Their mother, Mary Ann, the primary teller of the old folktales, had died in 1921. Jim had served in the army in France during World War I, and was wounded four times. He signed up for a second tour of duty after the Armistice to disinter remains of casualties and ship them back to the States. Back home, Jim cut and logged timber and did some moonshining ("I have made whisky, enough to float all them sawlogs out of here"). He admitted also to doing some witch-doctoring, and he had worked in the mines, where he lost a leg in an accident in 1943. He then became an expert lumber grader. He also maintained a farm while working in the lumber business.[14]

In addition to the many tales and other material, Jim gave Roberts detailed information about all the jobs he had done. However, Leonard found out that Jim could be elusive on the days he wasn't working. As his son said, "We don't know when he's going to come back in the door when he takes off. He goes down there in that town [Harlan] and stands around joking with ever'body, and he shoots pool all over the place, and then he might wind up in the picture show and not come in until the bus runs . . . or somebody brings him in."[15]

Dave was the main banjo picker and singer and had the best memory for the material folk culture, about how things used to be, and how they made a living while he was growing up. He thought that life and living had been better then than in the present. He talked about the natural fruits and nuts and how they had grown and preserved these and other things to eat, almost everything they needed. He told how he could stand in their garden and throw a fishing line into the Cumberland River to catch a mess of fish. During the winter they supplemented their table with wild game they killed on their frequent hunts. He said he never made moonshine while his mother, a good Christian woman, was alive, but when she died, he went to live with his brother Jim, and they made whiskey for several years. When he took a job with the C&O Railroad near Hazard, he brought moonshine and sold it to the railroad workers. He later worked in the mines, and then took a job at Pine Mountain Settlement School, where there was a considerable interest in the folklore of the mountains, especially in the songs and dances, although I doubt that anyone at the school was aware of his folkloric knowledge and abilities.

Jim and Dave Couch had scant schooling in one-teacher schools, but both had commodious memories, with a vast store of ballads, hymns, lyric songs, folktales, riddles, and jokes, as did others of their kin. They may not have known much about the printed literature that was taught in other parts of the country, but they had an oral literature of their own that they presented clearly and colorfully in their native speech. The old ballads, love songs, and hymns were presented usually with banjo accompaniment.

Sang Branch Settlers was reviewed widely and became a model for how folklore should be presented as part of the lives of those living in the culture. Folklorist Henry Glassie wrote recently in a letter to me (undated but April 2015) that "Leonard Roberts, along with Vance Randolph and George Korson, anticipated modern folklore scholarship study with his attention to individuals and their settings."

Carl Lindahl, the folklorist who most admired Roberts and his work, especially his collecting among the schoolchildren in eastern Kentucky schools and the enormous collection from the Couch family, commented in an email to me (April 6, 2015) about the work Roberts had done:

> For lovers of folktales, Leonard Roberts is most famous for his recording of fantasy narratives, which constitute the richest and most diverse collection yet recorded by one man in the southern mountains. But this great achievement was in many ways only the gateway to something greater: in discovering folktales, he discovered that they were narrated as a part of the kind of culture pattern that we were not too aware of until we began to look for it. Roberts' quest for tales expanded to become a quest to record, describe, and ultimately understand the *whole* folk culture of the Kentucky mountains: their songs, music, games, dances, family and neighborhood history; their hunting, farming, and courtship traditions. *Sang Branch Settlers* is the fruit of Roberts's conviction that to truly know a folktale or a folksong, we need to truly understand the whole teller, the whole singer, and the whole traditional culture that created, preserves, and treasures it. *Sang Branch Settlers* is the most important exploration of Appalachian folklife yet to be contained within the covers of a single book.

As Lindahl has pointed out, Leonard collected almost all of his tape-recorded tales, hundreds of them, along with riddles, jokes, and songs, during one decade between 1949 and 1959, and that was pretty much the end of his fieldwork. He continued to work this material into books and kept his books in print, but after that time, his energies went into his work as a teacher and a college department head. By this time he was well known as a teller of tales, and he received many invitations to entertain audiences on campuses and at workshops and festivals.

Roberts was involved with the American Folklore Society and was president of both the Kentucky and West Virginia folklore societies. He also worked with fellow Kentuckian Sarah Gertrude Knott, who headed the National Folk Festival Association and founded its long-running festival; he served as the organization's vice president and president for four years. I had the pleasure of traveling to Nashville with Leonard to attend an annual session of the National Folk Festival, where I heard him mesmerize an audience with the magic tales. However, he eventually found himself in conflict with fellow board members because he stressed folk authenticity over artistic excellence when it came to selecting performers for the festival. He was often at odds with other folklorists over how folklore should be collected, preserved, and presented.

During his lifetime, Roberts published over fifty articles and folktales and forty-two book reviews in the *Journal of American Folklore*, the *Kentucky Folklore Record,* the *Tennessee Folklore Bulletin, Midwest Folklore, Mountain Life and Work,* and other folklore, state, and regional journals. In 1954, the Council of the Southern Mountains published his *I Bought Me a Dog: A Dozen Authentic Folktales from the Southern Mountains*, and in 1957 *Nippy and the Yankee Doodle: And More Folk Tales from the Southern Mountains.* The University of Kentucky Press published his dissertation as *South from Hell-fer-Sartin: Kentucky Mountain Folk Tales* in 1955. Other publications followed: *The Tales and Songs of the Couch Family* (Lexington: University of Kentucky Press, Kentucky Microcards ed., 1959; reprint, Salem, Wis.: Microcards, Inc., 1969); *Up Cutshin and Down Greasy: Folkways of a Kentucky Mountain Family* (Lexington: University of Kentucky Press, 1959); *Sang Branch Settlers: Folksongs and Tales of a Kentucky Mountain Family* (Austin: University of Texas Press for the American Folklore Society, 1974); *Old Greasybeard: Tales from the Cumberland Gap* (Detroit: Folklore Associates of Gale Research, 1969); and *In the Pine: Selected Kentucky Folksongs,* with Buell Agey, who did the musical notations (Pikeville, Ky.: Pikeville, College Press, 1980). He also contributed to fourteen books by other writers and editors, and he edited and published numerous books on regional subjects under the imprint of the Pikeville College Press.

A fatal traffic accident in 1983 silenced Leonard Roberts's storytelling voice and ended his monumental work in documenting the folklore of eastern Kentucky. Edith Roberts survived Leonard by twenty-seven years. She died in 2010. They are buried in the Davidson Memorial Gardens in Ivel, Kentucky. All of the Roberts children survive. Sue Carolyn became a teacher; Margaret Anne was a librarian; Rita Helen studied folklore and then became a certified nurse-midwife; and Lynneda Jane is an office worker and a genealogist. Leonard and Edith have six grandchildren and nineteen great-grandchildren.

In 1993, the Appalachian Center of Berea College issued a cassette recording, *Raglif Jaglif Tetartlif Pole [and Other Tales from Appalachian Tradition]*, produced by folklorist Steve Green, which contains several of Roberts's favorite tales and riddles along with some comments on storytelling, taken from public lectures and storytelling events. It is the only publicly available recording of Roberts himself.

In the summer of 2003, Carl Lindahl organized a workshop for students, teachers, storytellers, and researchers at Berea College, where the Roberts papers are archived. Dr. Lindahl and other folklorists from Indiana University and the University of North Carolina led the workshop in analyzing and transcribing from the sound recordings. The main purpose was to transcribe enough material for several projects of scholarly importance, including a republication of Roberts's *Old Greasybeard*, in its original format but "prefaced by about 200 pages of additions that would contextualize the original collection and bring it up to date." (This project has not come to fruition.) Jane Muncy Fugate, who in 1949, as an eleven-year-old schoolgirl, had recorded tales for Roberts, appeared for two days at the workshop to perform some of the tales that she has continued to tell over the years and to answer questions about Roberts. The participants also interviewed several of Muncy's cousins who knew the old tales.

In Lindahl's report on the workshop, he wrote this about the importance of Berea's Roberts Collection:

Scholars have asserted that the three major folktale collections of Leonard Roberts—*South from Hell-fer-Sartin* (1955), *Old Greasybeard* (1960), *Sang Branch Settlers* (1974)—constitute the most important published record of traditional British American narrative. Yet the Leonard Roberts Collection, housed in Berea College, constitutes an even more important resource, because it contains hundreds of additional narratives that were not published in any of his books. Many of the narratives, like most of those that Roberts did publish, are available in the collection in audio form. These recordings constitute the nation's best gauge of the stylistic range of British American traditional märchen, legends, tall tales, jokes, and anecdotes.

Beyond the content of Roberts' published and unpublished materials, his collection possesses incomparable importance for a third reason. Because Roberts recorded many young narrators in the mid-twentieth century, folklorists today are able to find and interview many of these narrators and many surviving members of their audiences. In so doing, we can obtain important information on the context, performances, and meanings of the tales. Such information allows us to study a cross-section of American narrative history stretching from the nineteenth century to the beginning of the twenty-first and to discover much more about the living oral traditions of the Appalachians than has yet appeared in 80 years of scholarly study.[16]

In 2008, the American Folklore Society invited Lindahl to give the Invited Plenary Address at the society's annual meeting in Louisville. The award-winning folklorist's talk was entitled "Leonard Roberts, the Farmer-Lewis-Muncy Family, and the Magic Circle of the Mountain Märchen." It was a splendid address. He examined the storytelling tradition of these intermarried families, which included Jane Muncy, the pre-teen girl whom Roberts had recorded so many years earlier, who had learned her tales from her grandmother, Sidney Farmer Muncy. Lindahl said:

> Leonard's commitment . . . led him to assemble North America's richest extant record of one small region's English-language märchen. I believe that the massive chorus of voices he recorded constitutes one of the most important contributions yet made to the understanding of how American communities share and reshape their tales of magic. The moment of performance is the instant of emergence, but it takes a profound knowledge . . . to comprehend from what, precisely, the performance is emerging. By recording so many earlier versions Leonard provided a store of otherwise unrecoverable past performances, ones rich enough to help us see how Sidney's and Jane's tales both faithfully echoed their past and simultaneously created entirely new narrative worlds.[17]

Lindahl organized two other sessions on Roberts at the meeting. At the second one, he again spoke of Roberts's work in collecting, and then he presented Jane Muncy Fugate to tell "Merrywise," the full-blown narrative learned from her grandmother that she had told to Roberts back in 1949. I followed her to do the best I could with Leonard's favorite tale, "Raglif Jaglif Tetartlif Pole." The second session was "Leonard Roberts and the Cumberland Mountains," with family members and others who had known Roberts contributing. Henry Glassie, emeritus professor of folklore at Indiana University and author of the prizewinning book *Passing the Time in Ballymenone*, spoke to the group.[18] Later, in an email message, he wrote that the two Appalachian people he first sought out to interview, as an undergraduate, were Bascom Lamar Lunsford and Leonard Roberts. He said, "That is, I had independently developed for myself, before graduate school, a genealogy of influence, and Bascom Lunsford and Leonard Roberts were big parts of it. [They] were with me when, at last, I did the work I longed to do—not in Appalachia but in Ireland."

In his talk at the meeting, Glassie said this about Roberts:

> I'd say that *Up Cutshin and Down Greasy* is really an amazing book, and if you read that book carefully you realize that inside that book is everything that folklore is going to develop into in the next thirty years after that book was published. [Roberts] understood what was important—the stories are important, but it's really the people who tell the story [that are] the most important. . . . And once we understood that what really mattered was the people and how they told the stories, and the people and how they thought about the stories, then that became a whole new orientation in folklore. . . . Leonard Roberts, it seems to me, was a great and tremendous pioneer in the development of modern folklore.[19]

Roberts lived an interesting life and was a pioneer scholar with unique insight, since he was a native of the region that he studied. While many other Appalachian scholars and governmental experts were looking at the big picture of Appalachia—economics, educational advancement, social improvement, and above all change—he was visiting families in the coves and ridges and valleys and documenting their inner lives: what they thought and said, how they entertained themselves, what was sacred, what was funny to them, and what was worth remembering and passing on to the next generations. It is this legacy that Leonard Roberts captured and preserved.

Tales, Riddles, Jokes, and Songs
from the Leonard Roberts Collection

✺ Raglif Jaglif Tetartlif Pole
Type 313C, the Girl as Helper and the Forgotten Fiancée

Leonard Roberts recorded his aunt Columbia Roberts telling this tale in 1950. This version came from a recording of Leonard Roberts in my course "Appalachian Oral Tradition: Ballads and Tales" at Berea College in January 1975. He first published this tale in Mountain Life and Work 28, no. 1 *(Winter 1952): 29–32; a shorter version appeared in* Old Greasybeard, *pp. 65–68. Another version can be found in Loyal Jones, ed.,* Appalachian Folk Tales *(Ashland, Ky.: Jesse Stuart Foundation, 2010), pp. 19–29. You can hear Roberts tell it on the cassette recording* Raglif Jaglif Tetartlif Pole *(1993; AC004, Appalachian Center, Berea College). Variants of this tale have been collected in several countries in Europe. Richard Chase includes "Jack and King Marock" in* The Jack Tales. *Note, too, the relationship to the Greek tale of Hercules' task of cleaning out the Augean Stables in Jack's first task. In 2009, anthropologist Richard Ramsay, a classmate of mine at Berea College, who researches and teaches in Mexico, sent me his book containing a variant that he had collected from Leonardo Antonio, told in the Indian Otomi language, and published in three languages—Otomi, Spanish, and English: Leonardo Antonio and Richard Ramsay,* Mänga ya b'ede!/¡Cuenta las historias!/Tell the Stories! *(Hidalgo, Mex.: Hmunts'a Hem'i—Centro de Documentación y Asesoría Hñähñu, 2009).*

Well, once upon a time there was an old man and an old woman, and they had two or three kids, and one of them was named Jack. Well, Jack was the oldest, and he was a smart-alecky kind of boy, and he got to runnin' away from home, an' he was goin' down to the forks of the creek and playin' with those old rough boys. 'Course they fussed with him and tried to get him to stay at home, but he kept on goin' down there, and after a while he learned to gamble. Now, think about that—awfullest thing to do. But still, he'd gamble with the boys and got so he could win. He learned to be very skillful. So one day when he was down there, a strange-like fellow come up and got in the game, and soon Jack was winning from him, and pretty soon he won all this old stranger had. Well, the stranger said, "I guess you've got all my wealth, but I've got a beautiful daughter, several daughters at home, so I'll just wager you my daughter, give or take." Well, Jack thought about it for a while. He didn't want to risk the pot he had, but he decided he would, and Jack won the daughter. That old man sort of clouded up, walked around a little bit. Jack stood up and looked around, and that old man disappeared. Well, Jack didn't know where he had gone.

So Jack set out to hunt for him. Days passed and nights passed, weeks passed, months passed, and he never could find out where he was. Jack was about ready to give up and go back home, and he got so lost. Pretty soon when he started back home, he ran into a big house out in the wilderness of a place. He helloed at the door, and an old man came out, and it was that old man he'd won the daughter off of. Jack said, "Aren't you the old man I won that daughter off of?" The old man said, "Ah, yes, I remember that, yes, sure." Jack said, "Well, let me have her so I can take her back home. I'll start back." That old fellow said, "Come on up on the porch, sit and rest. It's gettin' sorta late. Stay all night with me." Well, that suited Jack pretty well, and they went, and they had supper. He saw there were three or four pretty girls around there, and he picked out the prettiest one and he began to wink at her, and they all had a good night's sleep.

The next morning Jack got up and he said, "Well, I want to take my girl," told him the one he wanted. That old man said, "Oh, I don't know—I don't believe you won her fair in that game. I believe I have a job for you, and then maybe you can have her." Jack said, "What is that?" "Well," the old man said, "I've got a big barn down here. It's got about a hundred stalls in it, and it hasn't been cleaned out in seven years. You clean it out by tonight—or off comes your head."

He laid out an old shovel and a new shovel, and he disappeared again. Jack looked at those shovels, and he looked at that big barn down there, and so he picked up that new shovel and went on down there. He got in there, and he started to shoveling. Ever' time he'd shovel out one shovelful, two more would jump back in—filled the stall half full. He worked up into the afternoon, and he couldn't get it cleaned out at all. Now, what's goin' to happen to him that night? Said he's goin' to have his head cut off. Well, Jack sat down, and he was beginning to get lonesome, began to feel pretty sad, and he was about halfway goin' to cry, when he looked up toward the house and there come that beautiful girl down there, the one that he'd picked out.

She came sidlin' down there, said, "What're you been doin', Jack?" Jack said, "Aw, I don't know if it'd do any good to tell you or not." She said, "Well, go ahead and tell me. It wouldn't do any harm." "Well," he said, "that old man up there told me to clean out this barn, or he's goin' to cut off my head tonight. I can't get anywhere at all." She said, "Which one of those shovels are you usin'?" He said, "Well, I'm usin' that new shovel." She said, "Aw, you shouldn't do that. You should a used that old shovel." So she went up there and got the old shovel and said, "Now, use this." He went in there, and he started shovelin', and ever' time he'd shovel out one shovelful, a half dozen more'd fly out with it. And in about an hour, he had that barn cleaned out clean as a pin. He had time to talk to the girl a little.

Pretty soon it got dusky-dark, and they went up to the house, sat around a little, and the old man came in. He said, "Well, how'd you get along today, Jack?" "Oh, I got along just fine." "You cleaned out that barn?" "Yes, I cleaned out the barn." "No one ever helped you?" "No, nobody helped me." "I believe somebody helped you, and I'll catch you in it yet." And that scared Jack, and he sidled away, and the old man went into the house, and of course he spent another night with them. He threw sheep's eyes at the girl across the supper table.

Next morning, he said, "Well, I want to take my girl home." That old fellow said, "Aw, I don't know whether you did a good job with that barn or not. I've got another job for you to do." Jack said, "Well, I'd like to know what that is." He said, "Well, now that you've got the barn cleaned out, I've got a big herd of horses back in the mountains here. They haven't been in that barn for seven years, and they're wild back there with their leader, old Raglif Jaglif Tetartlif Pole. Now you get all those horses in the barn, or off comes your head tonight." He laid out an old torn-up bridle and a new bridle, and he disappeared.

Well, Jack should have been wiser now, but he'd heard about that big wild horse, and he looked at that old ragged bridle, and he picked up the new bridle, and he went up there, and he run those horses from hilltop to hilltop way up into the afternoon, couldn't catch a one of 'em.

He sat down and started cryin'. He looked up and saw that beautiful girl comin' up there. Oh, she was as pretty as a peach-tree blossom. She said, "Well, how're you doing' today, Jack?" He said, "Oh I don't know if it would do any good to tell you." "Go ahead and tell me. It won't do any harm." "Well, that old man told me to get that barn full of these horses, or he'd cut off my head tonight." She said, "Which bridle are you usin'?" "Why, I'm usin' this new bridle." She said, "Well, you should be usin' that old bridle." So she got the old bridle and handed it to him. Jack went up toward those horses, and they were standin' pretty still, held the bridle up, and old Raglif Jaglif came up and put his head in the bridle, and he put it on him, and he led him, and all the rest followed, and the two walked down to the barn, and they put all the horses in their stables. They had time to court a little while, too. So they sparked a little bit and went back to the house.

The old man came in, looking a little more fierce, said, "How'd you get along today, Jack?" "Got along just fine." "You get all my horses in the barn?" "Yes, sir." "Nobody helped you?" "No, sir, I did it myself." "Never mind. I'll catch you at it yet. I suspect someone is helpin' you."

Well, they had a good supper, and they got up the next mornin' and Jack said, "I'll take your daughter, and I've got to go home. I've been out for months now." The old man said, "I don't believe I can let you go. I've got one more job for you." Jack said, "I'd like to know what that is." The old man said, "Well, right down here is the Red Sea. 'Way across the Red Sea is a big forest over there, and up on that ridge is an old big tree about five hundred feet tall with not a limb on it until the very top. Right in top of that tree is a big old eagle's nest with eggs in it that haven't been collected in seven years. You get them eggs here tonight or off comes your head."

So he dragged out a little old boat and a clean new boat, and he disappeared. Well, Jack began to try to do that job. He went down and looked at those boats to see which one he was going to take. Well, that old leaky one was about ready to sink, and he knew he couldn't even start, so he got in that new boat and started paddlin', and a-paddlin' and a-paddlin', and when he looked back, he hadn't got away from the shore. He worked there until the afternoon, couldn't get away. Well, he looked up, and there came that beautiful girl. She said, "Well, where are you goin' today, Jack?" He said, "Aw, it won't do me any good to tell you." "Well, go ahead and tell me. It won't do any harm." "Well," he said, "I've been told to go across here and climb a tree five hundred feet high and get some eagle's eggs that haven't been got in seven years, or have my head cut off tonight, and I can't get away from shore." She said, "Which one of the boats were you usin'?" He said, "I was usin' this new boat." She said, "Get in this old boat, and I'll go with you." He got in the old boat and started paddlin', and they just flew across the Red Sea and landed on the other side in a little while—had time to court a little while on the seashore. They walked through the land and the timber, through the flowers and trees, and came to that old big tree, and Jack looked up and said, "Oh, I just don't know how in the world I'm going to get in the top of that tree." "Well," she said, "I'm goin' to help you this time." She pulled all ten of her fingers off, and said, "You just stick these in the tree and step on them one at a time and then climb right on up." So that's what he did. He put all of her ten fingers in the tree for ladder steps, and he stepped right on up, climbed to the top and started gathering eggs, got 'em all in his pockets, and he started back down, bringing her fingers down with him. He got to the bottom, stepped down and handed her the fingers—only nine of them there. She put 'em on—had one finger missing. He said, "I'm sorry about that. I must have left one in the tree." She said, "Well, I can do without it. When we get back home—as you know, that old man is not our father. He's got us all captured—we're goin' to have a masquerade party tonight, and we'll all be dressed alike. Now, if you want to see me, you come around, and I'll hold up this hand, and you'll see my finger's missin'." He said, "That'll be fine. If you'll take it that way, I'm be glad."

They got in the boat, and they paddled back across, and they sparked a little bit. They went up to the house, and it was about dark and cloudy then. That old man came up. "How'd you get along today, Jack?' "Oh, I got along just fine." "You get those eagle eggs?" "Yes, sir, I got 'em," and he started pulling them out of his pockets and handing them to the old man, and he got mad and tried to grab Jack and said, "I'll cut off your head tonight. Somebody's been helpin' you." So Jack ran around and hid behind the house. That old man pulled out and went in the house. Well, Jack didn't eat much for supper that night, and he waited until the dance got started, and he slipped down to the dance hall, and they were swinging around with something like the Virginia Reel and some good old square dance, moving all over the floor. Jack slipped in there, and he kept looking around, and they were all dressed just alike. Pretty soon he saw a girl hold up her hand, and it just had four fingers. So he just cut in and started dancing around with her, and they danced to one side, and he said, "That old man doesn't believe me, and he thinks you helped me, so I'm goin' to have to leave here tonight." So she said, "Let's dance some more," and Jack said, "What shall I do?" She said, "Will you take me with you?" Jack said, "Why, shore I'll take you with me. Let's go. We've got a big fine horse out there." So they slipped out of the hall. She went and got her clothes and tied them up in a little budget, and she came back there, and he got up on old Raglif Jaglif Tetartlif Pole, and she got up behind him, and they took off in the middle of the night.

They rode on and rode on, over hills and over vales, until way up in the mornin', and they slowed down and began to talk, sweet things, you know, and pretty soon Jack looked around. "Uh-oh, there's a little speck of dust back there, coming after us." She said, "Well, you look again later on and see what it is." They rode on a little longer, slowed the horse up a little bit. Jack said, "Looks like that old man ridin' after us." She said, "All right, you look in the horse's right ear and see what you see." Well, Jack peeped in that right ear and said, "I don't see a thing in there but a little stick." She said, "Oh, you take that stick with your right hand and throw it over your right shoulder and say, 'Good roads before us and briars and grapevines behind us.'" That's what Jack did. As the old man was ridin' toward them, he throwed that stick over his right shoulder: "Good roads before us and briars and grapevines behind us." As soon as that stick hit the ground, it began to grow up into a thicket of vines and shrubbery and bushes, and that old man rode into it and got stuck in there. The road leveled on before them, and they rode on like the wind on old Raglif Jaglif Tetartlif Pole.

They rode on through the afternoon and night and on down to the next morning. Jack began to slow down and look around to see if he was coming into his county yet. Couldn't see anything that could tell him. He looked back again. Uh-oh, he could see a little speck of dust again. "Could you look a little bit later and see what it is?" And so a little later, Jack looked back and said, "Ah, it's that old man ridin' down on us again." She said, "Look in that horse's left ear and see what you see in there." He looked in the horse's left ear and said, "I don't see anything but a little drop of water." "You take that little drop of water in your left hand and throw it over your left shoulder, and say, 'Good roads before us and the Red Sea behind us.'" Well, he just reached in there and got it on his finger and throwed it over his left shoulder, said, "Good roads before us and the Red Sea behind us." Just when it hit the ground, it began forming a great big old lake. They watched that old man ride in there and go out of sight a-gurglin'.

Of course, the road ahead of them stretched like a highway, and so they rode on like the wind on old Raglif Jaglif Tetartlif Pole. They rode on through the evening and night, and pretty soon in the morning, Jack looked around and saw he was coming into his territory, where he played and gambled and all that stuff. So he said, "I'm getting pretty close to my home. I've been away so long, I want to stop." She said, "No, I don't believe you ought to stop. I don't want you to stop." He said, "Why? I want to stop and see my folks, I've been gone so long, they've nearly forgot me." She said, "Well, now, if you stop and let somebody kiss you, you'll forget about me, and we'll never be together again. If you won't let any of them kiss you, I'll wait for you to go in for a little while." So Jack said, "All right, I'll go in, and you stay out here and hold the horse."

So Jack went on in, and his family came around like some mountain folks do, "Oh, Jack! Hello, Jack," and they kept trying to hug him, and he kept pushin' them back, but his little dog came around and bounced up and licked his lips, and Jack forgot what he was doin' and began to talk to them and sat down and ate dinner with them. Well, the girl was out there holdin' the horse, and he hadn't come back, and she realized that someone had kissed him and he had forgotten her. So she just took the horse and rode across a few hills and vales and got her a job as a servant maid with a family over there.

Jack settled down there with his family. He'd grown up now with all of his adventures, and he began to court, and right soon he got right thick with a beautiful girl there, and so they norated that they were goin' to marry that Friday in the church house at the forks of the creek. So that evenin' they assembled at the forks of the creek.

Of course the message got to the girl, and she made three magic boxes, and she got on Raglif Jaglif Tetartlif Pole, and she came to the church. She hitched up her horse and came in with her boxes, and just as she got to the door, the preacher had Jack and his new girl up on the floor. The preacher began, "Folks, we're gathered here this evenin' . . ." About that time, the girl threw her first magic box down. It broke open, and a rooster and a hen fell out. The rooster pecked the hen, and the hen said, "Cack-caa, you forgot about cleaning out the barn that hadn't been cleaned out in seven years, or off comes your head tonight!" Well, Jack began to look around to see what that was—sounded rather strange and familiar to him. The minister said, "Turn around here, Jack. Let's continue the ceremony. We're gathered here today to join this girl and this boy together . . ." The girl threw down another magic box. It broke open and, and a hen and a rooster popped out of it. The rooster pecked the hen, and the hen said, "Cack-caa, you forgot about catching those wild horses that hadn't been caught in seven years, or off comes your head tonight!" Jack's mind began to come back to him. He looked around. He saw a familiar girl back there, just as pretty as a speckled pup. The minister said, "Turn around here, Jack, let's finish this ceremony. Now I join you in . . ." She threw down the third magic box. It broke open. A rooster and a hen popped out. The rooster pecked the hen, and the hen said, "Cack-caa, you forgot about gettin' those eagle eggs that hadn't been got in seven years, or off comes your head tonight!" Jack heard that and remembered his life, remembered his story, and he turned around and saw that beautiful girl standing there, and so he handed that other girl over to the minister, and he went back and got his old girl, and they came out, and they got on old Raglif Jaglif Tetartlif Pole, and they got away from there, and they rode over seven hills and seven vales, and finally came to a courthouse, and he got a pair of licenses, and they got married, and they lived happily ever after.

✼ Scoonkin Huntin'

This tale was told to Roberts by Martin Ambrose, a student at the Berea Foundation School, who learned it from his father, Luther Ambrose. It is from the Roberts Collection, tape LR4, track 8. An Ozark version, "The R'arin'-Up, Tearin'-Up Scoonkin Hunt," can be found in Ozark Tall Tales, *edited by Richard Young and Judy Dockrey Young (Little Rock, Ark.: August House, 1989), p. 61.*

Me and my Paw, we lived together down on Red River about a mile, mile and a half, two mile apart. Now, one day my Paw, he told me, said, "Son, how'd you keer to go down and round up all the dogs?" And I axed him,

I didn't keer whether I did or not. Well, I went down and rounded up all the dogs, that is, all of 'em 'cept Ol' Loud, and of course then I rounded up Ol' Loud too. Well, then he told me, "How would you like to go larrapin' terrapin' scoonkin huntin'?" And I axed him that I didn't keer whether I did or not. Well, we set out, all them dogs a-follerin' us, 'cept Ol' Loud, and he's a-follerin' us too. They run down the valley up along the ridge, and we come down to our neighbors' barn, and all their barks come out and dogged at us, and we got started on a little ways, and heard our dogs a-carryin' on, and my Paw, he told me, said, "Son, how would you like to go and see if them dogs has got anything?" And I axed him that I didn't keer if I did or not.

Well, I went on up the road a piece, and we heard them dogs a-hollerin' an' a-carryin' on, and my Paw told me, "How'd you like to go on up there and find out if them dogs have got anything?" I axed him that I didn't keer if I did or not. Well, I went on up the road a piece, and there about twenty foot above the top of a great big oak saplin' I spied a coon a-settin' out there on a limb about two feet from the ground, way up there. Well, my Paw, he told me, said, "Son, how would you like to climb up there and get that there thang?" Well, I axed him that I didn't keer whether I did or not. Well, I grabbed me a limb and clumb up that tree, gettin' me about ten foot above the top of that big ol' oak saplin'. The coon was a-settin' on that limb about two foot from the ground, so I clumb up a little bit further, and I took a swing at 'im, and I missed 'im, and he went a little further out on the limb, and my Paw, he hollers at me, told me, "Son, how'd you keer to knock that thing down here to me? I'm gittin' impatient." I told him I didn' keer if I did or not. Well, we started shakin', and all them dogs was a-carryin' on, all them dogs 'ceptin' Ol' Loud, 'course he was carryin' on, too. My Paw, he started shakin' that tree, and the dogs was a-jumpin' up on the tree, and I was a-shakin' it at the same time, you know. Well, all of a sudden, I heard a crash and a thump, an' I figgered somethin' had fell, you know, like somethin' falling out of a tree. Well, sir, I looked around, and it was me. An' all them dogs, they began jumpin' on me, a-yappin' and a-barkin' and a-bitin', that is, all of 'em 'cept Ole Loud, and he jumped on me and started to yappin' and a-bitin' too. Well, I grabs him by the tail an' I cuts his tail off up around his ears, and I throws him over my shoulder.

When we gets home that day—let's see now, we gets home with two black eyes, a coonskin, a couple of barked-up shins, and all the dogs, 'ceptin' Ole Loud. 'Course I got him home, too.

❀ Big Time Huntin'

This concise tall tale, told by Ruth Hale of Buchanan County, Virginia, in 1969, has elements that appear in other hunting tales. This and the following stories are from the Roberts Collection, box 28, folders 1–4.

This ole man went a-huntin' with a muzzle loader gun. He had plenty of powder, but he only had lead to load one time. He looked up and saw a turkey settin' on a limb, then looked behind him and saw a deer. He heard a racket under his feet, and there laid a rattlesnake. Well, he couldn't make up his mind which way to shoot. Finally, he took a notion to shoot the turkey and try to jump back before the snake could bite him. He aimed a little too low and hit the limb with the turkey on it, and it fell on the deer. The fall killed the turkey, the limb killed the deer, the gun fell on the rattlesnake and killed it, the old man fell over backwards in a hole of water, and when he came out of the water, he had a fish in each hand. He skinned the rattlesnake and made him a belt. He had enough meat from the fish, turkey, and deer that he didn't have to go huntin' for a long time.

❀ 'Feared of the Lord

Flora Ballard of Jellico, Tennessee, gave this story to Roberts, as remembered from Winston Baird's telling.

Presbyterian churches are all over this section now, and the church has missions out in the woods, too, tryin' to save the folks from their evil, sinful, and wasteful ways.

There was a time, though, when Presbyterians were strangers. Winston Baird, of Jacksboro, Tennessee, told how Aunt Polly Baird, of Caryville, set one off one time.

He said it was in the summer of 1882. The railroad was being built between Caryville and Jellico. And into that section came a Presbyterian missionary. Baird heard that Aunt Polly gave him a drink of spring water, and pushed him a chair.

"Right warm today, it is," she said.

The missionary vowed that it was hot, and then he turned to his mission. "Aunty," he asked, "what religious denominations do you have in this section?"

"Well," she said, "we're mostly just good old-time Baptists."

"Well," he said, "aren't there any Methodists?"

"Since they've been a-buildin' that railroad through here, a lot of ferriners have come in. I reckon there might be a sprinklin' of Methodists 'mongst them."

The missionary turned to talkin' about the railroad. He asked how the people liked the building of the railroad.

Aunt Polly said, "We'ns don't like hit a-tall. They brought in a lot of ferriners, and the people had to run some of them out'n the country. Then, they're just a-shootin' big rocks and trees all over the farms, and they don't like it."

"Well," said the missionary, "where's your husband today?"

"He went back in the mountains a hog-huntin'," Aunt Polly answered.

"Not on a Sunday!" the missionary exclaimed.

"Yes, on a Sunday," answered Aunt Polly.

"Ain't he afraid of the devil?" he asked.

"I reckon he is," she said. "He took his gun along."

The missionary took another drink of water from the big dipper. Sittin' back in his rocking chair, his hat on his knee, he turned to Aunt Polly and asked: "Are there any Presbyterians in this section?"

She said thoughtfully: "The dogs last night got after somethin' down at the crick, and run it 'crost the valley and up to the foot of the mountain, and caught it and kilt it. The boys brought hit back, but they didn't know what hit was."

The missionary sat mum.

"Hit might be one, sir," Aunt Polly went on. "You can go 'round thar an' see for yerself."

❊ The Oxen That Ran Away

As told by Bob Kiffer, once of Floyd, now Boyd County, Kentucky.

Not long after the turn of the [twentieth] century an ole ox driver of some renown by the name of Bob Hatcher was stalled with a load of corn in the mud. He had worked, pried, dug and carried rocks to work under the wheels. He had urged his oxen until they had become tired, and he had about given up and quit about how he was to free his wagon. He sat on a rock to rest and figure some way to get his ox team to try again when Dr. Hughes came riding along and stopped to console the stranded oxen driver.

Bob explained his situation to the doctor and asked him if he knew a way to get his team to pull once more and free his wagon from the mud hole.

"Sure," replied the doctor. "Shell me an ear of corn and give me the cob."

Doc proceeded to rub each ox's rectum with the cob. Then he reached in his saddlebags for a bottle and rubbed each place with turpentine. The old oxen started bawling and ringing their tails. They gave such a big surge, they pulled the wagon out of the mud hole and ran off. The befuddled driver looked toward his runaway team and then back to the doctor and said, "Doc, you're gonna have t' turpentine me so I can catch 'em."

❀ These Steep Hillsides

Roberts collected this story and the following one from John Stringer of Wayne County, Kentucky, in 1956.

I was travelin' along the road one day and happened to notice a tater patch by the side of the road planted so that the rows ran straight up and down the hill. There was a man hoein' thereabout. Sez I, "Why on earth do you plant your taters up and down the hill?"

He replied, "You see, it saves a lot of time and trouble when diggin' time comes. All we have to do is dig the first hill of taters in each row and hold the basket below the hill."

❀ Rich Land

Leonard left a note on this one saying it "may have a known author but was passed on to me by word of mouth and I have never seen it in print."

A young man came to our neck of the road apparently lookin' for a place to settle down. He stopped at the country store, and in the course of conversation asked an old-timer, "Is this land very rich around here?"

The old-timer replied, "Son, let me tell you, this land is *so rich* and grows corn *so big* that it takes only three ears to make a dozen!"

Riddles

This first riddle was Leonard's favorite, and he learned versions from both his wife, Edith, and Dave Couch of Harlan County, Kentucky. These riddles are from the Roberts Collection, box 34, folders 8–11.

> As I went around my world of Wiglam Waglam,
> I spied old Tom Tiglam Taglam,
> I called old Hellum Bellum
> To run old Tom Tiglam Taglam
> Out of my world of Wiglam Waglam.

Answer: Wiglam Waglam is the old fellow's corn field. Tiglam Taglam is an old sow that got in his corn field. He called his dog, Hellum Bellum, to run the sow out of his corn field.

> In came two legs, sat down on three legs,
> Holding one leg on his lap.
> In came four legs, picked up one leg.
> Up jumped two legs, picked up three legs.
> Threw it at four legs, made four legs give one leg back.

Answer: a man sitting on a stool holding a leg of lamb on his lap. Dog got the leg of lamb. Man threw stool at dog.

Contributed by Clara J. Dickison, Greenup County, Kentucky.

There were two men passing on the street. One said to the other, "Give me one of your sheep and I will have as many as you've got." The other said, "No, give me one of your sheep and I will have twice as many as you." How many sheep did each man have?

  Answer: Five and seven.

Harry J. Wallace, Garrett, Floyd County, Kentucky.

> Runs all day but never walks,
> Often murmurs, never talks.
> Has a bed but never sleeps.
> Has a mouth but never eats.
> Answer: a river.

Nellie G. Hills, Greenup, Kentucky.

Crooked as a rainbow,
Smooth as a plate,
Ten thousand horses
Can't pull it straight.
Answer: A river.

Nellie G. Hills, Greenup, Kentucky.

A farmer had a chicken, a bag of grain, and a fox and wanted to transport them across the river in a boat, but he could take only one over at a time and only make three trips. If he took the grain over first and left the fox with the chicken, then the fox would eat the chicken, and he couldn't leave the chicken and the grain together because the chicken would eat the grain. How did he do it?

Answer: He took the chicken over first because the fox would not eat the grain. He went back and took the grain over and took the chicken back. He left the chicken by itself and took the fox over, then came back for the chicken.

Billy Jo Moon, Russell, Kentucky.

Round as a biscuit,
Busy as a bee,
Prettiest little thing you ever did see.
Answer: a watch.

Billy Jo Moon, Russell, Kentucky.

A man was to be hung by the king. Since it was the custom to let the condemned man tell a riddle, which if it could not be solved, would set him free, the man told the following riddle:

Good morning, Mr. King,
I've just had a warm drink from your spring.
Through gold it run, through palings it come,
If you can guess this riddle, I'll agree to be hung.
The king could not guess it.

Answer: The man had solicited the help of the queen, who put one of her breasts through a paling fence and put a ring on it, and he sucked it.

Iva Mae Enzor, Harlan County, Kentucky.

Irishmen or Pat and Mike Stories

Roberts collected many of these stories. They are typical "numbskull" jokes or stories about strangers who are assumed to be dumb because they are different and don't know about things the natives know. The Irish Potato Famine in the middle of the nineteenth century caused a million Irish to emigrate mostly to the United States, where they were looked down on by long-time natives. Pat and Mike jokes abounded and were told throughout the country. These are selected from the Roberts Collection, box 32, folders 1–3.

Pat and Mike were unaccustomed to the city. On the first occasion to sleep in a hotel room, Pat was awakened early the next morning by a funny noise. Out of bed he got and went to look out the window. Now, this was when fire engines were first invented, and they were still in the "spit and sputter" stage. Pat saw one go by. It was painted red of course and sparks flew out as it spit and sputtered by. Then another passed, and another, and another real fast. Pat woke Mike and said, "Get up, Mike, 'cause they're moving Hell—I just saw three loads go by."

This tale and the following one were told by Sam B. Turner of Booneville, Kentucky, and related to Roberts by Marshall and Bessie Sallee of Rowan County, Kentucky.

It grew dark as Pat and Mike were going along one evening. They were near the river and a big tree hung over the river. Suddenly, they saw something shining down in the water. "Look," says Pat to Mike, "the moon has done fell down in the water." They tried to think of some way to get it out. They thought and thought and thought. Finally, they saw a group of men nearby and asked if they would help them get something out of the water. They agreed to help Pat and Mike. Pat said he would climb out on the limb of the tree and hang on to the branches. The other men were to form a human rope to reach to the water—each man holding on to the fellow's feet above him. Mike was just ready to reach into the water when Pat yelled, "Hold everything, boys, while I spit on my hands." Of course, they all fell into the water. After they got out and were lying on the river bank, they happened to look up into the sky, and they all wondered how in the world the moon got back up into the sky.

This tale sometimes had a different ending. The men got to wondering whether or not they had all gotten out of the river. There were Pat and Mike and three other men, making five when they started to retrieve the moon. So Pat said, "I'll count us." He counted but forgot to count himself, and so he had only four. Mike said, "Let me count," and he did, but he also forgot to count himself. About then, a farmer came by and asked them what they were doing, and they explained that they were trying to find out whether or not they were all there. The farmer pointed to a fresh cow pile and said, "Each one of you come and stick your nose in this cow pile, and then count the impressions." So they all did that, counted five impressions, and concluded that they were all there.

Pat and Mike were out traveling. They came to a railroad, and they wondered what in the dickens it was. There was a tunnel down the road a little ways, but they didn't know it. They were walking along when all at once there came a train. It scared them, but they managed to get off the track. Pat took off after it, and it went into the tunnel. Pat came back all out of breath, and told Mike, "I didn't catch it, but it ran in a hole, and I'm going to get a mattock and dig it out."

As told by Andy Cox, Artemus, Kentucky.

One time Pat and Mike went bear hunting. Mike wanted a cub for a pet. They came to a cave where there were some cubs. Mike went in this big old cave and was trying to get one of the cubs. All at once the cave got real dark. The mother bear had come and was in the doorway. Pat grabbed her by the tail. Mike called, "What's knocking out all the light, Pat?" Pat answered, "If my tail-hold slips, you'll find out."

John R. Davis, Artemus, Kentucky.

When the Irishmen first come over here, one was tellin' a farmer that he wanted to raise a colt. The farmer gave him a puffball and told him to put it on a stump in the sunshine, and it would hatch a colt, for it was a colt egg. The Irishman put it on a stump and kept watching it. One day a rabbit jumped out from behind the stump, and he took after it hollerin', "Coltie, Coltie, here's your mammy! Coltie, Coltie, here's your mammy!"

Henry A. Oakland, Garrett County, Maryland.

Other Jokes and Stories

The following are from the Roberts Collection, box 27, folders 2–5.

A man came home drunk and thought he was going to die. He asked his wife to pray for him, and she said she didn't know how to pray. He got so sick that she got scared and started to pray for him. She said, "Lord, have mercy on my drunk husband." And he said, "Damn it, don't tell Him I'm drunk; tell Him I'm sick."

Omeda C. Rees, Perry County, Kentucky, told this joke and the following three in 1956.

A man came across an old man crying. The old man looked to be about 90 years old. He asked him why he was crying, and he said his pa had whipped him for throwing a rock at his grandpa. The man said, "You don't mean your grandpa is still living?" He said, "Sure. You can soak him in water for about 30 minutes and he can tell you things that happened 500 years ago."

A man and his son were sawing wood with a crosscut saw, and a man came along and thought that they were trying to take the saw away from each other. He took the saw away from the man and told him he was too big to be taking anything away from such a little fellow.

Two boys gathered some chestnuts from a chestnut tree in a graveyard. They were dividing the chestnuts. One would say. "You take this one and I'll take that one." It got dark, and along came a fellow who was drunk. This drunk man stopped at the gate and heard what the boys were saying. They'd got almost all of the chestnuts counted, and one said, "You take this one, and I'll take that one over by the gate." The drunk man ran off. He ran home and told them that the world had come to an end, and they asked him why, and he said, "I heard the Lord and the Devil separating the dead."

One time there was a farmer, and he raised a lot of crops each year to sell at markets. One year, he didn't raise very many things, and he didn't think he would make very much money, but when he took his crops to town, he made more than he thought, and he said, "I think I'll just surprise my wife and buy me a new suit of clothes." He bought his suit and put it under the seat in his wagon, but while he was finishing his shopping, somebody stole his new outfit. On his way home, he stopped at a bridge over the river and pulled his old clothes off and threw them one by one in the river and watched them float away. When he reached for his new clothes, he discovered they were gone. He sat and thought for a few minutes, and then said to his horse, "Git up, Jim, I'll just go home and surprise her anyhow."

Edd Hale, Harlan County, Kentucky.

Leander Castle was a mine foreman at Wilton, Kentucky. He was working in his garden one morning in 1911 when Aunt Puss Engle came along. Puss was quite a talker and would ask questions all in one breath. Aunt Puss: "Good mornin', Leander, how's all the folks, about what time of day is it, how deep is the ford, and what's butter worth at Wilton?" Leander: "Good mornin', Aunt Puss, folks all well, it's about half past eight—not hardly nine, ford's ass-hole deep, and butter's a dime."

Willie Steele, Menifee County, Kentucky.

A wagon full of people pulled up in front of the Grundy County Courthouse. In walked a young man to ask for a marriage license. When the clerk told him that he was in the right place, he said, "Well, make one out to John Brown to marry Mary Jones."
    "Are you John Brown?"
    "Yes, I'm him."
    "And is Mary of age?"
    "Naw, she ain't."
    "Do you have her paw's consent to marry her?"
    "I reckon. See that old man settin' out there in that wagon with a shotgun pointin' this way? That's her paw."

As told by Ruth Hale, Buchanan County, Virginia.

One time there'uz two girls went to have their picture made. They set down, and the photographer got his camera out, put in a film plate, spread a black cloth over his head, and started adjusting his lens.
    One said to the other, "What's he tryin' to do?"
    The second one said, "Why, he's a-fixin' to focus."
    The other one said, "Bof'us?"

James Goforth, Irwin, Tennessee.

These two boys went to visit a girl that lived way out in the country with her daddy and mama, and they got there for supper, but all the family had to eat was corn mush and buttermilk. One of the boys was bashful, and he didn't eat much. They set around talking with the girl 'til it got kinda late, and the old man invited them to stay the night. Well, this was a one-room cabin with only two beds, so the old couple and the girl got in one bed, and the two boys got in the other'n.

During the night, the boy that didn't eat much got hungry. They'd cooked the mush in the fireplace in a big pot. The fire was still a'flickerin' and he saw that the old womern had left the mush on the hearthstone. So he got up and went over, lifted the lid, and ate him a bait of mush. The other boy whispered, "Bring me some too." So he scooped up a big handful to take to him, but he went to the wrong bed, where the old man was a-sleepin' on his stomach with his bare butt shining in the firelight. When he leaned over, the old man he began breakin' wind. Thinkin' it was the other boy blowin' to cool the mush, he said, "Hit ain't hot, no need to blow," and he dumped the mush in what he thought was his brother's mouth. The old man came awake and rolled over and started holler'n to his wife, sayin', "Hey, old womern, I've done sumpin' I ain't done in fifty years." "What do you mean," she asked, and he said, "I've be-nastied myself."

A thunder-share had come up, and the old womern said, "Well, hit's rainin', go out there under the eve and warsh ye'self off." So he run and stuck his butt under the eve and started warshing hisself. The boy with mush on his hand decided he'd go out and wash his hands. When he got out on the porch, a big flash of lightning come, and he saw the old man's butt a-shinin', and he come down ker-whump and smacked that old man on the ass, and he started hollerin' at the top of his lungs, "I BEEN STRUCK BY LIGHT'NIN! I BEEN STRUCK BY LIGHT'NIN!"

Lem was an old country boy, and the limit of his ability was hitchin' up a team of horses and plowing. Ella Mae was about in the same category. Well, Lem was courtin' Ella Mae, and ever' Saturday night he would go over to see Ella Mae and stay for several hours. Well, one Monday morning Lem's papa had a heart-to-heart talk with him.

Poppy said, "Lem, you're foolin' a lot of time away over there at Ella Mae's house. Air ye' fixin' to get hitched?"

Lem said, "Yes, Pa, we air."

The next Saturday night he made his trip as usual, but he didn't come back. He didn't come back Sunday, nor Tuesday. Along about sundown on Friday, Lem come draggin' in just like a whupped pup, his tongue hangin' out, his eyes lookin' like two piss holes in the snow. His pa looked him over right good and said, "Lem, where have you been?"

"Why, over at Ella Mae's house, Pa."

"Well, you must a got married?"

"Yes, Pa, we did."

"Well, where have ya been so long? Did you take a bridal tour?"

"No, Pa, I just held her by the ears until she got used to it."

James Goforth, Irwin, Tennessee.

Ballads and Songs

✻ Lovin' Henry

Child 68, Roud 47, Roberts 14

This ballad came to Roberts in 1949 from the singing of Florence Lamb and Mary Rowe, both of Pike County, Kentucky. He published it in Roberts and Agey, In the Pine, *pp. 34–37. Child listed eleven texts and fragments, all from Scotland. It has a rather active tradition in the United States, and versions are found in most of the standard collections. Nimrod Workman sings it on* Mother Jones' Will *(Rounder 0076, 1976).*

Look down look down, lov-in' Hen-ry, she said, And stay all night with __ me; Your bed shall be made of dia-monds and gold, And your doors of i-vo-ry. And your doors of i-vo-ry.

2. I can't get down nor I shan't get down,
    Nor I won't stay all night with thee;
    For I have another girl in the ivy cliff,
    And tonight she's a-looking for me,
    And tonight she's a-looking for me.

3. He leaned over from his saddle stirrup
   For to kiss her snow white cheek;
   And in her hand she held an awful knife,
   And she stobbed him both wide and deep,
   And she stobbed him both wide and deep.

4. O shall I ride east or shall I ride west,
   Or anyways under the sun;
   To bring a doctor here,
   For to cure this wounded one,
   For to cure this wounded one.

5. You needn't to ride east,
   You needn't to ride west,
   Nor no ways under the sun;
   There's just one good God above us all,
   That can cure this wounded one,
   That can cure this wounded one.

6. He gave a few more dyin' groans,
   Said, Little girl, you've treated me wrong;
   I'm going to a better world,
   Where you can never come,
   Where you can never come.

7. She took him by his brown curly locks,
   And her sister by his feet;
   They carried him down to the deep stonewall well,
   Where the water was so cold and deep,
   Where the water was so cold and deep.

8. Lay there, lay there, Lovin' Henry, she cried,
   Till the meat drops off your bones;
   For that girl that you have in the ivy cliff,
   Thinks you're a long time comin' home,
   Thinks you're a long time comin' home.

9. As she return-ed to go back home,
   A little bird sat on a limb;
   Said Go home, go home, you cruel-hearted girl,
   There's another boy for thee,
   There's another boy for thee.

10. Fly down, fly down, you purty little bird,
    And rest upon my knee;
    Your cage shall be made of yaller-beaten gold,
    And hung on a willow tree,
    And hung on a willow tree.

11. I can't fly down, nor I shan't fly down,
    Nor I won't rest upon your knee;
    For you have murdered your own true love,
    And perhaps you'll murder me,
    And perhaps you'll murder me.

12. Said, if I had my cedar bow,
    My arrow and my string;
    I'd shoot you right through the heart,
    And no more would you sit there and sing.
    And no more would you sit there and sing.

13. If you had your cedar bow,
    Your arrow and your string,
    I would fly to the top of some tall tree,
    And there I'd sit and sing,
    And there I'd sit and sing,

❋ The Cherry Tree Carol
Child 54, Roud 453, Roberts 13

This text came from Mary Gick of Rowan County, Kentucky, in 1959. Her husband contributed the tune. This carol may go back as early as the fifteenth century, and it is the most popular of the three carols that Francis Child had in his collection. Several variants have been collected, the most in Kentucky. Usually in American versions, Jesus announces His birth on January 5 or 6. This is because the folk kept Old Christmas after the English adopted the Gregorian calendar in 1752, which had the effect of moving the date of Christmas. See the notes on this carol in Roberts and Agey, In the Pine, *pp. 31–32. Jean Ritchie recorded it on her* Carols for All Seasons *on Tradition (TLP 1031, 1959).*

When Jo-seph was an old man, An old man was he; He mar-ried Vir-gin Ma-ry, The Queen of Gal-i-lee, He mar-ried Vir-gin Ma-ry, the Queen of Gal-i-lee.

2. Then Mary spoke to Joseph,
   So sweet and so mild:
   "Joseph, gather me some cherries,
   For I am with child,
   Joseph, gather me some cherries,
   For I am with child."

3. Then Joseph flew in anger,
   In anger flew he;
   "Let the father of the baby
   Gather cherries for thee . . ."

4. Then Jesus spoke a few words,
   A few words spoke he,
   "Let my mother have some cherries,
   Bow down low, cherry tree . . ."

5. The cherry tree bowed low down,
   Bowed low down to the ground,
   And Mary gathered cherries,
   While Joseph stood around . . .

6. Then Joseph took Mary
   Upon his right knee,
   "What have I done, Lord?
   Have mercy on me . . ."

7. Then Joseph took Mary
   Upon his left knee;
   "Oh, tell me little baby,
   When your birthday will be? . . ."

8. "The sixth day of January
   My birthday will be,
   When the stars in the heavens
   Shall tremble with glee . . ."

❀ Pap's Old Billy Goat

Roud 4574, Roberts 104

This text was sung to Roberts by Henry Keeney in 1959, in Greenup County, Kentucky (In the Pine, pp. 293–94). A song on the same subject but not close in either text or tune is listed in Sigmund Spaeth's Read 'Em and Weep: The Songs You Forgot to Remember *(Garden City, N.Y.: Doubleday, Page and Co., 1926), credited to songwriters Harrigan and Hart. It has been collected in various versions across the United States. Fiddlin' John Carson recorded it on OKeh 4994-B in 1923, and Uncle Dave Macon recorded it on Vocalion 14848 in 1924.*

Dad brought home a great big bil-ly goat, Mom she washed 'most ev-'ry day; She hung her clothes out on the line, That dad-goned old goat he came that way.

2. He jerked down that red flannel shirt,
   You ought to have heard those buttons crack,
   But I'll get even with that son-of-a-gun,
   I'll tie him to the railroad track.

3. Well, I tied him across the railroad track,
   And the train was a-comin' at a powerful rate,
   He coughed up that old red shirt,
   He flagged down that darned old freight.

4. I went to the depot and bought me a ticket,
   Walked right in and sat right down,
   Stuck my ticket in the brim of my hat,
   The dad-goned wind blew it out on the ground.

5. The conductor came around and said gimme your ticket,
   Or you'll be left on the railroad track.
   I'll get even with that son-of-a-gun,
   Got a one-way ticket and I ain't a-comin' back.

✹ The Orphant Girl

Roud 457, Roberts, 23

*Roberts got this sentimental song from Dave Couch, Leslie County, Kentucky, in 1955 (*Sang Branch Settlers, *pp. 116–17). It was published in the 1902 edition of* Sacred Harp *and was reprinted by George Pullen Jackson in* Spiritual Folk-Songs of Early America *(New York: J. J. Augustin, 1937), pp. 48–49, with the tune credited to Elder C. J. Keith. It was recorded by Fiddlin' John Carson (OKeh 7006) in 1924; by Riley Puckett (Columbia 15050-D) and Ernest Stoneman (OKeh 45044) in 1926; and by Buell Kazee (Brunswick 211) in 1928.*

2. Her clothes were thin, her feet were bare,
   The snow had covered her hair;
   "Oh give me a home," so feeble she cried,
   "A home and a piece of bread."

3. The night was dark and the snow still fell,
   The rich man closed the door.
   His proud lips quivered, so scornful he said,
   "No room, no bread for the poor."

4. The night rolled over like a midnight storm,
   Rolled over like a funeral song,
   The sky were white as a linen sheet,
   And drifts of snow still fell.

5. The rich man lies on his velvet sheets,
   He was dreaming of his silver and his gold,
   While the orphant lies on a bed of snow,
   And cries, "So cold, so cold."

6. The morning light shoned over the earth,
   She was a-lying at the rich man's door,
   Her soul had fled to the heavens above,
   Where they's room and bread for the poor.

❀ The Lifeboat Is Coming

Roud 2287, Roberts 42

Jim Couch of Leslie County, Kentucky, sang this hymn, which he had learned from his mother, in 1955 (Sang Branch Settlers, p. 137). It has been popular with gospel groups all over the South. Some sources credit John R. Bryant as the author, but it was published and copyrighted by J. A. Lee in his Greatest and Lasting Hymns: A Collection of the World's Best Songs *(Glencoe, Ky.: John A. Lee, 1906). Versions can be heard online.*

Float - ing down the __ stream of time we __ have not long to stay,

Storm clouds of dark - ness will turn ____ to bright - est day;

Let us all take cour - age __ for __ we're not left a - lone, The

life - boat soon is com - ing for to car - ry her je - wels home.

2. Then cheer, my brothers, cheer, our trials will soon be o'er,
   Our loved ones we shall meet, shall meet upon that golden shore;
   Let us all take courage, for we're not left alone,
   The lifeboat soon is coming to carry her jewels home.

3. Sometimes the devil tempts me, he says it's all in vain,
   Trying to live a Christian life and walk in Jesus' name,
   But then I hear the Master say I'll give you a helping hand,
   If you will but trust me, I'll guide you to that land.

4. Then cheer, my brothers, cheer, our trials will soon be o'er,
   Our loved ones we shall meet, shall meet, upon that golden shore;
   We're pilgrims and we're strangers here, we're seeking a city to come,
   The lifeboat soon is coming to gather her jewels home.

5. The lifeboat soon is coming by a higher faith I see,
   As she splashes through the water to rescue you and me.
   The fairest peace for one and all the Master bids you come,
   Get on board the lifeboat, she'll carry you safely home.

6. Then cheer, my brothers, cheer (etc. as in stanza 4)

7. Get on board the lifeboat while she is passing by,
   If you stand and wait too long you must forever die.
   She'll carry you safely to the port and friends you love so dear,
   O love, love, the lifeboat, O, love, she's almost here.

8. So cheer, my brothers, cheer (etc. as in stanza 4)

❋ Bright and Shining City

Roud 3401, Roberts 38

*Sung by Jim Couch, Leslie County, Kentucky, in 1955 (*Sang Branch Settlers, *pp. 133–34). This hymn was composed by George F. Root (1820–1895), a composer of popular music more than of hymns. Wade Mainer sings it on* Early and Great, *Volume 2 (Old Homestead Records, OHCS 150, 1983).*

Chorus. We are drifting, yes, we're drifting and our days are passing by.
We are drifting down the rugged streams of time,
Jesus suffered and died on Calvary for the opening of the way,
Yes, I'm drifting to the happy home of mine.

2. O, sinners, take this warning, Christ is pleading now for you,
   As he warns the end of time will surely come.
   You'll have to face the Judgment on the Resurrection morn,
   You will have to meet the deeds that you have done.

   Chorus

3. You will have to face the Judgment on that Resurrection morn,
   When your sinful life here on earth is o'er.
   You will look to him for mercy, but he'll only shake his head,
   And say, "Depart from me forever more."

   Chorus

FIGURE 16. Leonard in 1939, the year he graduated from Berea College. Courtesy of the Leonard Ward Roberts Collection, SAA 57, Southern Appalachian Archives, Hutchins Library, Berea College, Berea, Kentucky.

FIGURE 17. Leonard at his typewriter at Pikeville College, with the books he had published behind him. Courtesy of the Leonard Ward Roberts Collection, SAA 57, Southern Appalachian Archives, Hutchins Library, Berea College, Berea, Kentucky.

FIGURE 18. Leonard Roberts telling one of his great tales. Courtesy of the Leonard Ward Roberts Collection, SAA 57, Southern Appalachian Archives, Hutchins Library, Berea College, Berea, Kentucky.

FIGURE 19. Leonard and Edith Roberts. Courtesy of the Leonard Ward Roberts Collection, SAA 57, Southern Appalachian Archives, Hutchins Library, Berea College, Berea, Kentucky.

FIGURE 20. Dave Couch, one of Roberts's primary sources for his book *Sang Branch Settlers: Folksongs and Tales of a Kentucky Mountain Family*. Courtesy of the Leonard Ward Roberts Collection, SAA 57, Southern Appalachian Archives, Hutchins Library, Berea College, Berea, Kentucky.

Notes

Bascom Lamar Lunsford

An earlier version of this essay appeared as Loyal Jones, "Bascom Lamar Lunsford: A Herald of Appalachian Studies," *Appalachian Journal* 42, no. 3–4 (2015): 232–49.

1. For additional information on the Lunsford and Deaver families, see Jones, *Minstrel of the Appalachians*, pp. 1–10. This essay is based on that book. However, much of the information about Lunsford came from the voluminous Bascom Lamar Lunsford Collection at Mars Hill University, Mars Hill, North Carolina, and from personal interviews and correspondence with some forty-nine persons who knew or knew about him, as well as from books and other sources. These materials are in the Bascom Lamar Lunsford Collection, SAA 29, Southern Appalachian Archives, Hutchins Library, Berea College, Berea, Kentucky [hereafter Lunsford Collection, Berea College].

2. Beard, "The Personal Folk Song Collection of Bascom Lamar Lunsford," p. 3, Lunsford Collection, Berea College, series V, box 4; Jones, *Minstrel of the Appalachians*, p. 6.

3. Jones, *Minstrel of the Appalachians*, pp. 6–7, quote from p. 7; Beard, "The Personal Folk Song Collection of Bascom Lamar Lunsford," p. 4.

4. Beard, "The Personal Folk Song Collection of Bascom Lamar Lunsford," p. 7; Jones, *Minstrel of the Appalachians*, p. 8.

5. The original typescript is in the Lunsford Collection at Mars Hill University. A copy is in the Lunsford Collection at Berea College.

6. Beard, "The Personal Folk Song Collection of Bascom Lamar Lunsford," p. 13; Jones, *Minstrel of the Appalachians*, p. 14.

7. Jones, *Minstrel of the Appalachians*, pp. 20–22.

8. Beard, "The Personal Folk Song Collection of Bascom Lamar Lunsford," p. 20; Jones, *Minstrel of the Appalachians*, p. 23.

9. Jones, *Minstrel of the Appalachians*, p. 36.

10. Letter from Scott Wiseman to me, dated December 3, 1973, Lunsford Collection, Berea College, box 1, folder 3.

11. For a complete listing of Lunsford's recordings, see Jones, *Minstrel of the Appalachians*, appendixes I–VI, pp. 151–82 of Norm Cohen's discography.

12. Scarborough, *A Song Catcher in Southern Mountains*, p. 53.

13. Jones, *Minstrel of the Appalachians*, p. 66.

14. Ibid., pp. 70–71, from an author recording of Lair.

15. Entry dated March 27, in *Journal of the Indiana Field Trip, March 26 to April 16, 1938*, John A. and Alan Lomax Manuscript Collection, American Folklife Center, Library of Congress, AFC 1933/001 and 2004/004.

16. John Lair Papers, SAA 66, Southern Appalachian Archives, Hutchins Library, Berea College, Berea, Kentucky, box 7, folder 3.

17. Jones, *Minstrel of the Appalachians*, p. 129.

18. Williams, *Staging Tradition*, p. 101.

19. Telephone interview with Roger Sprung, July 1974, Berea College Archives, AC-CT-001-024.

20. Williams, *Staging Tradition*, pp. 153–54.

21. Finger, "Bascom Lamar Lunsford," pp. 35, 33. See also Jones, *Minstrel of the Appalachians*, chap. 6, "Bouquets and Arrows," pp. 89–116, for more opinions on Lunsford's work.

22. Jones, *Minstrel of the Appalachians*, appendixes, Norm Cohen's discography. In addition to the Lunsford Collection at Columbia University, copies of these recordings are in the collections at Berea College and Mars Hill University, and in the Southern Historical Collection at the University of North Carolina at Chapel Hill.

23. "Carolina Minstrel Heard in Concert at Columbia: Lunsford Sings Hill Melodies for Students of Folklore," *New York Herald Tribune*, March 2, 1935, p. 6.

24. Charles Seeger, "On Proletarian Music," *Modern Music* 11 (1934): 121–22, as cited in Jones, *Minstrel of the Appalachians*, p. 120.

25. Author interview with John Lair, April 30, 1974, Lunsford Collection, Berea College, AC-CT-001-028.

26. Lily May Ledford, recorded presentation to Appalachian Studies Workshop, June 25, 1975, Berea College SAA, AC-OR-052-001.

27. Jones, *Minstrel of the Appalachians*, p. 73.

28. Williams, *Staging Tradition*, p. 86.

29. Among Sharp's works are *English Folk Songs from the Southern Appalachians* (with Olive Dame Campbell; New York: G. P. Putnam's Sons, 1917; 2nd enlarged ed., New York: Oxford University Press, 1932), as well as several volumes of dance instructions.

30. McLeod, "Minstrel of the Appalachians," p. 26. A typescript of this unpublished biography is available in the Appalachian Room in the Mars Hill College Archives.

31. For a fuller discussion of *Music Makers of the Blue Ridge*, see Jones, *Minstrel of the Appalachians*, pp. 83–84.

32. Ibid., p. 114.

33. Whisnant, "Finding the Way between the Old and the New," 135–36.

34. Online at https://www.youtube.com/watch?v=h0Vpuzyn33E, or it can be downloaded from http://www.kazoofilms.org/if-i-had-wings-to-fly/download/.

35. Greil Marcus, "Real Life Rock Top 10," *Village Voice*, February 18, 1986, https://greilmarcus.net/2014/07/07/real-life-rock-top-10-21886/.

Josiah H. Combs

1. Combs, "Some Kentucky Highland Stories," p. 46.

2. Combs, "Quare Women of the Mountains," pp. 25–27.

3. G. L. Kittredge, "Ballads and Rhymes from Kentucky," *Journal of American Folklore* 20, no. 79 (1907): 251–77.

4. Combs, *Folk-Songs of the Southern United States*, pp. ix–x.

5. Combs, "Quare Women of the Mountains," p. 27.

6. Ibid., p. 47.

7. Wilgus, "Leaders of Kentucky Folklore," p. 68.

8. Combs, "Quare Women of the Mountains," p. 27.

9. Shearin and Combs, *A Syllabus of Kentucky Folk-Songs*, p. 3.

10. Ibid.

11. The preceding information is from the Josiah Combs Papers, SAA 71, Southern Appalachian Archives, Hutchins Library, Berea College, Berea, Kentucky [hereafter Combs Papers].

12. Combs Papers, series IV, box 1, folder 31.

13. Ibid., box 1.

14. Author conversations with Norris Combs.

15. John and Ruby Lomax 1940 Southern States Recordings Collection, Library of Congress, AFC 1940/003.

16. Combs, *Folk-Songs of the Southern United States*, p. xiv.

17. Ibid., ix, xi–xii.

18. "La musique du Highlander des États-Unis," *Vient de paraître: Revue mensuelle des lettres et des arts* 6, no. 50 (1926): 24–26.

19. Copy of *Folk-Songs of the Southern United States*, Combs Papers, box 1.

20. Ibid., p. xv.

21. Ibid., pp. xiv–xvii.

22. Ibid., pp. 96–106, quotes here from pp. 98 and 99.

23. H. L. Mencken, *The American Language*, 4th ed. (New York: Alfred A. Knopf, 1965), p. 53. Over the course of Combs's work, Mencken's book had grown into

three volumes, four editions, and sixteen printings (New York: Alfred A. Knopf, 1919, 1921, 1923, 1936).

24. This story comes from one of Charlotte Combs's handwritten notes in the copy of *Folk-Songs of the Southern United States* in the Combs Papers.

25. Norris Combs wrote a short biography of his uncle, *Josiah: The Story of Dr. Josiah H. Combs from the Mountains of Kentucky*, which he self-published in 1994. It can be found in a group of unprocessed Norris Combs material in the Combs Papers, box 926 [hereafter Norris Combs Papers]. This and other items there reflect on the Mencken-Combs relationship.

26. Combs, *Folk-Songs of the Southern United States*, p. xiii.

27. Norris Combs Papers.

28. Combs Papers, series V, box 1, folder 26.

29. Ibid.

30. Combs, *Folk-Songs of the Southern United States*, p. xiv.

31. "Decretum Est," Combs Papers, box 3, folder 4.

32. According to Nick Offerman, Carol Burnett has a sign over her bathroom that reads "Euphemism." Offerman, *Gumption: Relighting the Torch of Freedom with America's Gutsiest Troublemakers* (New York: Dutton, 2015), p. 260.

Cratis D. Williams

Much of the information for this essay came from Loyal Jones, "A Complete Mountaineer," *Appalachian Journal* 13, no. 3 (1986): 288–96.

1. Weatherford, who was arranging for scholars from universities and colleges throughout Southern Appalachia to write about different aspects of life in the region for a more diversified study, had heard of Williams's work and wanted to see how it might fit into his project. No doubt it was too massive to be considered, but the study that Weatherford directed was subsequently published as *The Southern Appalachian Region: A Survey*, ed. Thomas R. Ford (Lexington: University Press of Kentucky, 1962). The two works were major additions to scholarship on the region.

2. Williams, *Tales from Sacred Wind*, p. 4.

3. Ibid., p. 48; Robert M. Rennick, *Kentucky Place Names* (Lexington: University Press of Kentucky, 1984), p. 260.

4. I remembered this from Williams's lectures.

5. This story was told to me by Dr. William Lightfoot, folklorist and emeritus professor of English at Appalachian State University, during an interview in Boone, North Carolina, on July 28, 2012.

6. Williams, *Tales from Sacred Wind*, chap. 3, "Beyond the Big Sandy . . . and Home Again," pp. 126–67.

7. Ibid., pp. 239–43.

8. Ibid., pp. 244–46.

9. Ibid., pp. 250–52.

10. Williams, *William H. Vaughan*, pp. 17–27, quotation from p. 27.

11. Williams, "Ballads and Songs."

12. Cratis Williams Papers, SAA 56, Southern Appalachian Archives, Hutchins Library, Berea College, Berea, Kentucky.

13. Williams, *The Cratis Williams Chronicles*, pp. xiii–xiv.

14. Ibid., p. xiv.

15. Information on the most difficult period in his life can be found ibid., pp. xvii–xx.

16. Williams, *William H. Vaughan*, pp. 51, 52.

17. Williams, *The Cratis Williams Chronicles*, chap. 2, "Arriving in Boone: A New Beginning," pp. 11–28.

18. Interviews with David Cratis Williams, October 12, 2012, by phone, and Sophie Williams, November 5, 2012, Boone, N.C.

19. Williams, *The Cratis Williams Chronicles*, pp. xxiv–xxvii.

20. This version, with a foreword by poet, novelist, and historian Robert Morgan, is now available on CD-ROM from the *Appalachian Journal*, Belk Library, Appalachian State University, Boone NC 28608.

21. "Cratis Williams' Top Dozen," *Appalachian Mountain Books* 1, no. 3 (May–June 1985). *Appalachian Mountain Books* was a bimonthly publication written and produced by George Brosi, who owned the Appalachian Bookstore in Berea.

22. Email from David Cratis Williams, dated April 7, 2016.

23. Notes from conversations with Bobby McMillon in Berea, Kentucky, October 25–26, 1985.

24. Copied from an article written about Williams by Grace Toney Edwards. Unfortunately the article is now lost, but this quote was verified by Edwards in a phone conversation, November 30, 2016.

25. Williams, *William H. Vaughan*, p. 70.

26. Ibid., p. 72.

Leonard Ward Roberts

An earlier version of this essay appeared as Loyal Jones, "Leonard Roberts (1912–1983)," in *Hidden Heroes of the Big Sandy Valley*, comp. and ed. James M. Gifford (Ashland, Ky.: Jesse Stuart Foundation, 2015), pp. 171–88. I am grateful to Rita Roberts Kelly for the extensive bibliography of her father that she contributed to the Leonard Roberts Memorial Issue, *Appalachian Heritage* 15, no. 2 (1987): 56–65. I am also grateful for advice and materials, especially on the Roberts genealogy, from Lynneda Roberts Stansbury, and for other materials and advice from Dr. Carl Lindahl, who is working on a forthcoming book about Leonard Roberts.

1. Genealogical information on the Roberts and related families was supplied by Lynneda Roberts Stansbury, Henrico, Va.

2. Leonard Ward Roberts, "My Life" (unpublished ms.), Leonard Ward Roberts Collection (27.8 linear feet, 44 cassette tapes, 99 reel tapes), SAA 57, Southern Appalachian Archives, Hutchins Library, Berea College, Berea, Kentucky [hereafter

Roberts Collection], box 1, log no. 973 (unprocessed). Most of the information for this essay came from the Roberts Collection.

3. Ibid., p. 256.

4. Ibid., p. 273.

5. Lawrence Edward Bowling, "My Friend: Leonard Ward Roberts," *Appalachian Heritage* 15, no. 2 (1987): 10.

6. Leonard Roberts, "A Night with Jesse Stuart," *Wind Magazine* 6 (1956): 75–81.

7. From a July 1980 interview with Roberts by Joyce Hancock, quoted in Lindahl, "Leonard Roberts," p. 253. Dr. Hancock's recorded interview is in the Roberts Collection.

8. Ibid., p. 253.

9. Ibid., p. 265. *Märchen* is a German word meaning "fairy story" or "tall tale."

10. Ibid., p. 254.

11. The information in this and the following paragraphs comes from various sources in the Roberts Collection, box 1, folder 2.

12. Roberts, *Up Cutshin and Down Greasy*, p. vii.

13. Ibid., p. viii.

14. Ibid., p. 10.

15. Ibid., p. 19.

16. Hutchins Library–Indiana University Folktale Workshop Collection, Berea College Special Collections and Archives, Berea, Kentucky, BCA 0245, box 1, folder 1.

17. Lindahl, "Leonard Roberts," p. 260.

18. Henry Glassie, *Passing the Time in Ballymenone: Culture and History of an Ulster Community* (Bloomington: Indiana University Press, 1982). Winner of the Chicago Folklore Prize and the Haney Prize in the Social Sciences, this is a splendid study of the people of this place in Ireland, employing the same convictions and techniques that were dear to the heart of Leonard Roberts.

19. From a transcription of Glassie's remarks that Carl Lindahl sent to me by email on March 6, 2015.

Sources

Beard, Anne Winsmore. "The Personal Folk Song Collection of Bascom Lamar Lunsford." Master's thesis, Miami University, 1959.

Buxton, Barry M., ed. *The Cratis Williams Symposium Proceedings: A Memorial and Examination of the State of Regional Studies in Appalachia*. Boone, N.C.: Appalachian Consortium Press and the Faculty Development and Instructional Services Center and Cratis D. Williams Graduate School, Appalachian State University, 1990.

Combs, Josiah H., comp. *Folk-Songs from the Kentucky Highlands*. With piano accompaniments by Keith Mixson. Schirmer's American Folk-Song Series, set 1. New York: G. Schirmer, 1939.

———. *Folk-Songs of the Southern United States*. Edited by D. K. Wilgus. Austin: University of Texas Press for the American Folklore Society, 1967.

———. "Quare Women of the Mountains: The Story of the Founding of the Hindman Settlement School." *Kentucky Explorer*, January 1991, pp. 25–27.

———. "Some Kentucky Highland Stories." Introduction and notes by Herbert Halpert. *Kentucky Folklore Record* 4, no. 2 (1958): 45–61.

Finger, Bill. "Bascom Lamar Lunsford: The Limits of a Folk Hero." *Southern Exposure* 2, no. 1 (1974): 27–37.

Jones, Loyal. "A Complete Mountaineer." *Appalachian Journal* 13, no. 3 (1986): 288–96.

———. *Minstrel of the Appalachians: The Story of Bascom Lamar Lunsford*. 1984. Reprint, Lexington: University Press of Kentucky, 2002.

Lindahl, Carl. "Leonard Roberts, the Farmer-Lewis-Muncy Family, and the Magic Circle of the Mountain Märchen (American Folklore Society Fellows Invited

Plenary Address, October 2008)." *Journal of American Folklore* 123, no. 489 (2010): 251–75.

———. *Perspectives on the Jack Tales and Other North American Märchen*. Bloomington: Indiana University Press, 2001.

McLeod, John Angus. "Minstrel of the Appalachians: An Interpretative Biography of Bascom Lamar Lunsford." Unpublished ms., 1973.

Roberts, Leonard W. *Old Greasybeard: Tales from the Cumberland Gap*. 1969. Reprint, Pikeville, Ky.: Pikeville College Press, 1990.

———. *Sang Branch Settlers: Folkways of a Kentucky Mountain Family*. Music transcribed by C. Buell Agey. 1974. Reprint, Pikeville, Ky.: Pikeville College Press, 1980.

———. *South from Hell-fer-Sartin: Kentucky Mountain Folk Tales*. 1955. Reprints, Berea, Ky.: Council of the Southern Mountains, 1964; Pikeville, Ky.: Pikeville College Press, 1970.

———. *Up Cutshin and Down Greasy: Folkways of a Kentucky Mountain Family*. 1959. Reprint, Lexington: University of Kentucky Press, 1988.

Scarborough, Dorothy. *A Song Catcher in Southern Mountains: American Folk Songs of British Ancestry*. New York: Columbia University Press, 1937.

Shearin, Hubert G., and Josiah H. Combs. *A Syllabus of Kentucky Folk-Songs*. Lexington, Ky.: Transylvania Printing Co., 1911.

Whisnant, David E. "Finding the Way between the Old and the New: The Mountain Dance and Folk Festival and Bascom Lamar Lunsford's Work as a Citizen." *Appalachian Journal* 7, no. 1–2 (1979–80): 135–54.

Wilgus, D. K. "Leaders of Kentucky Folklore: Josiah H. Combs." *Kentucky Folklore Record* 3, no. 2 (1957): 67–69.

Williams, Cratis Dearl. "Ballads and Songs." Master's thesis, University of Kentucky, 1937. Kentucky Microcards ed., series A, no. 15, 1937; reprint, West Salem, Wis.: Microfilms, Inc., 1969.

———. *The Cratis Williams Chronicles: I Come to Boone*. Edited by David Cratis Williams and Patricia D. Beaver. Boone, N.C.: Appalachian Consortium Press, 1999.

———. *I Become a Teacher*. Edited by James M. Gifford, Ashland, Ky.: Jesse Stuart Foundation, 1995.

———. "The Southern Mountaineer in Fact and Fiction." Ph.D. diss., New York University, 1961. 3 vols.

———. *Tales from Sacred Wind: Coming of Age in Appalachia*. Edited by David Cratis Williams and Patricia D. Beaver. The Cratis Williams Chronicles. Jefferson, N.C.: McFarland & Company, 2003.

———. *William H. Vaughan: A Better Man Than I Ever Wanted to Be*. Edited by James M. Gifford. 1983. 2nd ed., Morehead, Ky.: Appalachian Development Center, Morehead State University, 1985.

Williams, Michael Ann. *Staging Tradition: John Lair and Sarah Gertrude Knott*. Urbana: University of Illinois Press, 2006.

Index

LOYAL JONES is the author of numerous books on Appalachian culture, including *Country Music Humorists and Comedians*. He served as director of the Appalachian Center at Berea College for twenty-three years.

The University of Illinois Press
is a founding member of the
Association of American University Presses.

Composed in 10.25/14 Chaparral Pro
by Kirsten Dennison
at the University of Illinois Press
Cover designed by Jennifer S. Holzner
Cover illustration: Cratis Williams, courtesy of
Dr. James Gifford, the Jesse Stuart Foundation;
Josiah Combs and Leonard Roberts, courtesy of
Berea College Special Collections and Archives,
Berea, KY; Bascom Lamar Lunsford, courtesy of
Southern Appalachian Archives, Mars Hill
University, Mars Hill, NC

University of Illinois Press
1325 South Oak Street
Champaign, IL 61820-6903
www.press.uillinois.edu